THE LEXICOLOGIST'S HANDBOOK:

A DICTIONARY OF UNUSUAL WORDS

DANE COBAIN

Edited by Pam Elise Harris
Cover Design by Larch Gallagher

INTRODUCTION

THERE ARE TWO INTRODUCTIONS to this book.

This one was written while the world was in the grip of the coronavirus crisis and I was working like crazy getting manuscripts ready to send over to my editor. This is a project that I started working on over ten years ago when I first took up writing. I kept a notebook in which I jotted down words that I liked and which I wanted to remember.

That slowly evolved into what became *The Lexicologist's Handbook*, the book that you're holding in your hands. But it's undergone major upgrades since it was first "published."

Technically, it predates *No Rest for the Wicked*, the first book that I released. I don't count this book – nor a handful of others that I wrote – as official releases because I only ever had a dozen copies printed for myself and for my immediate family.

By a strange quirk of fate, one of these rare early copies (I don't even have any myself) made it into the hands of one of my friends, Amanda de Grey. Amanda read it and enjoyed it, and she encouraged me to publish it for real. That was about five years ago.

I sat on it for a while, but eventually, I thought it was about time to dust this project off and to introduce it to the light of day. So that's exactly what I've done. Enjoy.

Dane Cobain
27th March, 2021

***

The Lexicologist's Handbook is a dictionary of the bizarre and the obscure, a collection of the interesting, atypical and idiosyncratic.

Some words are here because of the way that they sound, while others qualify because of their definition or association. They're presented alphabetically with phonetic spellings, alongside a definition and an example. The work is an experiment with language and a natural extension of my studies at university and beyond.

You can use this book in many ways. You can look up entries alphabetically, dip in at random for a word of the day or flick through it for inspiration. For a challenge, see how many words you can drop into day-to-day conversation.

The words are ours. Help me to share them with the world.

Dane Cobain
27th March, 2012

AUTHOR'S NOTE

PRONUNCIATION: I avoid using standard pronunciation systems, such as the International Phonetic Alphabetic, in favour of a personalised approach. I tried to spell the words phonetically in a way that reflects the way that I pronounce them, although if you're from a different part of the world then you might pronounce them differently. If in doubt, Google the word and let them pronounce it for you.

EXAMPLES: The words that are being defined are in bold in the examples to distinguish them from the rest of the sentence.

MULTIPLE EXAMPLES: When a word can be two or more different "types" (i.e. – an adjective and an adverb), the types are alphabetised and the numbered examples run in this order.

SELF-REFERENCE: *The Lexicologist's Handbook* is self-referential. If you see a dagger (one of these: †) after a word, it means that it's defined elsewhere in the handbook. To find out more about the word, simply locate the appropriate entry alphabetically.

WORKS OF ART: All works of art, music or literature are italicised, like so: *The Lord of the Rings*.

CONTENTS

0-9

1337

Pronunciation: Leet   **Type**: Adjective

Definition: Formidable; skilled or accomplished. Evolved from the word 'elite' and occasionally spelled 'leet,' the word is often used in online and gaming communities.

Example: Because of Bob's **1337** computer skills, he was able to restore the data from the crashed computer.

A

Abandonware

Pronunciation: A-band-un-wear   **Type**: Noun

Definition: Computer software that's no longer supported by the manufacturer, usually because the product is discontinued or the company is bankrupt.

Example: Although the manufacturer went out of business, its **abandonware** was still available online.

Aberrant

Pronunciation: Ab-eh-rant   **Type**: Adjective

Definition: Deviating from the norm; different.

Example: Her brightly coloured outfits were **aberrant** when compared to her more conservative peers.

Abjure

Pronunciation: Ab-jor   **Type**: Verb

Definition: To solemnly and completely renounce a belief, cause or claim.

Example: After the priest lost his faith, he decided to **abjure** his religion.

Abnegate

Pronunciation: Ab-ni-gate   **Type**: Verb

Definition: To refuse, deny, reject or renounce; to relinquish or to give something up.

Example: There's a protest march on Tuesday to prompt the government to **abnegate** their proposed tax hike.

Abortifacient

Pronunciation: Ab-or-ti-fass-ee-unt   **Type**: Noun

Definition: A drug that causes abortion during pregnancy.

Example: The drug addict took an **abortifacient** because she knew she couldn't raise a child.

Abreaction

Pronunciation: Ab-ree-ack-shun   **Type**: Noun

Definition: A psychoanalytical term used to describe the process of reliving an experience to release a previously repressed emotion.

Example: John experienced **abreaction** during his struggle with pancreatic cancer and found himself reliving the passing of his father from the same disease.

Abrogate

Pronunciation: Ab-ro-gate   **Type**: Verb

Definition: To repeal, abolish or do away with a law, a right or other formal agreement.

Example: The boss decided to **abrogate** his employees' birthday bonuses, and two of them resigned as a result of it.

Abscond

Pronunciation: Abs-cond   **Type**: Verb

Definition: To disappear, vanish or leave with something that doesn't belong to you. This verb is often used to describe the actions of a criminal.

Example: The witness saw the thief **abscond** with the jewellery after the heist.

Absolution

Pronunciation: Ab-so-loo-shun   **Type**: Noun

Definition: A formal release from guilt or punishment for a deed that was previously committed. Absolution is often granted by a higher religious power, such as a priest.

Example: Every night, the young Christian prayed for **absolution** for his sins.

Absquatulate

Pronunciation: Ab-skwot-yoo-late   **Type**: Verb

Definition: To leave quickly and abruptly; to depart in a hurry.

Example: When the locals found out my real identity, I knew I'd have to **absquatulate**, so I made sure I was ready to go at a moment's notice.

Abstemious

Pronunciation: Ab-stee-me-uss   **Type**: Adjective

Definition: Not self-indulgent; given to abstaining. This adjective is usually used in reference to food or drink.

Example: The **abstemious** gentleman refused to visit the nightclub with his contemporaries.

Abutment

Pronunciation: A-but-munt   **Type**: Noun

Definition: The point where two objects or structures meet, particularly the part of a structure that supports an arch or a bridge.

Example: The **abutment** stuck out like an imposing statue, but it stopped the bridge from collapsing.

Accoutrement

Pronunciation: A-coot-rim-unt   **Type**: Noun

Definition: Additional items of clothing or equipment, usually worn or carried for a specific purpose.

Example: The soldier inspected his fallen opponent's **accoutrement** and decided to take his ammunition.

Acephalous

Pronunciation: A-seff-al-us   **Type**: Adjective

Definition: Without a head.

Example: The ghost was **acephalous**.

Acolyte

Pronunciation: Ack-oh-lite   **Type**: Noun

Definition: A person who assists in or who follows a religious service or procession.

Example: The **acolyte** prepared to receive a blessing.

Acromegaly

Pronunciation: Ack-rom-eh-ga-lee   **Type**: Noun

Definition: A hormonal disorder leading to abnormal growth of the hands, feet and face. A rare and potentially life-threatening condition.

Example: Kevin says the Elephant Man had **acromegaly**.

Acumen

Pronunciation: Ack-yoo-men   **Type**: Noun

Definition: The ability to make good judgements and fast decisions in a particular field.

Example: Kendra's business **acumen** helped her to spot the good deals from the bad.

Adage

Pronunciation: Ade-ij   **Type**: Noun

Definition: A proverb, saying or short statement that expresses a generally held truth.

Example: The shopkeeper muttered an old **adage** about patience in the face of adversity and turned around to face the customer.

Adamant

Pronunciation: A-dam-ant   **Type**: Adjective, Noun

Definition: The adjective describes someone who's firmly convinced of something and reluctant to change their mind. The noun refers to a mythical mineral with extreme strength, chiefly used in the creation of armour and weaponry.

Example:
#1: I was **adamant** that my orders were to be obeyed.
#2: The barbarian's sword was made of **adamant** and was said to be unbreakable.

Adrenaline

Pronunciation: Ad-ren-a-lin   **Type**: Noun

Definition: A hormone and neurotransmitter that increases the heart rate and aids the fight-or-flight response.

Example: After my first bungee jump, my heart was racing from the **adrenaline**.

Adroit

Pronunciation: Ad-royt   **Type**: Adjective

Definition: Clever, skilled or adept with the hands or the mind.

Example: Things were going badly for the chancellor. Fortunately, he was an **adroit** public speaker and managed to diffuse the situation.

Adumbrate

Pronunciation: Ad-um-brate   **Type**: Verb

Definition: To sketch or represent something in an outline.

Example: Before writing his story, Stephen chose to **adumbrate** the plot.

Adventitious

Pronunciation: Ad-vent-ish-uss   **Type**: Adjective

Definition: Fortunate.

Example: The heavy snow was **adventitious** to the defending army as it impaired their enemies.

Affix

Pronunciation: Aff-icks   **Type**: Verb

Definition: To attach one object to another.

Example: My neighbour has only just moved in and still needs to **affix** his posters to the walls.

Aficionado

Pronunciation: Aff-iss-ee-un-arr-do   **Type**: Noun

Definition: A person with a particular interest, enthusiasm and knowledge of an activity, subject or pastime.

Example: The music **aficionado** refused to listen to albums on anything other than vinyl.

Agglomerate

Pronunciation: Agg-lom-ur-ate   **Type**: Noun, Verb

Definition: The noun refers to a group or a collection, while the verb refers to the act of gathering such a group.

Example:
#1: The village's **agglomerate** decided what was best for the inhabitants.
#2: The company knew it had to **agglomerate** all of its outlets under the same brand name.

Aggrandise

Pronunciation: Ag-ran-dize   **Type**: Verb

Definition: To embroider or add details to; to make something greater than it was before.

Example: We need to **aggrandise** the statistics to hide the low numbers.

Ague

Pronunciation: Ayg-yoo   **Type**: Noun

Definition: Any illness involving fevers and shivering, particularly malaria.

Example: Phillip went travelling through Africa and was struck down by a bad case of **ague**.

Alate

Pronunciation: Ay-late   **Type**: Adjective

Definition: Possessing wings or appendages† that resemble wings.

Example: The mayfly is an **alate** insect.

Aleatory

Pronunciation: Al-ee-ate-or-ee   **Type**: Adjective

Definition: Dependent upon chance. This adjective is often applied to pieces of art or literature that are affected by randomness.

Example: The poem was **aleatory**. The writer based the number of syllables on the results of a dice roll.

Algorithm

Pronunciation: Al-guh-rith-um   **Type**: Noun

Definition: A step-by-step procedure or set of rules that's designed to be followed in calculations or other problem-solving operations. The word is often used to describe a complex piece of computer software or code.

Example: The code breaker struggled with the **algorithm**.

Allegory

Pronunciation: Al-la-gor-ree   **Type**: Noun

Definition: A type of creative expression in which a story, poem or picture can be interpreted to have a hidden meaning.

Example: *The Lord of the Rings* trilogy has been viewed as an **allegory** of the Second World War.

Alliteration

Pronunciation: Al-lit-ter-ray-shun   **Type**: Noun

Definition: This noun is used to refer to a sequence of closely connected words that begin with the same sound.

Example: "Can Karen kill canned cats or con canny kittens?" is a sentence that uses **alliteration**.

Alphabetise

Pronunciation: Al-fa-bet-ize   **Type**: Verb

Definition: To sort something into alphabetical order.

Example: I had to **alphabetise** all the entries in *The Lexicologist's Handbook*.

Amalgam

Pronunciation: Am-al-gum   **Type**: Noun

Definition: A mixture or blend of different things that forms a new composite whole.

Example: The United States of America is an **amalgam** of independent territories.

Amanuensis

Pronunciation: Am-an-yoo-en-sis   **Type**: Noun

Definition: A literary, musical or artistic assistant, particularly one who takes down notes or copies manuscripts.

Example: Darran would never have finished his novel without Julie, his **amanuensis,** who typed his manuscript.

Ambergris

Pronunciation: Am-bur-gris   **Type**: Noun

Definition: A waxy substance that's secreted from the digestive system of the sperm whale and which is often used to create perfume.

Example: In *Futurama*, Kif is arrested after accidentally stealing the **ambergris** contained in whale vomit.

Ambiguity

Pronunciation: Am-big-yoo-it-ee   **Type**: Noun

Definition: The (often deliberate) use of words that leads to uncertainty of meaning. An ambiguous sentence can typically be read to have multiple meanings with no clue as to the intended or actual meaning.

Example: "I saw her duck" is an example of **ambiguity**. Did she duck, or does she have a duck?

Ambivalent

Pronunciation: Am-biv-al-unt   **Type**: Adjective

Definition: Possessing mixed or contradictory feelings about someone or something.

Example: Mr. Rombach's great uncle died and left him £10,000, making him feel **ambivalent**.

Ambulatory

Pronunciation: Am-bew-la-tor-ee   **Type**: Adjective, Noun

Definition: The adjective describes a person who's walking, while the noun refers to a place that's specifically created for people to walk in, often an aisle in a church or a monastery.

Example:
#1: The woman was **ambulatory** and able to do her own errands.
#2: The priest walked down the **ambulatory** towards the altar.

Amenorrhea

Pronunciation: Ah-men-or-ee-a   **Type**: Noun

Definition: Not to be confused with the menopause, amenorrhea is the unexpected absence of menstrual bleeding in a woman of reproductive age.

Example: Laura's period didn't come, and she thought she was pregnant. Turns out it was **amenorrhea**.

Amorphous

Pronunciation: Ah-morf-uss   **Type**: Adjective

Definition: Without a clearly-defined shape, body or form.

Example: "Harold," shouted Mabel. "What on earth is that **amorphous** globule[†] in your nose?"

Ampitheatre

Pronunciation: Am-pee-thee-it-ur   **Type**: Noun

Definition: A sloping gallery with rows of seats, designed to allow large numbers of people to watch a production or play.

Example: Last week, Joey saw *Romeo and Juliet* at the **amphitheatre**.

Andante

Pronunciation: An-dan-tay   **Type**: Adjective, Adverb

Definition: The adjective describes a piece of slow music, while the adverb describes the action of playing music slowly.

Example:
#1: Many of Mozart's concertos have an **andante** middle movement.
#2: Harry wrote a new song that's played **andante**.

Androgynous

Pronunciation: An-drodge-in-uss   **Type**: Adjective

Definition: Possessing characteristics that aren't gender-specific.

Example: Ann Widdecombe's short haircut is **androgynous**.

Anechoic

Pronunciation: An-eck-oh-ick   **Type**: Adjective

Definition: Free from echo.

Example: According to a popular urban legend, the quack of a duck is **anechoic**. Scientists have been able to disprove it by listening to recordings of quacks and pinpointing their echo.

Ankh

Pronunciation: Ank   **Type**: Noun

Definition: An Ancient Egyptian hieroglyphic symbol that represents life, formed of a cross with a loop at the top.

Example: The stonemason carved an **ankh** into the obelisk[†].

Animatronic

Pronunciation: An-im-at-ron-ic   **Type**: Adjective

Definition: A description applied to robotic devices that have been designed to look like animals, rather than machines.

Example: Laura's favourite part of Cadbury World was the **animatronic** gorilla because it looked so realistic.

Annihilate

Pronunciation: An-I-ill-ate   **Type**: Verb

Definition: To totally destroy or eradicate.

Example: The emperor swore to **annihilate** his enemies.

Anomaly

Pronunciation: Ah-nom-al-ee   **Type**: Noun

Definition: Something that deviates from the norm. This noun is often used to describe a piece of data or a result that was different to what was expected.

Example: Apart from one **anomaly**, the results of the experiment proved the scientist's theorem[†].

Anomie

Pronunciation: An-om-ee   **Type**: Noun

Definition: A lack of the usual social or ethical norms and considerations in a person, a group or an organisation.

Example: The councillor fought against plans for a new housing estate in case having a lower class of tenant led to **anomie**.

Anserine

Pronunciation: An-sir-een   **Type**: Adjective

Definition: Resembling a goose. Often used as an insult to mean "foolish" or "stupid".

Example: George W. Bush is **anserine** in the eyes of much of the left-wing public.

Antagonist

Pronunciation: An-tag-an-ist   **Type**: Noun

Definition: A person who actively opposes something. Synonymic[†] with "foe" or "adversary," it's used in film and literary circles to refer to the "bad guy", i.e. the person who opposes the protagonist[†], the hero of the narrative.

Example: It's a well-known rule of storytelling that the **antagonist** is never victorious.

Antediluvian

Pronunciation: An-tee-di-loo-vee-an   **Type**: Adjective

Definition: This adjective is used to describe a time before the flood in the Bible. By extension, it can also describe anything that's ridiculously old-fashioned or outdated.

Example: I went to my grandparents' house on Tuesday and listened to their **antediluvian** radio.

Anthropomorphism

Pronunciation: Anth-ro-po-morf-iz-um   **Type**: Noun

Definition: The attribution of human characteristics to something non-human, such as a god, an animal, an object or a concept[†].

Example: Walt Disney might have been inspired by **anthropomorphism** when he created Bugs Bunny and Mickey Mouse.

Antibodies

Pronunciation: An-tee-bod-ees   **Type**: Noun

Definition: Blood proteins that are produced by the immune system to defend the body from attack.

Example: The COVID-19 vaccine helps people to develop **antibodies** to fight the virus.

Antidisestablishmentarianism

Pronunciation: An-tee-dis-ist-ab-lish-munt-air-ee-an-is-um   **Type**: Noun

Definition: This noun is often believed to be the longest word in the English language. It refers to a political position originating in Britain in the 1800s, directly opposing the belief that there should no longer be an official church for the country.

Example: Mr. Willis, a staunch[†] Anglican, was a firm supporter of **antidisestablishmentarianism**.

Antimatter

Pronunciation: An-tee-mat-tur   **Type**: Noun

Definition: The opposite of matter: molecules formed of antiprotons, antineutrons and positrons. It reacts violently when it comes into contact with normal matter and doesn't exist in a stable form in our universe.

Example: When the **antimatter** collided with matter, they annihilated[†] each other and gave off vast amounts of energy.

Antinomian

Pronunciation: An-tee-no-me-an   **Type**: Adjective

Definition: A term coined by Martin Luther to describe the view that Christians don't need to obey moral and religious laws because their faith and their god's forgiveness releases them from the obligation.

Example: Ian was a religious pacifist until he became **antinomian** and joined the army to fulfil his violent blood-lust.

Antiquated

Pronunciation: An-tee-kway-tid   **Type**: Adjective

Definition: Extremely old-fashioned or out-of-date.

Example: Joe couldn't understand his mother's **antiquated** cassette player.

Antiscorbutic

Pronunciation: An-tee-scorb-yoo-tick   **Type**: Adjective, Noun

Definition: This adjective is usually used to describe a drug or a foodstuff and means it possesses the ability to prevent or cure scurvy. The noun refers directly to such a foodstuff.

Example:
#1: The **antiscorbutic** tablets were used to stop the sailors from growing ill on the journey.
#2: Citrus fruits are an effective **antiscorbutic**.

Antispasmodic

Pronunciation: An-tee-spazz-mod-ick   **Type**: Adjective, Noun

Definition: The adjective is used to describe something that has the ability to relieve involuntary spasms and twitches. The noun refers to a chemical or a drug that has this effect.

Example:
#1: The **antispasmodic** medicine helped the epileptic to recover.
#2: The doctor asked the nurse to fetch him an **antispasmodic** to stop the patient's seizures.

Aphasia

Pronunciation: Ay-fay-zee-ah   **Type**: Noun

Definition: The loss of the ability to understand, express or communicate through speech, usually caused by head trauma or damage to the parts of the brain that control language.

Example: After the tragic accident, John suffered from **aphasia** and had to undergo therapy to relearn how to communicate.

Aphrodisiac

Pronunciation: Af-ro-dizz-zee-ack   **Type**: Noun

Definition: A substance that stimulates sexual desire and arousal. The name comes from Aphrodite, Greek goddess of love.

Example: Oysters are often believed to be an **aphrodisiac**.

Aphorism

Pronunciation: Ayf-or-iz-um   **Type**: Noun

Definition: A short phrase or observation that expresses a well-known or generally held truth.

Example: Henry's favourite **aphorism** is, "Nothing great was ever achieved without enthusiasm."

Apoplexy

Pronunciation: Ap-oh-plex-ee   **Type**: Noun

Definition: Incapacity or speechlessness resulting from a cerebral haemorrhage or stroke. The noun can also be used to refer to the same symptoms when caused by extreme anger.

Example: The veins throbbed in his head as he was struck down by **apoplexy**.

Apotropaic

Pronunciation: Ap-oh-tra-pay-ick   **Type**: Adjective

Definition: Possessing the power to ward off evil influences or bad luck.

Example: Jenny has always been superstitious. That's why she wears an **apotropaic** necklace.

Apparel

Pronunciation: App-ah-rel   **Type**: Noun

Definition: Items of clothing.

Example: I went shopping for **apparel** yesterday and came back with two new T-shirts, a pair of jeans and a new jacket.

Apparition

Pronunciation: App-ah-rish-un   **Type**: Noun

Definition: A ghost or a ghost-like image of a person. It can also be defined as the sudden appearance of something unexpected, unusual or remarkable.

Example: I was woken in the middle of the night by a sudden chill and saw an **apparition** passing through the bedroom wall.

Appendage

Pronunciation: Ah-pen-didge   **Type**: Noun

Definition: An external body part that protrudes from an organism.

Example: Followers of the Church of the Flying Spaghetti Monster often believe that they've been touched by his noodly **appendage**.

Aquiline

Pronunciation: Ack-will-line   **Type**: Adjective

Definition: Like or resembling an eagle. This adjective is often used to describe a person's face when they have a hooked nose.

Example: Bram Stoker described Count Dracula's nose as "**aquiline**, with high bridge of the thin nose and peculiarly arched nostrils."

Arbiter

Pronunciation: Arr-bit-ur   **Type**: Noun

Definition: A settler of disputes; any judge, moderator or other person with the power to have the final say in a matter.

Example: The industrial **arbiter** forced the factory owner to give his workers time and a half if they worked in the evenings.

Arboreal

Pronunciation: Arr-bore-ee-al   **Type**: Adjective

Definition: Tree-like or related to trees.

Example: When he was on holiday, Stephen took photos of the **arboreal** garden to capture the vibrant colour of the leaves.

Archaic

Pronunciation: Arr-kay-ick   **Type**: Adjective

Definition: Old or out-dated; often used to describe habits or spellings.

Example: The Olde Sweete Shoppe was Laura's favourite **archaic** purveyor[†] of confectionery.

Archipelago

Pronunciation: Arr-chi-pel-ah-go   **Type**: Noun

Definition: A group of islands or a stretch of water containing such a group. The UK, the Philippines and New Zealand are all archipelagos.

Example: The world's largest **archipelago** by area is Indonesia, with over seventeen thousand islands.

Arcuate

Pronunciation: Arr-cue-ate   **Type**: Adjective

Definition: Curved in the shape of a bow; arched.

Example: The façade of the building was **arcuate**, and from above it looked like the letter C.

Argentiferous

Pronunciation: Arr-jent-if-er-uss   **Type**: Adjective

Definition: Containing silver. This adjective is usually used to describe minerals or rocks.

Example: The miners saw the rock deposits as a problem until they realised they were **argentiferous**.

Argot

Pronunciation: Arr-go   **Type**: Noun

Definition: The jargon, slang and vernacular[†] of a particular group or socio-economic class.

Example: The policeman had trouble understanding the youngsters because of their working-class **argot**.

Arpeggio

Pronunciation: Ar-pej-ee-oh   **Type**: Noun

Definition: The notes of a chord played or sung in sequence, in either ascending or descending order.

Example: An **arpeggio** in the key of C Major would hit the notes C, E and G.

Arrestable

Pronunciation: Ah-rest-ah-bull   **Type**: Adjective

Definition: This adjective is used to describe a person who could legally and morally be arrested.

Example: When Kelly stole a microwave during the riots, her actions made her **arrestable**.

Arterial

Pronunciation: Arr-teer-ee-al   **Type**: Adjective

Definition: Of or relating to the arteries.

Example: The heart attack was caused by an **arterial** blockage.

Articular

Pronunciation: Ar-tick-yoo-lar   **Type**: Adjective

Definition: Of, similar to or relating to a joint or the joints.

Example: Since his retirement, John was forced to put up with constant **articular** pain when climbing stairs.

Assiduity

Pronunciation: Ass-sid-yoo-it-tee   **Type**: Noun

Definition: Constant close attention to an activity.

Example: Alex painted his masterpiece with **assiduity**.

Assimilate

Pronunciation: Ass-sim-ill-ate   **Type**: Verb

Definition: To take in information, ideas, a people or their culture and to absorb them into something larger.

Example: Modern bands usually **assimilate** the music and ideologies of their predecessors to form new genres.

Askance

Pronunciation: Ass-kance   **Type**: Adverb

Definition: With a bearing, attitude or appearance of suspicion, disapproval or condemnation.

Example: Jonathan looked **askance** at his wife when she asked him what he'd been doing on Sunday night.

Assonance

Pronunciation: Ass-oh-nance   **Type**: Noun

Definition: The repetition of vowel sounds to create internal rhyming within phrases. Often used in poetry and rap lyrics.

Example: The lyrics to *Triumph* by the Wu-Tang Clan are an example of **assonance**: "I bomb atomically – Socrates' philosophies and hypotheses can't define how I be droppin' these mockeries."

Astringent

Pronunciation: Ah-strin-junt   **Type**: Adjective, Noun

Definition: The adjective refers to something that causes bodily tissue (often skin) to contract. The noun refers to a substance with this effect.

Example:
#1: The lotion smelled of coconut and was mildly **astringent**.
#2: The doctors used an **astringent** on the leper's lesions.

Atoll

Pronunciation: At-ol   **Type**: Noun

Definition: An island or group of islands formed of coral.

Example: The scientists discovered a new species of butterfly on the Australian **atoll**.

Atrocity

Pronunciation: At-ross-it-ee   **Type**: Noun

Definition: A highly unpleasant, evil, cruel or immoral act.

Example: The Holocaust is considered by most to be history's greatest **atrocity**.

Attenuate

Pronunciation: At-ten-yoo-ate   **Type**: Verb

Definition: To reduce the force, value, density or effect of something.

Example: The mechanism used oil to **attenuate** friction to keep it from accelerating too fast.

Augean

Pronunciation: Or-jee-an   **Type**: Adjective

Definition: Requiring a massive amount of effort, so much so that the task seems impossible.

Example: After the crazy house party, Phil began the **augean** job of cleaning up the debris[†].

Augur

Pronunciation: Or-gur   **Type**: Noun, Verb

Definition: In ancient times, an augur was a religious figure like a prophet who interpreted events or circumstances as indications of a divine approval or disapproval of a proposed course of action. The verb refers to the act of indicating such approval or disapproval.

Example:
#1: The **augur** said that the shooting star meant a plague would sweep the land.
#2: The philosopher said that the end of the war seemed to **augur** a period of happiness and prosperity.

Aureole

Pronunciation: Or-ee-ole   **Type**: Noun

Definition: A circle of light or an area of brightness surrounding something, often used in art and literature to depict[†] holiness.

Example: The streetlight formed an **aureole** around the shoulders of the sleeping wino.

Autarchy

Pronunciation: Or-tar-key   **Type**: Noun

Definition: This word has two meanings. It can either describe a state of absolute rule or power, or a state in which a country doesn't require any trade, subsidy or outside help from any other country.

Example: The citizens of the **autarchy** were unaware that they lived in a state of poverty compared to their immediate neighbours.

Autochthon

Pronunciation: Or-tock-thun   **Type**: Noun

Definition: A native or aborigine; the earliest known inhabitant of a location.

Example: The archaeologist won an award for discovering the fossilised remains of an **autochthon**.

Autodidact

Pronunciation: Or-toh-di-dact   **Type**: Noun

Definition: A person who taught themselves a skill, a language or an area of study.

Example: Jimmy, the band's lead guitarist, was an **autodidact**, who learned to play from watching YouTube videos.

Avoirdupois

Pronunciation: Av-ur-duh-poi   **Type**: Noun

Definition: A system of weights used widely in English-speaking countries, where a pound is equal to sixteen ounces.

Example: The grocer had never heard of **avoirdupois**, despite the fact that he weighed fruits on a daily basis.

Avuncular

Pronunciation: Ay-vun-cue-lah   **Type**: Adjective

Definition: Of, characterised by or relating to an uncle. By extension, the word has taken on a second meaning and can be used to describe anyone who's kind and friendly towards a younger or less experienced person.

Example: All of the employees got on with Terry because of his **avuncular** manner.

Axolotl

Pronunciation: Ax-ah-lot-tul   **Type**: Noun

Definition: A type of salamander, originally from Mexico. Axolotls are often used for scientific research because of their ability to regenerate limbs.

Example: Barry bought an **axolotl** from the pet shop, but his mother made him take it back because of her aversion to amphibians.

B

Baccalaureate

Pronunciation: Back-ka-loh-ree-ut   **Type**: Noun

Definition: An educational qualification attained upon completion of a bachelor's degree.

Example: After three years of drinking and studying, Laura finally received her **baccalaureate**.

Backwash

Pronunciation: Back-wash   **Type**: Noun, Verb

Definition: The result of drinking from a bottle. The backwash is the liquid that comes out of the mouth and goes back into the bottle, a mixture of the drink and the drinker's saliva. The verb refers to the act of drinking and allowing the backwash to return to the receptacle[†].

Example:
#1: Jeremy refused to take his lemonade back because it was full of Stephen's **backwash**.
#2: Before he handed him the drink, Jeremy said, "Make sure you don't **backwash**."

Bagatelle

Pronunciation: Bag-at-ell   **Type**: Noun

Definition: A game that's similar to billiards in which small balls are hit with a cue and allowed to roll down a sloping board. The aim is to knock them into holes that are numbered and guarded by wooden pins.

Example: The gentlemen retired to the games room to play **bagatelle** and smoke pipes beside the fireplace.

Baldrick

Pronunciation: Ball-drick   **Type**: Noun

Definition: A belt worn over the shoulder to support a sword by the hip.

Example: The warrior drew his sword from the **baldrick** and charged into battle.

Ballsy

Pronunciation: Ball-zee   **Type**: Adjective

Definition: Brave or daring.

Example: Tony Hawk won the championship with a **ballsy** kickflip.

Balustrade

Pronunciation: Bal-uss-trade   **Type**: Noun

Definition: A railing at the side of a staircase or a balcony that's designed to stop people from falling.

Example: Keith leant over the **balustrade** and waved at the people below.

Ballyhoo

Pronunciation: Ba-lee-hoo   **Type**: Noun, Verb

Definition: The noun refers to a type of publicity that praises something blatantly or sensationally. The verb refers to the action of making a fuss of something or to provide this type of publicity.

Example:
#1: Despite the **ballyhoo**, there was a disappointing turnout for the opening night.
#2: The newspapers promised to **ballyhoo** the singer's new album.

Bamboozle

Pronunciation: Bam-boo-zull   **Type**: Verb

Definition: To confuse or thwart someone, usually with a piece of clever trickery.

Example: I knew the hypnotist was trying to **bamboozle** me when he asked me to close my eyes and empty my wallet.

Banal

Pronunciation: Bah-narl   **Type**: Adjective

Definition: Lacking in originality or freshness; stale and boring.

Example: The non-conformist hated the **banal** pop music of the new millennium.

Banshee

Pronunciation: Ban-she   **Type**: Noun

Definition: A (usually) female spirit with an unearthly[†] wail that warns of impending† death.

Example: The old woman was so superstitious that when she heard the creaking of the eaves, she thought it was a **banshee**. She died three days later.

Banzai

Pronunciation: Banz-eye   **Type**: Adjective, Exclamation

Definition: Originating in Japan, the adjective describes a type of fierce and reckless charge, while the exclamation is used as a battle cry before such an attack.

Example:
#1: The Japanese soldiers fought back bravely with a **banzai** charge.
#2: Yoshiko shouted "**banzai!**" and ran towards the bully with his fists raised.

Bathos

Pronunciation: Bay-thos   **Type**: Noun

Definition: This noun is usually used to refer to a piece of literature or film. An unintentional anti-climax created by a sudden shift from the sublime† to the ridiculous.

Example: Jimmy was enjoying the movie until the character broke the fourth wall with bad exposition and **bathos**.

Bayou

Pronunciation: Bi-yew   **Type**: Noun

Definition: An American term for a low-lying expanse of water, typically home to a large population of fish, plankton and vegetation.

Example: In the summer, the flies flocked to the **bayou**.

Beatnik

Pronunciation: Beet-nick   **Type**: Noun

Definition: A member of a counter-culture movement from the 1950s that's closely associated with the beat generation of authors and poets. Beatniks are often considered to be the forerunners of hippies.

Example: Allen Ginsberg was a figurehead for the **beatnik** generation.

Belligerent

Pronunciation: Bil-ij-uh-runt   **Type**: Adjective

Definition: Hostile and aggressive; eager to fight.

Example: The patient's mood turned increasingly **belligerent** as the conversation continued, and the doctors knew they had to sedate him.

Benediction

Pronunciation: Ben-uh-dick-shun   **Type**: Noun

Definition: The bestowing of a blessing, particularly at the end of a religious service. It can also refer to the service itself.

Example: The church offered **benediction** to all comers.

Benzedrine

Pronunciation: Ben-zuh-dreen   **Type**: Noun

Definition: The trade name for a form of amphetamine, often used in an inhaler and colloquially referred to as "Bennies." Jack Kerouac and other key members of the beatnik[†] community were firm advocates of Benzedrine.

Example: Allegedly fuelled by **Benzedrine**, Jack Kerouac wrote *On the Road* in three weeks.

Benzene

Pronunciation: Ben-zeen   **Type**: Noun

Definition: A colourless, flammable liquid obtained from distilling petroleum.

Example: The water was unsafe to drink because it had been polluted by **benzene** from the industrial plant.

Besmirch

Pronunciation: Biss-murch   **Type**: Verb

Definition: Either to damage the reputation of something or to make something dirty or discoloured.

Example: Joe stopped taking heroin because he didn't want to **besmirch** the good name of his family.

Bibliobibuli

Pronunciation: Bib-lee-oh-bib-yoo-lie   **Type**: Noun

Definition: A person who reads too much.

Example: Dane is a **bibliobibuli** and has six bookcases full of books. He's read all of them, too.

Bigamy

Pronunciation: Big-am-ee   **Type**: Noun

Definition: The act of marrying someone while legally married to another person.

Example: Fred committed **bigamy** when he married Betty while still married to Wilma.

Billabong

Pronunciation: Bill-la-bong   **Type**: Noun

Definition: An Australian-English word meaning a small lake or pool.

Example: The explorer paused to refill his flask from the **billabong**.

Binge

Pronunciation: Binj   **Type**: Noun, Verb

Definition: To indulge heavily in or to overindulge in something, particularly after a period of abstinence. The noun refers to a session of binging. The verb is commonly used to refer to a session of heavy drinking or of watching episodes of a TV show back-to-back.

Example:
#1: Gerald put on half a stone because of his eating **binge**.
#2: I decided to **binge** the new season of *Stranger Things*.

Biorhythm

Pronunciation: By-oh-ri-thum   **Type**: Noun

Definition: A recurring cycle of activity or emotion in a living thing, such as the eat-drink-sleep-repeat cycle.

Example: Flying across the world upset Jamie's **biorhythm** and left him feeling jet-lagged.

Blackshirt

Pronunciation: Black-shirt   **Type**: Noun

Definition: A member of a fascist organisation, particularly the paramilitary group that was founded by Mussolini.

Example: The **blackshirt** murdered the socialist under cover of darkness.

Blag

Pronunciation: Blag   **Type**: Verb

Definition: The act of talking your way through or around a problem, particularly when feigning⁺ expertise in a subject that you have no prior knowledge of.

Example: Dave didn't think he'd get into the club, but he managed to **blag** his way past security.

Blurb

Pronunciation: Blurb   **Type**: Noun

Definition: A short section of descriptive text on the back of a book, DVD or CD that describes roughly what to expect inside.

Example: Juliet told everybody that her favourite book was *A Brief History of Time*, but she'd never got past the **blurb**.

Boatswain

Pronunciation: Boat-swayne   **Type**: Noun

Definition: A sailor in charge of the crew and supplies.

Example: The captain ordered the **boatswain** to make sure that nobody was missing before they set sail.

Bodge

Pronunciation: Bodge   **Type**: Verb

Definition: To complete a task, usually a construction or repair, with a low level of skill. The finished product is usually somewhat faulty or physically unattractive, but still usable. The process is often carried out quickly to provide a short-term fix. The term originally related specifically to woodworking and referred to a technique used in furniture making.

Example: The plumber quoted me £180, so I decided to **bodge** it myself.

Bodkin

Pronunciation: Bod-kin   **Type**: Noun

Definition: A small, blunt needle with a large eye, designed for pulling tape or thread through a hem.

Example: The tailor used his **bodkin** to thread elastic through the dress.

Bohemian

Pronunciation: Bo-hee-me-un   **Type**: Adjective

Definition: This adjective is used to describe someone who has an alternative lifestyle, not conforming to any of society's standards. Bohemian people usually mix and match fashions, tastes and interests, inventing new ones on the way.

Example: Oscar Wilde is probably the most famous **bohemian** to have lived.

Bolshevik

Pronunciation: Bol-shuv-ick   **Type**: Noun

Definition: A member of the Russian Social Democratic Party, which became the Communist Party after seizing power.

Example: Did you see the old **Bolshevik** who was spouting propaganda[†] in the park?

Bonhomie

Pronunciation: Bon-om-ee   **Type**: Noun

Definition: Cheerful cordiality, geniality or friendliness. From the French phrase "bon homme," meaning "good man."

Example: The students sat around the campfire singing songs in a state of **bonhomie**.

Bordello

Pronunciation: Bore-dell-oh   **Type**: Noun

Definition: An alternative name for a brothel.

Example: I can't wait to go to Amsterdam. My brother told me about a great **bordello**.

Bovine

Pronunciation: Bo-vine   **Type**: Adjective

Definition: Of or related to cows.
Example: Janice bit into the meat and said, "This tastes **bovine**."

Bowdlerise

Pronunciation: Bowd-luh-rise   **Type**: Verb

Definition: To remove text that's considered lewd[†] or profane, often to the detriment of the overall piece of work.

Example: I had to **bowdlerise** my first novel before my grandmother would read it.

Brachial

Pronunciation: Bray-key-ul   **Type**: Adjective

Definition: Of, similar to or related to the arm. This adjective is often used to describe something arm-shaped.

Example: The tree's **brachial** appendages[†] waved in the wind.

Braggart

Pronunciation: Brag-art   **Type**: Noun

Definition: A person who boasts about their skills or possessions; someone who likes to brag.

Example: Emily is such a **braggart**. She won't shut up about the pony that her parents bought her for Christmas.

Brevity

Pronunciation: Brev-it-ee   **Type**: Noun

Definition: The precise and concise use of words in language, either when writing or when speaking.

Example: Phillip was in demand as an after-dinner speaker because of his renowned **brevity**.

Brigantine

Pronunciation: Brig-an-teen   **Type**: Noun

Definition: A type of two-masted sailing ship.

Example: The **brigantine** was a favourite vessel of Mediterranean pirates.

Brilliantine

Pronunciation: Brill-ee-an-teen   **Type**: Noun

Definition: Scented oil used on men's hair (including beards and moustaches) to make it look glossy.

Example: It was hard to see the man's face through the shine of the **brilliantine** in his hair.

Brindled

Pronunciation: Brin-duld   **Type**: Adjective

Definition: A brownish-greyish colour, usually used to describe the patterned fur of animal coats.

Example: Jenny stroked the **brindled** fur of the Yorkshire Terrier.

Brobdingnagian

Pronunciation: Brob-ding-nag-ee-un   **Type**: Adjective, Noun

Definition: The adjective refers to anything that's huge or gigantic, while the noun describes a giant. The word stems from the land of Brobdingnag from *Gulliver's Travels* by Jonathan Swift. Opposite in meaning to Lilliputian[†].

Example:
#1: The building was **Brobdingnagian**. It took fifteen minutes to climb the stairs.
#2: Jill saw the **Brobdingnagian** and ran for her life.

Brogues

Pronunciation: Broe-gs   **Type**: Noun

Definition: A pair of strong shoes made from leather.

Example: I bought a new pair of **brogues** before the big presentation.

Brouhaha

Pronunciation: Brew-ha-ha   **Type**: Noun

Definition: A noisy commotion[†] or overexcited reaction in response to something.

Example: After Chelsea scored, the stewards struggled to deal with the **brouhaha** in the away team's stand.

Bunkum

Pronunciation: Bun-cum   **Type**: Noun

Definition: Nonsense.

Example: My grandfather kept talking **bunkum** at the family meal, and none of us knew what he was talking about.

Bourgeoisie

Pronunciation: Bur-shwah-zee   **Type**: Noun

Definition: The middle class.

Example: During the protest, the socialists chanted, "Down with the **bourgeoisie!**"

Byword

Pronunciation: By-word   **Type**: Noun

Definition: A word, expression or phrase that summarises either the characteristics of something or a person's beliefs or principles.

Example: Because of his inadequacies, the builder's name became a **byword** for clumsiness.

C

Capitulate

Pronunciation: Ca-pit-yoo-late   **Type**: Verb

Definition: To cease resistance to an unwelcome demand. Synonymic[†] with "surrender."

Example: The enemy soldier refused to **capitulate** and went down fighting.

Capricious

Pronunciation: Cap-rish-uss   **Type**: Adjective

Definition: Prone to sudden and inexplicable mood swings or erratic behaviour.

Example: Lola's **capricious** behaviour made it difficult for her to make friends.

Carapace

Pronunciation: Cah-rap-ace   **Type**: Noun

Definition: The hard upper shell of animals like turtles and tortoises or crustaceans.

Example: The old tortoise had paint stains on his **carapace**.

Caravanserai

Pronunciation: Cah-rav-ann-suh-rye   **Type**: Noun

Definition: An inn with a large courtyard designed to provide accommodation for caravans, often found in eastern countries such as Syria or Turkey.

Example: The tired merchants spent the night at the **caravanserai**.

Carcinogens

Pronunciation: Car-sin-oh-jens   **Type**: Noun

Definition: Substances that cause cancer in living tissue.

Example: Cigarette smoke is full of **carcinogens**.

Cartel

Pronunciation: Car-tell   **Type**: Noun

Definition: A group of manufacturers or suppliers who keep prices at artificially high levels, restricting competition and maximising profit.

Example: The **cartel** controlled the country's supply of the drug by forcefully limiting the competition.

Cartesian

Pronunciation: Car-tee-shun   **Type**: Adjective

Definition: Of or relating to Descartes and/or his ideas.

Example: Michael's philosophy coursework was often **Cartesian**.

Cartouche

Pronunciation: Car-toosh   **Type**: Noun

Definition: An oval enclosing a group of Ancient Egyptian hieroglyphs to represent the name and title of a monarch.

Example: The **cartouche** was supposed to protect the pharaoh[†] from evil spirits in life and death.

Cassock

Pronunciation: Cass-uck   **Type**: Noun

Definition: A full-length robe of a single colour, often black or grey, worn by the clerics of various churches.

Example: The priest murmured a prayer after spilling tea on his **cassock**.

Castrate

Pronunciation: Cass-trate   **Type**: Verb

Definition: To remove the testicles of a male animal or person.

Example: When her husband saw me, he shouted, "I'm going to **castrate** you when I catch you."

Catamite

Pronunciation: Cat-ah-mite   **Type**: Noun

Definition: A boy kept for homosexual practices. Stemming from Greek/Roman tradition, this noun is more commonly used to describe a man's younger male lover.

Example: Herbert was in love with Chris and wanted him to be his **catamite**.

Caterwaul

Pronunciation: Cat-ur-wall   **Type**: Verb

Definition: To make a shrill, wailing noise like the sound of a dying cat.

Example: We could barely hear the film over the **caterwaul** of the woman going into labour.

Catharsis

Pronunciation: Kath-arr-sis   **Type**: Noun

Definition: The process by which you purge negative repressed emotions by releasing them.

Example: The patient was completely changed after his **catharsis**. He opened up to his therapist and was able to start coming to terms with his trauma.

Cauterise

Pronunciation: Corr-ter-ize   **Type**: Verb

Definition: To burn or freeze tissue, usually for the purpose of a medical operation.

Example: When John lost his finger, the hospital had to **cauterise** the wound.

Cavalcade

Pronunciation: Ca-vul-cade   **Type**: Noun

Definition: A formal, often ceremonial procession of people who are either walking, on horseback or riding in vehicles.

Example: The villagers raised their caps as the **cavalcade** drove past.

Cedilla

Pronunciation: Sid-ill-la   **Type**: Noun

Definition: A small mark that's written under the letter 'C' to show that it has an 's' sound, rather than a 'k' sound. Cedillas are particularly common in French.

Example: The word "garçon" uses a **cedilla**.

Cenotaph

Pronunciation: Sen-oh-taff   **Type**: Noun

Definition: A monument, often in the form of a tomb, to someone who's buried elsewhere.

Example: Unveiled in 1953, the **cenotaph** is the centrepiece to the annual Remembrance Sunday service.

Cephalic

Pronunciation: Seff-al-ick   **Type**: Adjective

Definition: Of, in or related to the head.

Example: The potato looked **cephalic**.

Cerulean

Pronunciation: Suh-rule-ee-un   **Type**: Adjective

Definition: A deep blue colour.

Example: The beggar boy's **cerulean** eyes were as clear as the morning sky.

Chiminea

Pronunciation: Chim-in-ee-ah   **Type**: Noun

Definition: A self-standing fireplace for outdoor use, usually made of clay or terra cotta and with a vent or a chimney.

Example: It was cold at the barbecue, so Will lit the **chiminea** and the family gathered round.

Cimmerian

Pronunciation: Sim-air-ee-un   **Type**: Adjective, Noun

Definition: The adjective can be used to describe something dark and gloomy. The noun refers to a member of a mythological race who lived in darkness and mist near the land of the dead.

Example:
#1: The cave was **Cimmerian**, and Philip was scared to go near it.
#2: As she passed through the mist, she trembled at the sight of the Cimmerian.

Circumlocution

Pronunciation: Sir-cum-lo-cue-shun   **Type**: Noun

Definition: The use of more words than are strictly necessary, particularly in an attempt to be vague.

Example: The senator was guilty of **circumlocution** when he delivered his overly long lecture on the environment.

Clergy

Pronunciation: Clurr-jee   **Type**: Noun

Definition: The collection of people who have been sanctioned to carry out official duty within a religion, particularly the Catholic Church.

Example: The archbishop surveyed the members of the **clergy** and prepared to address them.

Coeliac

Pronunciation: See-lee-ack   **Type**: Noun

Definition: A sufferer of an autoimmune disorder of the small intestine that leads to an allergy to wheat and gluten.

Example: My dad's a **coeliac**, and he can't eat pizza.

Commotion

Pronunciation: Cum-oh-shun   **Type**: Noun

Definition: A state of noise and confusion.

Example: My parents came home in the middle of the party and wanted to know what the **commotion** was about.

Concept

Pronunciation: Kon-sept   **Type**: Noun

Definition: An abstract idea or general notion; the formation of something before the planning stage.

Example: Terry liked the **concept** of communism, but he didn't like how it worked in practice.

Concubine

Pronunciation: Con-cue-bine   **Type**: Noun

Definition: A female servant or slave who lives with a man but has a lower status than his wife or wives.

Example: The pharaoh[†] loved his wife, but not as much as his favourite **concubine**.

Congeal

Pronunciation: Con-jee-ul   **Type**: Verb

Definition: To coagulate or solidify, particularly by cooling.

Example: Sarah always washed up straight away, so that the food didn't **congeal** on the dishes.

Contumacy

Pronunciation: Con-choo-mass-ee   **Type**: Noun

Definition: A refusal to comply with authority, particularly when it comes in the form of a court order or summons.

Example: The dog used the carpet as a toilet with its usual **contumacy**, despite its owner's constant negative reinforcement.

Convolute

Pronunciation: Con-vo-loot   **Type**: Adjective

Definition: Rolled, twisted or curled up on itself.

Example: The leaf was **convolute** and wobbled in the wind.

Copywriter

Pronunciation: Cop-ee-rite-ur   **Type**: Noun

Definition: Someone who writes the text (or copy) for advertisements or publicity material.

Example: I graduated from university with a degree in English and ambitions to become a **copywriter**.

Coquette

Pronunciation: Kock-et   **Type**: Noun

Definition: A flirtatious woman.

Example: Josie was a **coquette** before I met her.

Corporeal

Pronunciation: Cor-por-ee-ul   **Type**: Adjective

Definition: This adjective is usually used to describe something with a physical body. It can also refer to something belonging to a body, particularly when opposed to the spirit or soul.

Example: The ghost was so **corporeal** that she thought it was a person.

Corrigible

Pronunciation: Coh-rij-ib-ull   **Type**: Adjective

Definition: Capable of being fixed, repaired, corrected, rectified or reformed.

Example: The judge believed the accused was a **corrigible** criminal and sentenced him to community work.

Corroborate

Pronunciation: Coh-rob-or-ate   **Type**: Verb

Definition: To supply new evidence that helps someone's argument, case or proposal.

Example: The witness's evidence helped to **corroborate** the defendant's story.

Coterie

Pronunciation: Ko-tuh-ree   **Type**: Noun

Definition: A small, exclusive group of people with shared tastes or interests.

Example: The Harry Potter fans formed a **coterie** in the playground.

Countenance

Pronunciation: Count-uh-nunce   **Type**: Noun

Definition: A person's face or expression – synonymic[†] with visage[†].

Example: Janet pretended to be happy, but her **countenance** betrayed her true feelings.

Coup d'état

Pronunciation: Coo Deh-tah   **Type**: Noun

Definition: A sudden unconstitutional removal and replacement of a government, usually with force from a small group inside the establishment such as the military.

Example: The citizens were worried about what would happen when the new government took over after the **coup d'état**.

Cowcatcher

Pronunciation: Cow-cat-chur   **Type**: Noun

Definition: A metal frame attached to the front of a train or tram to prevent it from killing a large animal like a cow or a sheep. Usually angled, the device pushes the animals (and other obstacles) away from the line.

Example: Doris was interrupted mid-chew by the **cowcatcher** on the front of the steam train, which nudged her off the tracks and back towards the field.

Crampon

Pronunciation: Cram-pon   **Type**: Noun

Definition: A plate of spikes that's fixed to a boot to help the wearer to traverse difficult terrain like ice or rock.

Example: Sir Edmund Hillary asked Santa for a new **crampon** for his next trip up the mountain.

Creed

Pronunciation: Kreed   **Type**: Noun

Definition: A statement of the beliefs or attitudes that guide someone's actions.

Example: The barbarians were fearless enemies: they followed the **creed** of victory or death.

Crenellate

Pronunciation: Kren-ul-ate   **Type**: Verb

Definition: To provide a wall with battlements.

Example: During the war, the duke decided to **crenellate** his fortress.

Crepitate

Pronunciation: Krep-it-ate   **Type**: Verb

Definition: To make a crackling sound, like the sound of electricity.

Example: The phone line began to **crepitate** as the rain built up and the line went dead.

Crepuscular

Pronunciation: Kri-pus-cu-la   **Type**: Adjective

Definition: Of, resembling or related to twilight.

Example: The **crepuscular** moon hovered on the horizon as the sun began to set.

Cretin

Pronunciation: Creh-tin   **Type**: Noun

Definition: A stupid, slow, uneducated person.

Example: Adam's never read *To Kill a Mockingbird*. He's such a **cretin**.

Crotchety

Pronunciation: Crot-che-tee   **Type**: Adjective

Definition: Irritable.

Example: The **crotchety** old man at Number Twelve won't give me my ball back.

Crud

Pronunciation: Krud   **Type**: Noun

Definition: Any substance that's considered disgusting or unpleasant, typically because of its dirtiness and potential threat to hygiene.

Example: The housemates all helped to keep the place clean, but no one was willing to tackle the **crud** under the sink.

Cuboid

Pronunciation: Kyoo-boyd   **Type**: Adjective, Noun

Definition: The adjective describes something that's cuboid in shape, while the noun refers to the shape itself. A cuboid is a solid shape with six rectangular faces at right angles to each other.

Example:
#1: The soap had a **cuboid** shape and smelled of lavender.
#2: The mathematician picked up the **cuboid** and stared at it.

Cudgel

Pronunciation: Cuj-ul   **Type**: Noun, Verb

Definition: The noun describes a short, heavy stick that's used as a weapon, while the verb refers to the act of beating someone with such a weapon.

Example:
#1: The assassin raised his **cudgel** and brought it down heavily on his target's skull.
#2: The protesters claimed that the police had tried to **cudgel** them into submission with their truncheons.

Cul-de-sac

Pronunciation: Kull-de-sack   **Type**: Noun

Definition: Originally meaning "bottom of bag" in French, this term is now applied to a residential dead end with one combined entrance and exit.

Example: The car pulled into the **cul-de-sac** and parked in front of a garage.

Cummerbund

Pronunciation: Cum-er-bund   **Type**: Noun

Definition: A type of belt or sash that's worn around the waist, usually as part of a male's formal evening dress.

Example: "Martha!" cried George. "Bring me my **cummerbund**. I don't want to be late for the wedding."

Curmudgeon

Pronunciation: Cur-muj-ee-un   **Type**: Noun

Definition: A person with a bad temper.

Example: When I joined the darts team, they warned me not to talk to Old John, the **curmudgeon**.

Cushy

Pronunciation: Cush-ee   **Type**: Adjective

Definition: The exact meaning of this word depends upon its usage. It can refer to something that's easy, comfortable or both.

Example: John has a **cushy** new job where he gets to fly off to California every month.

Cutaneous

Pronunciation: Cue-tay-nee-uss   **Type**: Adjective

Definition: Of, related to or directly affecting the skin.

Example: Melissa impressed everyone when she got the job as a scientist at the Centre for **Cutaneous** Research, specialising in melanomas.

Cyberflâneur

Pronunciation: Cy-bur-flan-urr   **Type**: Noun

Definition: A person who idly surfs the internet for pleasure.

Example: The **cyberflâneur** quickly found himself joining web forums and signing up for social networking sites.

Cymric

Pronunciation: Sim-rick   **Type**: Adjective, Noun

Definition: The adjective is used to describe anything Welsh or with a strong tie or connection to the country. As a noun, it refers to the Welsh language.

Example:
#1: The Dragon Inn, with its Welsh flags and dishes, was Glynn's favourite

Cymric pub.
#2: Glynn was Welsh through and through and could only speak **Cymric**.

Cynosure

Pronunciation: Sine-oh-shore   **Type**: Noun

Definition: Someone or something that's the centre of attention.

Example: At the wedding, the bride's dress was a **cynosure**.

D

Dais

Pronunciation: Day-iss   **Type**: Noun

Definition: A raised platform that's often fitted with seats and designed to be occupied by a person or a group of people of importance.

Example: The visiting dignitary took his place on the **dais** and prepared to watch the ceremony.

Dandy

Pronunciation: Dan-dee   **Type**: Adjective, Noun

Definition: The adjective is used to describe a man who's devoted to style and fashion, particularly in dress and appearance. The noun is used to refer directly to such a man.

Example:
#1: The **dandy** gentleman was overdressed in a top hat and tails.
#2: The **dandy** paid a visit to the city for a new suit.

Dapper

Pronunciation: Dap-per   **Type**: Adjective

Definition: This adjective is usually used to describe a man who's neat in dress and appearance and who possesses a gentlemanly bearing.

Example: "You're looking **dapper** tonight," said Sanchez, pleased to see his friend had made an effort with his appearance.

Dastard

Pronunciation: Das-turd   **Type**: Noun

Definition: A despicable person; someone dishonourable and disgusting.

Example: Captain Hook is the most well-known **dastard** in children's literature.

Dauphin

Pronunciation: Doh-fan   **Type**: Noun

Definition: A title held by the eldest son of the king of France.

Example: Louis-Antoine, eldest son of Charles X, was the last **dauphin** of France.

Dearth

Pronunciation: Durth   **Type**: Noun

Definition: A lack of something; vaguely synonymic[†] with deficiency.

Example: They couldn't convict the criminal because of the **dearth** of evidence.

Debauchery

Pronunciation: Di-baw-chuh-ree   **Type**: Noun

Definition: An excessive indulgence in pleasures of the senses, particularly for long periods of time. Often associated with alcohol use and sexual activity.

Example: Captain Jack Sparrow has had his fair share of **debauchery**.

Debonair

Pronunciation: Deh-bun-air   **Type**: Adjective

Definition: Usually used to describe a man, this adjective depicts[†] the combined qualities of confidence, charm and style.

Example: When Thomas walked into the room, all the women were taken with him because he was so debonair.

Debris

Pronunciation: Day-bree   **Type**: Noun

Definition: Fragments of material, found naturally or as the remnants of something that's been shattered or destroyed.

Example: As the asteroid broke apart in the atmosphere, the Earth was pelted by falling **debris**.

Decay

Pronunciation: Di-kay   **Type**: Noun, Verb

Definition: The noun refers to organic matter that's rotted or decomposed due to bacteria, while the verb refers to the process of decomposition.

Example:
#1: The dentist said to his patient, "It looks like you have tooth **decay**."
#2: The researchers studied how long it took the body to **decay**.

Decompose

Pronunciation: Dee-comp-oze   **Type**: Verb

Definition: This verb is synonymic[†] with decay[†] and is usually used to describe the process by which the dead body of an organism starts to rot.

Example: The human body starts to **decompose** after burial, so you might as well donate your organs.

Décolletage

Pronunciation: Day-coll-et-tardge   **Type**: Noun

Definition: The upper part of a woman's body between her waist and her neck, specifically the part of it which is exposed and accentuated by her style of clothing. The noun can also be used to refer to a low-cut neckline on a woman's dress which emphasises her cleavage.

Example: When Janet went out in the evenings, the men could hardly keep their eyes off her **décolletage**.

Décor

Pronunciation: Day-core   **Type**: Noun

Definition: The decoration, furnishing and general appearance of a place, particularly a room or a stage.

Example: Gemma loved the location of the bungalow but wasn't convinced about the **décor**.

Defecate

Pronunciation: Def-fur-kate   **Type**: Verb

Definition: The act of expelling faeces through the bowels and anus.

Example: The greasy food made Terry need to **defecate**.

Defenestration

Pronunciation: De-fen-uss-tray-shun   **Type**: Noun

Definition: The act of throwing something out of or through a window.

Example: "That's the third **defenestration** in this book," Dane said. "It's like he only enters rooms through windows."

Deleterious

Pronunciation: Del-eh-tee-ree-uss   **Type**: Adjective

Definition: Capable of causing harm or damage.

Example: Smoking cigarettes is **deleterious** to your health.

Delinquent

Pronunciation: De-lin-kwunt   **Type**: Adjective, Noun

Definition: The adjective is used to describe the behaviour of a youngster who has a tendency to break the law, particularly by committing minor crimes. The noun refers to someone who exhibits this behaviour.

Example:
#1: The children showed they were **delinquent** by stealing sweets from the tuck shop.
#2: The young **delinquent** was caught breaking into a house.

Demagogue

Pronunciation: Dem-ag-og   **Type**: Noun

Definition: A political leader who tries to gather support by appealing to popular desires, biases or prejudices, rather than with rational argument.

Example: Nick Griffin's scare tactics as the leader of the BNP established him as the foremost **demagogue** in the country.

Dendrochronology

Pronunciation: Den-dro-kron-ol-oh-gee   **Type**: Noun

Definition: The science of dating things, including environmental change and historical artefacts, based on the rings that form inside the trunks of trees.

Example: The historians resorted to **dendrochronology** to date the shield.

Denouement

Pronunciation: Di-noo-mon   **Type**: Noun

Definition: The final part of a narrative in which the different parts of the plot are pulled together, paving the way for a resolution.

Example: Frodo and Sam's adventure came to a climactic **denouement** as Frodo attempted to rid himself of the ring.

Depict

Pronunciation: Dip-ict   **Type**: Verb

Definition: To show something through an art form.

Example: Howard wasn't sure how to **depict** Sir Arthur Conan Doyle in his piece of historical fiction.

Depravity

Pronunciation: Dip-rav-it-ee   **Type**: Noun

Definition: Extreme moral corruption or a wicked, immoral act.

Example: The enemy soldiers sunk to a new level of **depravity** when they started removing the faces of their enemies.

Desideratum

Pronunciation: Des-id-ur-ate-um   **Type**: Noun

Definition: Something that's desired, needed or wanted.

Example: After a long day at work, a pint of lager was Josh's **desideratum**.

Destitute

Pronunciation: Dess-tich-oot   **Type**: Adjective

Definition: Without the means to look after oneself; lacking food, water, clothing or shelter.

Example: The **destitute** woman took to shoplifting to feed her family.

Desuetude

Pronunciation: Deh-swuh-chood   **Type**: Noun

Definition: A state of abandonment and disuse.

Example: After the emergency services were relocated, the old fire station fell into **desuetude**.

Detritivore

Pronunciation: De-try-ti-vor   **Type**: Noun

Definition: Any organic life form that survives by absorbing nutrients from decaying[†] plant and animal parts, contributing to the decomposition cycle.

Example: The worm is a natural **detritivore**, helping to turn plant matter into compost.

Detritus

Pronunciation: De-try-tuss   **Type**: Noun

Definition: Synonymic[†] with waste and debris[†]; a collection of solid material brought together arbitrarily.

Example: After falling over, Billy brushed the fine **detritus** from his knees and climbed back on his bicycle.

Deucedly

Pronunciation: Jew-sid-lee   **Type**: Adverb

Definition: This adverb is used to describe something extreme and has a similar meaning to devilishly.

Example: The exam paper was **deucedly** hard.

Diacritics

Pronunciation: Die-ack-rit-icks   **Type**: Noun

Definition: Symbols or marks that are added to letters to change the way they sound.

Example: The characters á, í, ó, ú, ý, and ø all have **diacritics**.

Dieresis

Pronunciation: Die-uh-ree-siss   **Type**: Noun

Definition: A linguistic occurrence where two adjacent vowels are pronounced in separate syllables with no intervening consonant.

Example: The words hiatus and **dieresis** are examples of **dieresis**.

Diatribe

Pronunciation: Die-at-ribe   **Type**: Noun

Definition: A long and forceful verbal or written attack.

Example: The mistress penned a **diatribe** against the widow to be read at the funeral.

Dichotomy

Pronunciation: Die-kot-oh-mee   **Type**: Noun

Definition: The splitting of something into two separate parts which are mutually exclusive. To choose one option rules the other one out.

Example: Phillip puzzled over Hamlet's **dichotomy** – "to be or not to be," that was the question.

Digraph

Pronunciation: Die-graff   **Type**: Noun

Definition: A linguistic occurrence whereby two characters or letters are placed side by side to represent a single sound.

Example: The combinations 'sh', 'th' and 'ch' are examples of the **digraph**.

Dilapidated

Pronunciation: Dill-app-id-ate-id   **Type**: Adjective

Definition: This adjective is used to describe buildings, sites or objects that are worn down or in a state of disrepair.

Example: The door hung off the hinges of the **dilapidated** shed.

Dilettante

Pronunciation: Dil-let-ant-ee   **Type**: Noun

Definition: A person who claims a certain level of expertise and interest in a subject without having any prior knowledge of it. This noun is occasionally used derogatorily to refer to an amateur.

Example: Alex claimed to be a fan of Graham Greene's work, but he hasn't read any of his books. He's such a **dilettante**.

Dionysian

Pronunciation: Die-on-ee-shun   **Type**: Adjective

Definition: Characterised by or relating to the Greek god Dionysus. This adjective is often used to refer to the sensual, emotional and spontaneous aspects of human nature.

Example: Harry quit his job and built a **Dionysian** sex dungeon.

Diphthong

Pronunciation: Diff-thong   **Type**: Noun

Definition: A sound that's formed by combining two vowels into a single syllable.

Example: The vowel sounds in 'loud', 'loin' and 'lean' are examples of the **diphthong**.

Dipsomania

Pronunciation: Dip-so-may-nee-ah   **Type**: Noun

Definition: Alcoholism.

Example: The beggar with **dipsomania** always had a bottle in his hand.

Dirigible

Pronunciation: Dih-rij-ib-ul   **Type**: Adjective, Noun

Definition: The adjective can be used to refer to a floating object that's capable of being steered. The noun describes an aircraft of this type.

Example:
#1: The **dirigible** blimp was remote-controlled, and Jerry flew it around the office.
#2: The couple climbed aboard the **dirigible** and flew to Paris.

Discography

Pronunciation: Diss-cog-raff-ee   **Type**: Noun

Definition: A collection of all the recordings by a band or artist. This can either be a physical collection or a digital collection on a computer or mp3 player.

Example: For Christmas, Alice got the Jefferson Airplane **discography**.

Discombobulated

Pronunciation: Diss-com-bob-yoo-late-id   **Type**: Adjective

Definition: Confused or disconcerted.

Example: Gary was too **discombobulated** to concentrate on the test.

Disconsolate

Pronunciation: Diss-con-suh-lut   **Type**: Adjective

Definition: Without consolation or comfort.

Example: John was **disconsolate** after his mother died.

Discord

Pronunciation: Diss-kord   **Type**: Noun

Definition: A disagreement between two or more people.

Example: The marital **discord** was obvious when Peter and Jenny danced together.

Discrepancy

Pronunciation: Diss-crep-un-see   **Type**: Noun

Definition: A lack of compatibility or a conflict between two statements that are both presumed to be facts.

Example: Matt noticed a **discrepancy** when he checked the results of his experiments and quickly realised that one of them had been carried out incorrectly.

Discursive

Pronunciation: Diss-cur-siv   **Type**: Adjective

Definition: This adjective is used to describe a piece of speech or writing which digresses or switches rapidly from subject to subject.

Example: It was hard to follow the **discursive** essay, and the academic quickly gave up on it.

Distrain

Pronunciation: Diss-trane   **Type**: Verb

Definition: To seize property or possessions to ensure that any money owed is repaid.

Example: Jeannie's ex-husband had to **distrain** her car to get his child support.

Diuretic

Pronunciation: Die-ur-et-ick   **Type**: Adjective, Noun

Definition: The adjective refers to the ability of something to increase the flow of urine, while the noun refers to a drug that has this effect.

Example:
#1: The **diuretic** drink helped the young woman to pass water.
#2: The doctor prescribed a common **diuretic** to help Phillip with his "problem".

Dodecahedron

Pronunciation: Doh-deck-ah-he-dron   **Type**: Noun

Definition: A three-dimensional shape with twelve faces.

Example: Carl bought a silver **dodecahedron** because he needed a new 12-sided die for Dungeons & Dragons.

Dogma

Pronunciation: Dog-ma   **Type**: Noun

Definition: Something laid down by an authority figure as irreversibly true. The technique is often used by oppressive religions or political tyrants.

Example: David became an atheist because he could no longer put up with religious **dogma**.

Doldrums

Pronunciation: Doll-drums   **Type**: Noun

Definition: Low morale or a feeling of boredom, stagnation and depression.

Example: Bored with his life, Jack had a case of the **doldrums** and made a New Year's resolution to do more in the coming year.

Dolorifuge

Pronunciation: Doll-or-if-yooj   **Type**: Noun

Definition: A pain-killer.

Example: The patient was begging for a **dolorifuge** to ease his chronic pain.

Dolorous

Pronunciation: Doll-uh-rus   **Type**: Adjective

Definition: Sorrowful.

Example: After Kristy's father died, her eyes grew **dolorous**.

Dosser

Pronunciation: Doss-ur **Type**: Noun

Definition: Someone who doesn't have a proper job and who survives on the kindness of others. Often on the dole, a typical dosser doesn't contribute to society and lives to laze around.

Example: Stephen's been on the dole for five years and hasn't even tried to get a job – what a **dosser**.

Dotage

Pronunciation: Doh-tij **Type**: Noun

Definition: The period of life in which people are intellectually or physically impaired due to old age.

Example: I'm going to become rich and famous to look after my mother in her **dotage**.

Doyen

Pronunciation: Doy-en **Type**: Noun

Definition: The most prominent, iconic or well-respected person in a particular field.

Example: Allen Ginsberg is the **doyen** of beat poetry.

Draconian

Pronunciation: Drack-oh-nee-un   **Type**: Adjective

Definition: Excessively harsh or severe. This adjective is usually used to describe rules and laws or the punishments for breaking them.

Example: The **draconian** legal system sentenced Jamie to six months in jail for a tweet.

Dram

Pronunciation: Dram   **Type**: Noun

Definition: A small measure of whiskey or any other alcoholic spirit.

Example: Laura had a **dram** of whiskey to ward off the winter cold.

Dressage

Pronunciation: Dress-arge   **Type**: Noun

Definition: The art of training a horse to obey the rider.

Example: Zoe blew off steam at the weekend by visiting the stables and practising **dressage**.

Dubious

Pronunciation: Jew-be-uss   **Type**: Adjective

Definition: Unconvincing – of doubtful quality or origin.

Example: As they were unable to discover where it came from, the new evidence was deemed **dubious** and inadmissible.

Dulcet

Pronunciation: Dull-sit   **Type**: Adjective

Definition: Soothing or calming.

Example: I fell asleep listening to the **dulcet** sound of Stephen Fry reading *Harry Potter and the Goblet of Fire*.

Dysphasia

Pronunciation: Diss-faze-ee-a   **Type**: Noun

Definition: A language disorder that leads to speech difficulties and problems comprehending the speech of others. Dysphasia is usually brought on by brain disease or damage.

Example: After his stroke, Stephen developed **dysphasia** and had difficulty communicating.

E

Ebullient

Pronunciation: Ee-bull-ee-unt   **Type**: Adjective

Definition: Happy and lively; full of energy.

Example: When Janice learned that she'd passed her exams, she was **ebullient**.

Echelon

Pronunciation: Esh-uh-lon   **Type**: Noun

Definition: A level or rank in an (often military) organisation.

Example: Gary was promoted to a higher **echelon**.

Eclampsia

Pronunciation: Ek-lamp-see-ah   **Type**: Noun

Definition: A medical condition in which a pregnant woman with high blood pressure suffers from convulsions. These convulsions can be followed by a coma and even death, posing a threat to the health of both the mother and the child.

Example: Jimmy panicked when his pregnant wife was taken to hospital with **eclampsia**.

Edict

Pronunciation: Ee-dickt   **Type**: Noun

Definition: An official decree, order or proclamation by a high office.

Example: King Charles's **edict** forced all citizens to eat potatoes on a Tuesday.

Effervescent

Pronunciation: Eff-ur-vess-unt   **Type**: Adjective

Definition: This adjective means "bubbly" and is usually used to describe a liquid.

Example: The sparkling wine was **effervescent**.

Effete

Pronunciation: Eff-eet   **Type**: Adjective

Definition: Ineffectual or marked by weakness and decadence; no longer capable of taking positive and effective action.

Example: The gentleman was **effete** and had never worked a day in his life.

Efficacious

Pronunciation: Eff-ick-ay-shuss   **Type**: Adjective

Definition: Effective.

Example: The cream was **efficacious** at curing acne.

Effluvium

Pronunciation: Eff-loo-vee-um   **Type**: Noun

Definition: An unpleasant and often harmful smell or discharge.

Example: Janet's daughter was taken ill after coming into contact with **effluvium**.

Egalitarian

Pronunciation: Ee-gal-it-air-ee-un   **Type**: Adjective, Noun

Definition: The adjective can be used to describe anything that's related to the idea that everyone's created equal. The noun refers to a person who supports and believes in this principle.

Example:
#1: Sarah believed in the **egalitarian** idea that job vacancies should be filled on individual merit, rather than by race or creed[†].
#2: Because of her beliefs, Sarah was an **egalitarian**.

Egregious

Pronunciation: Ee-gree-jee-uss   **Type**: Adjective

Definition: Extraordinary in some way, usually by being either conspicuously bad or outstandingly good.

Example: During the recital, the pianist made an **egregious** error and the orchestra had to start all over again.

Ekphrasis

Pronunciation: Eck-frass-iss   **Type**: Noun

Definition: A literary or artistic technique whereby something is translated from one medium to another. Examples include a painting of a story, a poem about a sculpture or a song about a film.

Example: Harry's lecturer said his painting of Ginsberg's *Howl* was a masterful piece of **ekphrasis**.

El Dorado

Pronunciation: El Duh-rard-oh   **Type**: Noun

Definition: A fictional place of wealth and prosperity, sought in South America by colonial explorers.

Example: Mr. Bates searched for **El Dorado** for forty years and died destitute and disappointed.

Eldritch

Pronunciation: El-dritch   **Type**: Adjective

Definition: Occult – magical and eerie.

Example: The old woman's cottage was filled with **eldritch** symbols and strange instruments.

Elegy

Pronunciation: El-uh-jee   **Type**: Noun

Definition: A piece of creative work, often a poem or a piece of music, with a mournful style and tone. Elegies are usually created as a lament for the dead and shouldn't be confused with eulogies.

Example: When Ian died, Peter wrote a poem as an **elegy**.

Elision

Pronunciation: El-iz-yun   **Type**: Noun

Definition: An omission, particularly the omission of a sound or a syllable during speech.

Example: 'O'er the hills' is an example of **elision**.

Elocution

Pronunciation: El-oh-cue-shun   **Type**: Noun

Definition: The art and skill of expressing oneself with clear speech, particularly when using clean and distinct pronunciation and articulation.

Example: Luan is an **elocution** expert who teaches his clients to deliver speeches and presentations effectively.

Eloquence

Pronunciation: El-oh-kwunce   **Type**: Noun

Definition: The art of persuasive speech or writing.

Example: The orator addressed her audience with typical **eloquence**.

Elysian

Pronunciation: Ill-iz-yun   **Type**: Adjective

Definition: This adjective is used to describe any idyllic[†] representation of the afterlife.

Example: When Karen died, her soul travelled to the **Elysian** Fields.

Emaciated

Pronunciation: Im-may-see-ate-id   **Type**: Adjective

Definition: Extremely frail and thin, particularly from cold or hunger.

Example: The beggar boy was so **emaciated** that I could see his ribcage through his T-shirt.

Embargo

Pronunciation: Im-bar-go   **Type**: Noun, Verb

Definition: An official ban on trade with a particular country. In journalism and public relations circles, it can also describe a ban on releasing information before a certain date or time.

Example: The journalist knew all about the takeover, but he couldn't tell anyone because of the **embargo**.

Emeritus

Pronunciation: Ee-meh-rit-uss   **Type**: Adjective

Definition: This adjective is used to refer to a title or position, particularly that of a professor, when it's kept as an honour after retirement.

Example: The dean stood up and announced, "We're pleased to welcome Mr. John Darby, **Emeritus** Professor of Geology."

Émigré

Pronunciation: Em-ig-ray   **Type**: Noun

Definition: A person who has emigrated, leaving one country to settle in and live in another.

Example: The **émigré** struggled to get on the career ladder in America and ended up working at a bowling alley.

Emporium

Pronunciation: Emp-or-ee-um   **Type**: Noun

Definition: A large shop selling a variety of goods.

Example: I spent way too much money in the **emporium**.

Encapsulate

Pronunciation: In-caps-yoo-late   **Type**: Verb

Definition: To enclose or capture something, as if inside a capsule.

Example: It was difficult, but the photographer managed to **encapsulate** everything his client represented in the photograph.

Endemic

Pronunciation: En-dem-ick   **Type**: Adjective, Noun

Definition: The adjective is used to describe a disease or condition that occurs often in a particular geographic location but that's rarely found outside of it. The noun refers to such a condition.

Example:
#1: The **endemic** disease spread quickly through the people of Nigeria.
#2: The World Health Organisation was keeping a close eye on the spread of the **endemic**.

Enema

Pronunciation: En-uh-ma   **Type**: Noun

Definition: The process of injecting a liquid or gas into the rectum[†], either to clean it or to introduce drugs into the system. The noun is also the name of a device that's designed to carry out the procedure.

Example: Melissa was supposed to go to the hospital for an **enema**, but she wasn't looking forward to it.

Enervate

Pronunciation: En-ur-vate   **Type**: Verb

Definition: The act of making someone feel drained of energy.

Example: The fundraiser knew that the marathon would **enervate** him, but it was worth it to raise money for a good cause.

Enhancement

Pronunciation: In-hance-munt   **Type**: Noun

Definition: Something that improves an object or a process.

Example: Billy used Adobe Photoshop when his photographs needed **enhancement**.

Ennui

Pronunciation: En-wee   **Type**: Noun

Definition: A feeling of weariness and discontent resulting from boredom.

Example: Jason doesn't go to lectures anymore because of his unending **ennui**.

Entrails

Pronunciation: En-tray-ulls   **Type**: Noun

Definition: The intestines or internal organs of a person or animal, particularly when they've been removed or exposed.

Example: The horror film was unsuitable for children because of the gore and **entrails**.

Enunciate

Pronunciation: Ee-nun-see-ate   **Type**: Verb

Definition: This verb refers to the action of pronouncing something clearly.

Example: Pierre speaks limited English. You have to **enunciate** so he can understand you.

Epaulette

Pronunciation: Ep-all-et   **Type**: Noun

Definition: A shoulder adornment used to signify rank in military organisations.

Example: After the Burmese campaign, the soldier was rewarded with an **epaulette** of a higher rank.

Ephemera

Pronunciation: If-em-uh-ra   **Type**: Noun

Definition: Things that exist for a short period of time.

Example: As he aged, Stanley watched the **ephemera** come and go.

Epidermis

Pronunciation: Ep-id-ur-miss   **Type**: Noun

Definition: The outer layer of an animal's skin.

Example: The paper sliced through her **epidermis** and made Marissa cry.

Epilepsy

Pronunciation: Ep-ill-ep-see   **Type**: Noun

Definition: A neurological disorder that's characterised by recurring bouts of convulsions, loss of consciousness or sensory disturbance, often caused by flashing lights.

Example: Pauline was diagnosed with **epilepsy** and wasn't allowed to take her driving test for fear that she might have a seizure behind the wheel.

Epiphanic

Pronunciation: Ep-if-an-ick   **Type**: Adjective

Definition: This adjective is used to describe something that possesses the quality of an epiphany. An epiphany is the sudden manifestation of a divine being or a moment of revelation or insight.

Example: The old statue at the back of the museum seemed to speak to Sean in a moment of **epiphanic** clarity.

Episcopal

Pronunciation: Ip-iss-co-pull   **Type**: Adjective

Definition: Of, characterised by or related to bishops.

Example: The **Episcopal** Church opens its doors to tourists for the first time on Monday.

Episiotomy

Pronunciation: Ep-iz-ee-ot-oh-me   **Type**: Noun

Definition: A surgical cut made at the opening of the vagina. This medical procedure aims to ease the delivery of children and to prevent tissue damage.

Example: An **episiotomy** was necessary to aid in the baby's delivery.

Epistemology

Pronunciation: Ep-ist-uh-mol-oh-gee   **Type**: Noun

Definition: The theory and practice of studying knowledge to justify beliefs.

Example: Joe was a practitioner of **epistemology** and didn't believe in a god because of the lack of evidence.

Epitaph

Pronunciation: Ep-it-aff   **Type**: Noun

Definition: A (usually short) phrase or statement written in memory of the dead, usually in the form of an inscription on a tombstone.

Example: John's **epitaph** read, "I told you I was sick."

Equinoctial

Pronunciation: Eck-win-ock-tee-ul   **Type**: Adjective

Definition: Occurring during an equinox[†] or relating to the concept[†] of an equal day and night.

Example: The **equinoctial** winds blew hard against the sails of the merchant ship.

Equinox

Pronunciation: Ek-win-ox   **Type**: Noun

Definition: An **equinox** occurs twice a year when the day and night are of equal length.

Example: Billy didn't agree with the Gregorian calendar. He thought the New Year should start on the Winter **Equinox**.

Erogenous

Pronunciation: Ih-roj-in-uss   **Type**: Adjective

Definition: This adjective is used to describe a part of the body that's sensitive to sexual stimulation.

Example: Phyllis loves it when her boyfriend massages her **erogenous** zones.

Erudite

Pronunciation: Eh-rud-ite   **Type**: Adjective

Definition: Displaying or exemplified by a large amount of knowledge, learning or intellect.

Example: The professor's speech was **erudite** and well-rehearsed.

Escritoire

Pronunciation: Ess-crit-wahr   **Type**: Noun

Definition: A small writing desk with drawers and compartments.

Example: The poet sat down at the **escritoire** and began to work on his manuscript.

Escutcheon

Pronunciation: Ess-cutch-un   **Type**: Noun

Definition: A shield or shield-shaped emblem that bears a coat of arms.

Example: The nobleman's **escutcheon** proudly displayed two lions and a lance.

Esperanto

Pronunciation: Ess-puh-rant-oh   **Type**: Noun

Definition: An artificial language that was created with the intention of making communication universal.

Example: Despite high initial hopes, **Esperanto** is rarely spoken.

Ethos

Pronunciation: Ee-thoss   **Type**: Noun

Definition: The mental and spiritual characteristics of a culture as demonstrated through its beliefs, goals and desires.

Example: Flower power formed the basis of the hippie **ethos**.

Etiolate

Pronunciation: Ee-tee-oh-late   **Type**: Verb

Definition: This verb refers to the act of growing a plant in the darkness, causing it to develop without chlorophyll.

Example: The botanist decided to see what would happen if he tried to **etiolate** the tropical plant, so he locked it in a cupboard.

Etymology

Pronunciation: Et-im-ol-oh-gee   **Type**: Noun

Definition: This noun is used to refer to the origin of a word and the way that it developed over time. It can also describe the study of this area of linguistics.

Example: The English professor was interested in **etymology** and loved to discover archaic[†] spellings.

Eucharist

Pronunciation: Yoo-ka-rist   **Type**: Noun

Definition: A Christian ceremony that commemorates the Last Supper by consecrating and consuming bread and wine. The bread represents the body of Christ, while the wine represents his blood.

Example: As a devout Catholic, Holly celebrated the **Eucharist** every Sunday.

Euphemism

Pronunciation: Yoo-fum-iz-um   **Type**: Noun

Definition: A euphemism occurs when someone uses an innocent word or phrase to refer to something more explicit, often something that's considered to be profane, lewd†, unpleasant or embarrassing.

Example: When John asked Lucy if she wanted to nibble on his turkey stick, she wondered if it was a **euphemism**.

Evanescent

Pronunciation: Ev-an-ess-unt   **Type**: Adjective

Definition: Quickly fading out of sight, memory or existence.

Example: To make sure that no one saw her, the ghost became **evanescent** when she heard people coming.

Eviscerate

Pronunciation: Iv-iss-ur-ate   **Type**: Verb

Definition: This verb refers to the act of removing the guts and intestines of an animal.

Example: The marauders† used kukri† knives to **eviscerate** the villagers.

Evocative

Pronunciation: Iv-ock-at-iv   **Type**: Adjective

Definition: Capable of bringing back memories or conjuring strong images or feelings.

Example: John's paintings were **evocative** of death and war.

Exacerbate

Pronunciation: Ekks-ass-ur-bate   **Type**: Verb

Definition: When you exacerbate something, you make a problem worse.

Example: Scratching the insect bite was enough to **exacerbate** the wound.

Exaltation

Pronunciation: Ekks-all-tay-shun   **Type**: Noun

Definition: The act of giving praise.

Example: The priest retired from his **exaltation** to read the newspaper.

Exasperated

Pronunciation: Ekks-ass-purr-ate-id   **Type**: Adjective

Definition: Irritated to the point of annoyance.

Example: Mr. Jenkins was **exasperated** when his son came home drunk again.

Excoriate

Pronunciation: Ekks-cor-ee-ate   **Type**: Verb

Definition: This verb refers to the act of expressing strong disapproval and originated as a term to refer to damage to the skin.

Example: The newspaper editor was quick to **excoriate** the latest untalented celebrity.

Exemplify

Pronunciation: Ekks-emp-lif-eye   **Type**: Verb

Definition: To exemplify something means to create an example of something.

Example: The chef used cumin and coriander when asked to create a dish to **exemplify** Indian cuisine.

Exeunt

Pronunciation: Ekks-ee-unt   **Type**: Verb

Definition: A stage direction in the script of a play meaning that a group of characters should leave the stage.

Example: In *Hamlet*, Shakespeare wrote, "**Exeunt** Hamlet and Polonius."

Exodus

Pronunciation: Ekks-ode-uss   **Type**: Noun

Definition: A mass physical movement or departure of people, particularly when a group emigrates from one country to another.

Example: The Bible tells of the **exodus** of the Israelites from Egypt.

Exorbitant

Pronunciation: Ekks-or-bit-unt   **Type**: Adjective

Definition: This adjective is used to describe a high price, particularly one that's excessive, unnecessary or unreasonable.

Example: "My god!" said David, looking at the menu. "Have you seen these **exorbitant** prices? Five quid for a cup of coffee!"

Exordium

Pronunciation: Ekks-or-dee-um   **Type**: Noun

Definition: The beginning or introduction of something, particularly a speech or a piece of prose.

Example: The assembled diplomats sat in silence as the speaker began her **exordium** to start the meeting.

Exoteric

Pronunciation: Ekks-oh-teh-rick   **Type**: Adjective

Definition: Suitable for consumption by the masses or the general public. This word is opposite in meaning to esoteric.

Example: The novelist tried to pen an **exoteric** best-seller that would appeal to everyone.

Expectorate

Pronunciation: Ekks-peck-tor-ate   **Type**: Verb

Definition: To cough or spit phlegm† from the lungs or the back of the throat.

Example: Janet missed everything about her ex-husband except the way that he used to **expectorate** on the floor.

Exploitation

Pronunciation: Ekks-ploy-tay-shun   **Type**: Noun

Definition: The act of using a person, an object or a situation to gain an (often unfair) advantage.

Example: The **exploitation** of sweatshop workers put Alex off the idea of buying Adidas trainers.

Exponent

Pronunciation: Ekks-po-nunt   **Type**: Noun

Definition: Someone who believes in and promotes a particular theory, technique or idea.

Example: Stephen was an early **exponent** of the Apple Mac.

Expurgate

Pronunciation: Ekks-purr-gate   **Type**: Verb

Definition: To purge or remove something deemed to be objectionable, scandalous or questionable, particularly from a book or some other written passage.

Example: When my mother asked to read my manuscript, I decided to **expurgate** parts before handing it over.

Extemporaneous

Pronunciation: Ekks-tem-pore-ain-ee-uss   **Type**: Adjective

Definition: This adjective is usually used to describe a speech that's delivered without any preparation.

Example: The lecturer said that **extemporaneous** speaking should be practiced and cultivated.

Extenuate

Pronunciation: Ekks-ten-yoo-ate   **Type**: Verb

Definition: To reduce the severity of an offence or action or to make it seem more forgivable.

Example: The criminal's heartfelt apology was enough to **extenuate** his crime in the eyes of the jurors.

Extirpate

Pronunciation: Ekks-tur-pate   **Type**: Verb

Definition: To hunt down and destroy all traces of something.

Example: Genocide attempts to **extirpate** entire races.

Extortionate

Pronunciation: Ekks-tor-shun-ut   **Type**: Adjective

Definition: Synonymic† with exorbitant†, this adjective is usually used to describe a price that's disproportionately high.

Example: Gerard refused to pay the bill because he thought it was **extortionate**.

Extraneous

Pronunciation: Ekks-train-ee-uss   **Type**: Adjective

Definition: Of external origin. This adjective is most commonly used to describe something that's completely irrelevant or unrelated to whatever's being dealt with.

Example: The band's demo album was ruined by the **extraneous** noise.

Extrapolate

Pronunciation: Ekks-trap-oh-late   **Type**: Verb

Definition: To estimate something unknown by using data from other sources.

Example: The scientist managed to **extrapolate** his theory from the results of dozens of other experiments.

Eyrie

Pronunciation: Ear-ee   **Type**: Noun

Definition: The nest of a bird of prey, particularly an eagle.

Example: The eagle flew back to the **eyrie** to feed its babies.

F

Façade

Pronunciation: Fass-ard   **Type**: Noun

Definition: The front of a building or a structure. This noun can also refer to a person's outward appearance and mannerisms when they're carefully crafted to conceal something.

Example: I couldn't keep up the **façade** anymore. My shoulders sagged, and I admitted everything.

Facetious

Pronunciation: Fa-see-shuss   **Type**: Adjective

Definition: This adjective is used to describe someone who treats serious issues and situations with inappropriate humour.

Example: Lisa angered her mother by being **facetious** when she was told to quit drinking before it killed her.

Facsimile

Pronunciation: Fack-sim-ill-ee   **Type**: Noun, Verb

Definition: An exact replica of something, particularly something written or printed. The verb refers to the process of making such a copy.

Example:
#1: The examiner handed everyone a **facsimile** of the question paper.
#2: I was asked to **facsimile** the notes from the meeting so everyone could have a copy.

Factotum

Pronunciation: Fac-toe-tum   **Type**: Noun

Definition: An employee who does multiple types of work.

Example: Hank was the office **factotum**. He could help out in any department, and the agency couldn't function without him.

Fallacy

Pronunciation: Fal-ass-ee   **Type**: Noun

Definition: Something that's untrue, particularly a belief that's based on an argument with errors in it.

Example: The atheist believed that Christianity was history's biggest **fallacy**.

Falsetto

Pronunciation: Fall-set-oh   **Type**: Noun

Definition: A vocal technique that allows people to sing high-pitched notes that would normally be out of their range.

Example: The judges were impressed by the contestant's **falsetto**.

Fantasise

Pronunciation: Fan-tah-size   **Type**: Verb

Definition: To indulge in one or more fantasies.
Example: John and Sally liked to **fantasise** that they were royalty.

Fantod

Pronunciation: Fan-tod   **Type**: Noun

Definition: A state of extreme nervousness, restlessness, uneasiness or unreasonableness.

Example: The lieutenant faced a serious **fantod** before the big battle.

Fathom

Pronunciation: Fath-um   **Type**: Noun, Verb

Definition: The noun refers to a unit of measurement that's used to measure the depth of water. One fathom is equal to six feet. The verb refers to the process of understanding a complex idea.

Example:
#1: The swimming pool was a **fathom** deep.
#2: Terry couldn't **fathom** how to put the bookshelf together.

Feasible

Pronunciation: Fee-zib-ull   **Type**: Adjective

Definition: Realistically possible.

Example: Peter knew that his dream of becoming a lawyer was **feasible**, if impractical.

Fecund

Pronunciation: Fee-cund   **Type**: Adjective

Definition: Fertile; capable of producing a large number of offspring or a lot of growth.

Example: The vegetation was **fecund** and continued to spread despite deforestation.

Feign

Pronunciation: Fain   **Type**: Verb

Definition: To fake an injury or feeling.

Example: I didn't know the deceased, so I had to **feign** sorrow at the funeral.

Felicitations

Pronunciation: Fuh-liss-it-ay-shuns   **Type**: Noun

Definition: An expression of praise or good wishes on a special occasion. Synonymic[†] with congratulations.

Example: When he came first in the big race, I gave my **felicitations** to my brother.

Fellatio

Pronunciation: Ful-ay-she-oh   **Type**: Noun

Definition: Oral stimulation of the penis.

Example: Ben refused to marry a woman who wouldn't perform **fellatio**.

Fenestration

Pronunciation: Fen-uss-tray-shun   **Type**: Noun

Definition: The way that the windows and doors are arranged on a building.

Example: The Joneses fell in love with the house when they saw the exterior **fenestration**.

Feral

Pronunciation: Fear-ul   **Type**: Adjective

Definition: Wild or like an animal.

Example: The **feral** child attacked everyone who approached him.

Fetter

Pronunciation: Fett-ur   **Type**: Noun, Verb

Definition: A chain or manacle that's used to restrict the movement of a prisoner. In a wider sense, it can also refer to any restraint or restriction on someone's freedom, particularly one that's considered unfair or over the top. The verb refers to the action of restricting or restraining someone in this way.

Example:
#1: When he entered the jail, the prisoner was fitted with a **fetter**.
#2: The warden knew that to refuse to **fetter** the new arrival would be seen as a sign of weakness by the other inmates.

Fickle

Pronunciation: Fick-ul   **Type**: Adjective

Definition: This adjective is used to describe a person or an animal that frequently changes loyalties, ethics, morals, interests or affections.

Example: The **fickle** girl moved from crush to crush, often several times in a week.

Fiefdom

Pronunciation: Feef-dum   **Type**: Noun

Definition: The land of a feudal lord. This word is often informally used to describe anything over which one dominant person or organisation has complete control.

Example: Anna ran the company like a **fiefdom**. No-one else got a say.

Filigree

Pronunciation: Fill-ig-ree   **Type**: Noun

Definition: A type of ornamental work consisting of fine wire bent into shapes or letters. The wire is typically made from a precious metal like gold or silver, and filigree is most often seen on pieces of jewellery.

Example: Leticia wore a beautiful **filigree** ring that her mother gave to her.

Finagle

Pronunciation: Fin-nay-gul   **Type**: Verb

Definition: To act in a devious or dishonest manner, particularly with the end goal of achieving or obtaining something.

Example: Ted managed to **finagle** a promotion, and everyone thought he'd slept with the boss.

Finesse

Pronunciation: Fin-ess   **Type**: Noun

Definition: A deeply subtle and refined delicacy.

Example: Susan made delicious cakes with natural **finesse**.

Finnimbrun

Pronunciation: Fin-im-brun   **Type**: Noun

Definition: A keepsake, a trinket[†] or a knick-knack.

Example: The cross that Jennifer wore around her neck was a **finnimbrun** that once belonged to her grandmother.

Fixation

Pronunciation: Fick-say-shun   **Type**: Noun

Definition: An obsessive focus, interest or feeling about something specific.

Example: Joe had a **fixation** about Jane and followed her everywhere.

Flagellant

Pronunciation: Flaj-ell-unt   **Type**: Noun

Definition: A person who flogs themselves or others, usually for sexual pleasure or as a form of religious discipline.

Example: The sadomasochistic[†] **flagellant** had an extensive collection of whips.

Flamboyant

Pronunciation: Flam-boy-unt   **Type**: Adjective

Definition: Attracting attention because of exuberance, colour, stylishness or confidence. This adjective is often used to describe a person's mannerisms, dress or behaviour.

Example: Oscar's wardrobe is filled with **flamboyant** clothes to make heads turn wherever he goes.

Flâneur

Pronunciation: Flan-urr   **Type**: Noun

Definition: A French word with no direct translation. Broadly speaking, it's used to refer to someone who wanders aimlessly through an urban environment; a leisurely stroller who observes the bustle of city life.

Example: The **flâneur** wrote haiku as he walked the streets.

Flapdoodle

Pronunciation: Flap-doo-dull   **Type**: Noun
Definition: Nonsense.

Example: Dave thought that the politician's big speech was a load of old **flapdoodle**. He didn't believe a word he said.

Flibbertigibbet

Pronunciation: Flib-ur-tee-jib-it   **Type**: Noun

Definition: A person who's frivolous and flighty, often a whimsical, excessively talkative young woman.

Example: The actress portrayed a **flibbertigibbet**, but off-camera she was quiet, thoughtful and polite.

Flippant

Pronunciation: Flip-unt   **Type**: Adjective

Definition: Not showing a respectful attitude.

Example: The schoolboy showed a lack of respect with his **flippant** remarks.

Flocculent

Pronunciation: Flock-yoo-lunt   **Type**: Adjective

Definition: This adjective is used to describe something with a fluffy or woolly texture, character or appearance.

Example: The summer clouds were **flocculent** and resembled sheep.

Flotsam

Pronunciation: Flot-sum   **Type**: Noun

Definition: Wreckage of a ship or its cargo that's found floating on the sea or washed up on the shore. This word is often coupled with jetsam[†], though the two words have slightly different meanings.

Example: The survivors hunted through the **flotsam** to look for supplies.

Flummox

Pronunciation: Flum-ux   **Type**: Verb

Definition: To confuse someone.

Example: The tricky exam paper was enough to **flummox** the students.

Flunk

Pronunciation: Flunk   **Type**: Verb

Definition: To fail to achieve a certain standard. This verb is often used to describe what happens when students are held back a year or kicked out of a class.

Example: Stuart knew he was going to **flunk** after failing to attend his exams.

Fluvial

Pronunciation: Floo-vee-ul   **Type**: Adjective

Definition: This word describes something that possesses the properties or qualities of a river or something that's likely to be found in one.

Example: The alleyway had a **fluvial** contour.

Flyleaf

Pronunciation: Fly-leef   **Type**: Noun

Definition: A blank page found at the beginning or the end of a book.

Example: Donna wrote her name in the **flyleaf** so she'd always know which textbook was hers.

Foetus

Pronunciation: Feet-us   **Type**: Noun

Definition: An unborn or unhatched person or animal in the later stages of development, showing at least some recognisable features of the adult.

Example: The doctors could tell the baby's sex before it was born by taking ultrasound scans of the **foetus**.

Foible

Pronunciation: Foy-bull   **Type**: Noun

Definition: A very slight weakness or peculiarity in someone's character.

Example: Every evening at eight o'clock, Peter treated himself to his **foible** of half a glass of wine.

Folklore

Pronunciation: Foke-lor   **Type**: Noun

Definition: The traditional beliefs, customs and stories of a community or civilisation, passed down by word of mouth.

Example: Mrs. Henderson studied Ancient Egyptian **folklore**.

Folksy

Pronunciation: Foke-see   **Type**: Adjective

Definition: Possessing the characteristics of traditional cultures and customs, particularly in an artificial manner.

Example: Percival looked around the **folksy** gift shop and came out with a hand-made candle and a book that was hand-stitched together.

Folly

Pronunciation: Foll-ee   **Type**: Noun

Definition: A lack of common sense or intelligence; foolishness. The word can also be used to refer to a bad idea or a foolish act.

Example: The gambler thought that betting on blackjack was **folly**.

Foolscap

Pronunciation: Fools-cap   **Type**: Noun

Definition: A type of paper that was popular before the rise of A4.

Example: The sailor wrote a letter home on a piece of **foolscap**.

Footpad

Pronunciation: Fut-pad   **Type**: Noun

Definition: A bandit, robber or highwayman who works on foot instead of on horseback.

Example: It used to be dangerous to travel through the mountains. You could fall victim to a **footpad** at any point.

Forceps

Pronunciation: For-seps   **Type**: Noun

Definition: A medical or scientific instrument consisting of a pair of pincers or tweezers.

Example: During the operation, the doctor asked for his **forceps**.

Forelock

Pronunciation: For-lock   **Type**: Noun

Definition: A lock of hair that grows just above the forehead. The noun can also be used to describe the part of the mane of an animal that's situated in a similar place.

Example: The driver touched the **forelock** on his head as the passenger climbed out of the carriage.

Fornicate

Pronunciation: For-nick-ate   **Type**: Verb

Definition: To have sexual intercourse with someone outside of marriage.

Example: It's a common misconception that students only drink and **fornicate** – they sometimes go to lectures, too.

Fortissimo

Pronunciation: For-tiss-im-oh   **Type**: Adverb, Noun

Definition: The adverb is a musical direction which instructs musicians to play loudly. The noun refers directly to a piece of loud music.

Example:
#1: At the concert, Darrel played **fortissimo** to replicate the sound of thunder.
#2: The choirmaster decided to conduct the **fortissimo**.

Fortuitous

Pronunciation: For-choo-it-uss   **Type**: Adjective

Definition: Happening by accident or by chance, rather than by organisation or design. This adjective is usually used to describe something positive and is synonymic[†] with fortunate or lucky.

Example: It was **fortuitous** that the rain drove back the infantry.

Foundling

Pronunciation: Found-ling   **Type**: Noun

Definition: An infant that was abandoned by its parents and cared for by others, often by the state.

Example: The **foundling** was fortuitous[†] and was adopted while she was still an infant

Franchise

Pronunciation: Fran-chize   **Type**: Noun

Definition: A type of business agreement in which a company lets others use its name, trademarks, recipes and formulae in exchange for a share of the profit. The word can refer to either the agreement itself or to an outlet that's a member of such a franchise.

Example: The McDonald's **franchise** has outlets all over the world.

Francophile

Pronunciation: Frank-oh-file   **Type**: Noun

Definition: A person who has a deep interest in or a love of France, from the country itself to its people, language, culture and history.

Example: Harry's dad is a **Francophile** and especially loves French movies.

Freeware

Pronunciation: Free-ware   **Type**: Noun

Definition: Computer software that's distributed for free. Freeware is different to abandonware[†] because it's still supported by the manufacturers, who often rely on donations, sponsorship or advertisements within the program to generate revenue.

Example: Audacity is a great piece of **freeware** for recording and editing sound clips and music.

Frippery

Pronunciation: Frip-ur-ee   **Type**: Noun

Definition: Showy or over-the-top decoration or style in architecture, dress or language.

Example: The old folk were unimpressed by the youngsters and weren't taken in by their **frippery**.

Frolicsome

Pronunciation: Frol-ick-sum   **Type**: Adjective

Definition: Lively and playful.

Example: The **frolicsome** children played in the street.

Frontispiece

Pronunciation: Frun-tis-peace   **Type**: Noun

Definition: An illustration facing the title page of book.

Example: The **frontispiece** depicted[†] the villain on a golden throne.

Fructify

Pronunciation: Fruck-tif-eye   **Type**: Verb

Definition: To make something fruitful or productive, or to reach such a state of productivity.

Example: Karen waited impatiently for her plans to **fructify**.

Frugal

Pronunciation: Froo-gul   **Type**: Adjective

Definition: This adjective is used to describe someone who's sparing or economical, particularly when dealing with money or food.

Example: Harry's family were **frugal** and he survived on hand-me-downs and leftovers.

Fulcrum

Pronunciation: Ful-krum   **Type**: Noun

Definition: The central point on which a lever rests. The noun can also be used to refer to something that's essential to an activity, event, situation or argument.

Example: The seesaw pivoted on the **fulcrum**.

Fulminate

Pronunciation: Full-min-ate   **Type**: Verb

Definition: This word has two meanings – it can either refer to the issuing of a verbal attack or rebuttal[†], or to the act of exploding or detonating with a loud bang.

Example: The protesters knew they had to **fulminate** against the war in Iraq.

Funambulist

Pronunciation: Fun-amb-yoo-list   **Type**: Noun

Definition: A tightrope walker.

Example: Jeremiah could never be a **funambulist**. He was afraid of heights.

Fungible

Pronunciation: Fun-jib-ul   **Type**: Adjective

Definition: This adjective is used to describe goods that are replaceable by an equal quantity of the same substance.

Example: Crude oil and grain are both **fungible**.

Futurology

Pronunciation: Few-chur-ol-oh-gee   **Type**: Noun

Definition: The art and science of predicting or forecasting the future, particularly when using present or past trends as a basis.

Example: Harold was a keen practitioner of **futurology** and spent most of his time analysing past and present trends to make his predictions.

G

Gallivant

Pronunciation: Gal-iv-ant   **Type**: Verb

Definition: To go from one place to another in the pursuit of pleasure or entertainment, usually in high spirits.

Example: For his eighteenth birthday, Jerry was happy to **gallivant** around town.

Gamin

Pronunciation: Gam-in   **Type**: Noun

Definition: A street urchin.

Example: The **gamin** followed the gentlemen around until they paid him to leave them alone.

Gammy

Pronunciation: Gam-ee   **Type**: Adjective

Definition: An old slang word used to describe a part of the body, particularly the leg, that's no longer functioning correctly because of an injury or chronic pain.

Example: My grandfather always used to talk about his **gammy** leg and how he got injured by shrapnel in the war.

Gamut

Pronunciation: Gam-ut   **Type**: Noun

Definition: The range or scope of something, often a voice or a musical instrument.

Example: The actress was renowned for portraying the whole **gamut** of human emotion.

Gander

Pronunciation: Gan-dur   **Type**: Noun, Verb

Definition: This word has two definitions – it can either refer to a male goose or to the act of taking a glance.

Example:
#1: John called me over to look at the **gander**.
#2: John called me over to have a **gander** at the male goose.

Gantry

Pronunciation: Gan-tree   **Type**: Noun

Definition: An overhead structure like a bridge that's used during the construction and servicing of buildings, rockets and ships.

Example: The security guard patrolled the **gantry** to get a better view from above.

Garble

Pronunciation: Gar-bul   **Type**: Verb

Definition: This verb refers to the action of reproducing a message or a signal in such a way that it becomes confused, distorted or unintelligible.

Example: Somehow, the transmitter managed to **garble** the signal, and we had to figure out what it meant.

Gargantuan

Pronunciation: Garr-gan-choo-an   **Type**: Adjective

Definition: Gigantic, huge or enormous.

Example: The builder had a **gargantuan** appetite. He had five large meals per day.

Garotte

Pronunciation: Gah-rot   **Type**: Noun, Verb

Definition: A weapon designed to commit murder or execution by strangulation. The verb refers to this type of assault.

Example:
#1: The thug pulled a **garrotte** from his trousers and bore down on his opponent's throat.
#2: The drunk threatened to **garrotte** the barman.

Gatefold

Pronunciation: Gate-fold   **Type**: Noun

Definition: An oversized page in a book, magazine or other printed publication that's folded down to be the same size as all the other pages.

Example: Alex examined the **gatefold** map in the tourist guide.

Gauleiter

Pronunciation: Gow-lie-tur   **Type**: Noun

Definition: The official governor of a district under Nazi rule.

Example: The **Gauleiter** was sentenced to death after the war.

Gazunder

Pronunciation: Gaz-und-ur   **Type**: Verb

Definition: This verb refers to the act of lowering the amount that's on offer for a property after agreeing to pay more, particularly just before contracts are exchanged.

Example: The deal on the house fell through because the buyer tried to **gazunder** the seller.

Gendarme

Pronunciation: Shyon-darm   **Type**: Noun

Definition: An armed police officer in France or another French-speaking country.

Example: The **gendarme** arrested the criminal when he surfaced at a bar in Paris.

Generalissimo

Pronunciation: Jen-uh-rul-iss-im-oh   **Type**: Noun

Definition: A military rank assigned to the commander of a combination of units from the army, navy and air force.

Example: The **generalissimo** asked not to be disturbed while he prepared for the assault.

Genteelism

Pronunciation: Jen-teel-iz-um   **Type**: Noun

Definition: A word, phrase or expression that's used in place of another to avoid vulgarity. Genteelisms are generally considered to be more acceptable in conversation than their alternatives.

Example: Gerry's grandmother couldn't stand impoliteness and often hid behind a **genteelism**.

Geriatric

Pronunciation: Jeh-ree-at-rick   **Type**: Adjective, Noun

Definition: Of, characterised by or relating to old people and the elderly, particularly when concerning healthcare. The noun refers to an old person, especially one who's receiving special care.

Example:
#1: The **geriatric** ward was severely underfunded and the nurses were forced to work long hours for poor pay.
#2: Gerald was the latest **geriatric** to arrive at the home.

Gerrymander

Pronunciation: Jeh-ree-man-da   **Type**: Verb

Definition: This verb refers to the process of manipulating the boundaries of an electoral constituency to favour a particular political party or class.

Example: The politician was only in power because he was willing to **gerrymander**.

Gestapo

Pronunciation: Guh-stap-oh   **Type**: Noun

Definition: The German secret police.

Example: As head of the **Gestapo**, Heinrich Himmler was responsible for countless atrocities.

Gestation

Pronunciation: Jess-tay-shun   **Type**: Noun

Definition: The process of carrying a child in the womb between its conception and birth.

Example: Human beings generally have a nine-month **gestation** period.

Gesticulate

Pronunciation: Jess-tick-yoo-late   **Type**: Verb

Definition: To use the hands to make gestures, particularly to emphasise a point.

Example: The young man liked to **gesticulate** when giving people directions.

Gibberish

Pronunciation: Jibb-ur-ish   **Type**: Noun

Definition: Meaningless speech or writing; synonymic[†] with gobbledegook and nonsense.

Example: "I don't understand," said Kimberley. "Stop speaking **gibberish**."

Gibbet

Pronunciation: Jibb-it   **Type**: Noun

Definition: A construction used to commit execution by hanging or to hang bodies from as a warning to others.

Example: The dead man grinned as he swung from the **gibbet**.

Gigolo

Pronunciation: Jig-a-lo   **Type**: Noun

Definition: An offensive or derogatory term used to refer to a young man who's financially supported or paid outright to be an older woman's escort or lover.

Example: Mother asked why grandma had a smile on her face, so I told her that she now has a **gigolo**.

Glitch

Pronunciation: Glitch   **Type**: Noun, Verb

Definition: A sudden minor error or setback. The noun can be used to refer to problems with equipment, plans or ideas, but it's more commonly used to refer to problems with computer software. The verb describes the action of causing something to glitch, particularly when doing so to gain an unfair advantage.

Example:
#1: There was a **glitch** on the video game's server, so Gary went outside to play football.
#2: When he got back online, Gary decided to **glitch** the game to get hold of unlimited gold.

Globule

Pronunciation: Glob-yool   **Type**: Noun

Definition: A small, round particle of a liquid substance.

Example: A **globule** of snot dribbled slowly from Charlie's nose.

Gluttony

Pronunciation: Glutt-un-ee   **Type**: Noun

Definition: Greed and/or excess when it comes to eating and drinking.

Example: It came as no surprise when the fat man confessed to **gluttony**.

Glyph

Pronunciation: Gliff   **Type**: Noun

Definition: A visual symbol, usually hieroglyphic or pictographic, used as an element of writing.

Example: The archaeologist examined the **glyph** on the cave wall, but he couldn't understand it.

Googlewhack

Pronunciation: Goo-gul-wack   **Type**: Noun

Definition: The result of a search on Google when two words are searched for and only one result is generated. Googlewhacks are hard to find, but there's a thriving[†] community of Googlewhackers online.

Example: Dave wasted three hours trying to find a **Googlewhack** when he should have been revising for his exam.

Goon

Pronunciation: Goon   **Type**: Noun

Definition: A bully or a thug, particularly one hired to be a bodyguard or to frighten away opposition. It's also a slang word for a foolish, stupid or unpleasant person.

Example: Gareth is such a **goon**. He thinks fist-fights and football are more important than his relationship with his wife and kids.

Gormandise

Pronunciation: Gor-mun-dize   **Type**: Verb

Definition: To binge† on food or to overeat.

Example: After six weeks on her diet, Janet decided to **gormandise** at the Chinese buffet.

Gormless

Pronunciation: Gorm-less   **Type**: Adjective

Definition: An informal description, usually of a person or an animal, meaning stupid, dull or clumsy.

Example: Anthony laughs at everything. He's so **gormless**.

Gound

Pronunciation: Gow-nd   **Type**: Noun

Definition: The thin mucous that's discharged from the eyes during sleep.

Example: They didn't give Peter the job because he turned up to the interview with **gound**.

Grandiloquent

Pronunciation: Gran-dil-oh-kwunt   **Type**: Adjective

Definition: Pompously extravagant in language, style, dress or manner.

Example: The old man was **grandiloquent** in his designer suit.

Gratuitous

Pronunciation: Grat-yoo-it-uss   **Type**: Adjective

Definition: This adjective is usually used to describe something that's given freely, but it can also be used to describe something that was uncalled for or unnecessary.

Example: The film was heavily censored because of its **gratuitous** nudity.

Graupel

Pronunciation: Gr-ow-pul   **Type**: Noun

Definition: Granular pellets of snow, somewhere between snowflakes and hailstones.

Example: The **graupel** crunched underfoot as the children ran across it.

Gravamen

Pronunciation: Grah-vay-mun   **Type**: Noun

Definition: The most serious part of a complaint, accusation or grievance. The noun can also be used to refer to the grievance itself.

Example: Harry's **gravamen** was the loud music that his loutish neighbours played throughout the night.

Gravid

Pronunciation: Grav-id   **Type**: Adjective

Definition: Pregnant. This adjective can be used to describe animals as well as humans, as long as the creature is carrying fertilised eggs, a foetus[†] or developing young.

Example: The security guard panicked when the **gravid** woman fell over clutching her belly.

Gregarious

Pronunciation: Greg-air-ee-uss   **Type**: Adjective

Definition: The definition of this adjective differs slightly depending upon whether the word is used to describe a human or an animal. When used to describe a person, it means that they're fond of company or at their best in a social situation. In most other circumstances, it's used to describe a group of animals that live in a community together, such as a flock of geese or a herd of sheep.

Example: The **gregarious** old man spent most of his retirement at posh parties and fancy ballroom dances.

Grilse

Pronunciation: Grill-ss   **Type**: Noun

Definition: A salmon that's returned to fresh water after spending the winter at sea.

Example: Harold took his grandson fishing for **grilse**.

Grotty

Pronunciation: Grot-ee   **Type**: Adjective

Definition: Unpleasant, particularly because of dirt or a lack of hygiene.

Example: Billy said to the manager, "I refuse to stay in this **grotty** hotel room! Don't you ever clean?"

Groupie

Pronunciation: Groo-pee   **Type**: Noun

Definition: A person, particularly a young woman, who follows a band, artist or other celebrity around in the hope of meeting them or having sex with them.

Example: The rock star had a smile on his face after the **groupie** left his hotel room.

Gruelling

Pronunciation: Grool-ing   **Type**: Adjective

Definition: Hard and arduous. This adjective is usually used to describe a task that's characterised by the huge amount of effort that's required to complete it.

Example: When his car wouldn't start, Harold began the **gruelling** task of pushing it home.

Grunge

Pronunciation: Grunj   **Type**: Noun

Definition: Originally meaning grime or dirt, this noun is also the name of a style of rock music that's characterised by a dirty guitar sound, heavy drumming and a lazy vocal delivery.

Example: Nirvana, Alice in Chains and Pearl Jam are my favourite **grunge** bands.

Guano

Pronunciation: Gwah-no   **Type**: Noun

Definition: The excrement of seabirds, bats and seals, often used as a fertiliser. Guano occurs naturally in thick deposits, notably on the islands off Peru and Chile.

Example: The mining of **guano** is a major plot device in *Dr. No*.

Guerrilla

Pronunciation: Guh-ril-la   **Type**: Adjective, Noun

Definition: The adjective is used to describe a type of warfare in which a weaker opponent fights a stronger one with tactics including ambushes, sabotage, raids and the element of surprise. The noun refers to someone who's engaged in this type of warfare.

Example:
#1: The rebel troops carried out a **guerrilla** operation against the military.
#2: The **guerrilla** picked up his rifle and fired at the soldiers.

Guesstimate

Pronunciation: Gess-tim-ate   **Type**: Noun, Verb

Definition: An estimate that's based on a combination of guesswork and intelligent calculation. The verb refers to the act of making this kind of estimate.

Example:
#1: When Johnny was asked how far away the village was, he said, "Three miles at a **guesstimate**."
#2: They couldn't be bothered to split the bill precisely, so Carol decided to **guesstimate**.

Gumption

Pronunciation: Gump-shun   **Type**: Noun

Definition: Initiative and resourcefulness.

Example: It took a lot of **gumption** for Steven to challenge his bosses' authority.

Gunge

Pronunciation: Gunj   **Type**: Noun

Definition: A thick, sticky substance of a similar consistency to paint. Also known as slime, it's commonly used on children's television programmes.

Example: The children laughed as the contestant was sprayed with paint-like **gunge**.

Gusset

Pronunciation: Guss-it   **Type**: Noun

Definition: A small piece of material that's sewn into a garment to strengthen part of it, particularly the crotch.

Example: The seamstress added a **gusset** to strengthen the crotch of the pants.

Guttural

Pronunciation: Gut-tur-al   **Type**: Adjective

Definition: This adjective is used to describe a type of harsh-sounding speech that's produced in the throat.

Example: If you want to sing in a metal band, you should master **guttural** vocals.

Gytrash

Pronunciation: Guy-trash   **Type**: Noun

Definition: A legendary black dog that was believed to haunt lonely roads in northern England, leading people astray.

Example: "Make sure you get a lift home," said Mrs. Warren. "They say the **Gytrash** is about."

H

Hacienda

Pronunciation: Ha-see-en-da   **Type**: Noun

Definition: A Spanish word that's used to describe a large estate or plantation. In everyday use, it's more commonly used to describe the main house on one of these estates.

Example: As the afternoon sun grew hotter, the farmer and his son decided to retire to the **hacienda**.

Hackneyed

Pronunciation: Hack-need   **Type**: Adjective

Definition: Insignificant through overuse. This adjective is usually used to describe a phrase or an idea.

Example: The marketing team didn't realise that their "new" idea was **hackneyed**.

Haemophilia

Pronunciation: He-mo-fill-ee-a   **Type**: Noun

Definition: A genetic disorder that leads to uncontrollable bleeding, usually passed from mother to son.

Example: Gary had **haemophilia** and often needed medical treatment for even the most minor scrapes to keep his bleeding under control.

Hag-ridden

Pronunciation: Hag-rid-un   **Type**: Adjective

Definition: Full of nightmares or anxiety, as if tormented by a witch. The condition of sleep paralysis was once dismissed as a symptom of being hag-ridden.

Example: Harold was **hag-ridden** after eating too much cheese.

Halcyon

Pronunciation: Hal-see-on   **Type**: Adjective

Definition: This adjective is used to describe a period in the past that was idyllic[†], peaceful and happy.

Example: Derek dreamt wistfully of the **halcyon** days of his childhood.

Halitosis

Pronunciation: Hal-it-oh-sis   **Type**: Noun

Definition: Bad breath.

Example: No amount of toothpaste could cover up Joan's **halitosis**.

Hallucinogen

Pronunciation: Hal-oo-sin-oh-jen   **Type**: Noun

Definition: A drug or substance that can cause hallucinations.

Example: LSD is Sid's favourite **hallucinogen**.

Hangdog

Pronunciation: Hang-dog   **Type**: Adjective

Definition: Possessing a guilty, ashamed or dejected appearance.

Example: Tania was concerned when her husband came home from work with a **hangdog** expression on his face.

Harangue

Pronunciation: Ha-rang   **Type**: Noun, Verb

Definition: The noun is used to describe a long, aggressive speech or lecture, while the verb means to speak to someone in this style.

Example:
#1: Harry's wife delivered a **harangue** about the evils of television.
#2: Lesley was a good orator, but when he felt passionate about a subject, he tended to **harangue** his audience.

Hara-Kiri

Pronunciation: Ha-ra-kih-ree   **Type**: Noun

Definition: This noun is an alternative word for seppuku[†], the ceremonial suicide formerly practiced in Japan by disgraced warriors or people who were sentenced to death. This method of suicide involves ripping open the abdomen with a dagger, sword or knife. These days, the noun can also be used to refer to any suicidal or self-destructive act or action.

Example: The politician committed political **hara-kiri** when he unveiled plans to turn the playground into a block of flats.

Harbinger

Pronunciation: Har-bin-jer   **Type**: Noun

Definition: Something that announces the approach or arrival of someone or something else.

Example: The Four Horsemen are a **harbinger** of the apocalypse.

Harem

Pronunciation: Harr-eem   **Type**: Noun

Definition: The part of a household that's reserved for wives, concubines[†] and female servants. The noun can also refer to the women themselves.

Example: The foreign diplomat was invited to visit the **harem,** and he was surprised by how many women were housed there.

Harlequin

Pronunciation: Harl-uh-kwin   **Type**: Adjective, Noun

Definition: The adjective describes something that comes in multiple colours, while the noun refers to a mute character in a pantomime, usually masked and dressed in a diamond-patterned costume.

Example:
#1: Kate looked stunning in her **harlequin**-patterned dress.
#2: The **harlequin** wore a black mask as he performed for the audience.

Harridan

Pronunciation: Ha-rid-un   **Type**: Noun

Definition: A strict, stern or bossy old woman.

Example: After she married her husband, Charlotte grew into a **harridan**, always telling him what to do.

Heathen

Pronunciation: He-thun   **Type**: Adjective, Noun

Definition: A person who doesn't belong to the established local religion. The adjective can be used to describe anything that's of or related to heathens.

Example:
#1: The priest said, "Destroy that **heathen** statue. It's an abomination to our god."
#2: The **heathen** was beheaded by the Christian invaders.

Hebdomadal

Pronunciation: Heb-dom-ad-ul   **Type**: Adjective

Definition: Weekly.

Example: It was Harry's turn to take the minutes for the team's **hebdomadal** status meeting.

Hedonistic

Pronunciation: He-don-iss-tick   **Type**: Adjective

Definition: Engaged in hedonism; devoted to the pursuit of sensual pleasure.

Example: Carol didn't go to nightclubs because she thought they were too **hedonistic**.

Hegemonic

Pronunciation: Hej-um-on-ick   **Type**: Adjective

Definition: Ruling, leading or dominant.

Example: The politician was **hegemonic** and highly influential.

Heliotropic

Pronunciation: He-lee-oh-tro-pic   **Type**: Adjective

Definition: Growing or moving towards or away from the light of the sun. This adjective is usually used to describe plant-life and vegetation.

Example: The **heliotropic** growth in the garden expanded to block out the sun, killing all the hydrangeas.

Hermeneutics

Pronunciation: Her-mun-yoo-ticks   **Type**: Noun

Definition: The art and science of interpreting text.

Example: The professor of **hermeneutics** loved nothing better than to sit in front of the fire with a good book in an ancient language.

Heterogeneous

Pronunciation: Het-uh-ro-gee-nee-uss   **Type**: Adjective

Definition: Diverse in character or content.

Example: My dad's album collection is **heterogeneous** with a wide range of musical styles represented.

Hibernicism

Pronunciation: Hi-bur-niss-iz-um   **Type**: Noun

Definition: A phrase, habit or characteristic that's unique to or peculiar to the Irish.

Example: True to his Irish roots, Harry's favourite **Hibernicism** was the heavy consumption of Guinness.

Hidalgo

Pronunciation: Hid-al-go   **Type**: Noun

Definition: This noun is used predominantly in Spanish-speaking areas and is used to refer to a gentleman.

Example: The **hidalgo** lost all his money at the races.

Highbrow

Pronunciation: Hi-brow   **Type**: Adjective, Noun

Definition: Scholarly, intellectual or elitist in taste. The noun refers to a person with these attributes.

Example:
#1: The poetry club was too **highbrow** for me, so I went to the movies instead.
#2: The **highbrow** on the train was reading Dostoyevsky's *War and Peace*.

Highfalutin

Pronunciation: Hi-fa-loo-tin   **Type**: Adjective

Definition: Pompous or pretentious. This adjective is usually used to describe a speech, a piece of writing, a concept[†] or an idea.

Example: After the presentation, the chairman shook his head and said, "We don't want any of that **highfalutin** nonsense around here."

Hinny

Pronunciation: Hin-nee   **Type**: Noun

Definition: The child of a female donkey and a male horse.

Example: The farmer felt like a proud grandparent after he bred a donkey and a horse to create a **hinny**.

Hinterland

Pronunciation: Hin-tur-land   **Type**: Noun

Definition: The (often unmapped) area beyond or behind a coast or the shoreline of a river. The noun can also be used to refer to the area surrounding and served by a town or a port.

Example: As soon as they landed, the sailors began to explore the **hinterland**.

Hirsute

Pronunciation: Her-sute   **Type**: Adjective

Definition: Hairy.

Example: Austin was notorious for his **hirsute** chest.

Histamine

Pronunciation: Hiss-ta-meen   **Type**: Noun

Definition: A chemical compound that's released by cells in response to an injury, often causing an allergic reaction.

Example: The patient's body produced too much **histamine** and caused his airways to inflame.

Histrionic

Pronunciation: Hiss-tree-on-ic   **Type**: Adjective

Definition: Overly melodramatic or theatrical in character or style.

Example: The old musician had been overlooked for so long that he adopted a **histrionic** dress code to get attention.

Hoarfrost

Pronunciation: Hor-frost   **Type**: Noun

Definition: A greyish-white coloured deposit of frozen vapour that forms in clear weather on inanimate objects such as fences and vegetation.

Example: When they woke up in the winter morning, the world was covered in beautiful **hoarfrost**.

Hoax

Pronunciation: Hokes   **Type**: Noun, Verb

Definition: A deliberate deception that's presented as the truth. The verb refers to the act of carrying out a deception in this manner.

Example:
#1: The **hoax** fooled hundreds of thousands of people after becoming a trending topic on Twitter.
#2: Johnny decided to **hoax** the general public by spreading the rumour that 5G towers caused veganism.

Hobbledehoy

Pronunciation: Ho-bull-dee-hoy   **Type**: Adjective, Noun

Definition: Awkward or clumsy. The noun refers to a youngster with these traits.

Example:
#1: His **hobbledehoy** hands dropped his phone every time he tried to use it.
#2: The **hobbledehoy** was terrible at sports because he always tripped over.

Hobnob

Pronunciation: Hob-nob   **Type**: Verb

Definition: To mix socially with people of a higher social status.

Example: Every Saturday, Karen put on her best suit to **hobnob** with the gentlefolk at the Savoy.

Hogmanay

Pronunciation: Hog-ma-nay   **Type**: Noun

Definition: New Year's Eve and the celebrations that take place to mark it, particularly in Scotland.

Example: The family marked **Hogmanay** with a huge party, inviting all of their relatives.

Hoi Polloi

Pronunciation: Hoy Pal-oy   **Type**: Noun

Definition: The masses; the common people as a whole.

Example: The royal advisors were concerned about the **hoi polloi** and didn't want the princess to mix with them.

Hoick

Pronunciation: Hoyk   **Type**: Verb

Definition: To move something quickly and with force.

Example: Dave looked at the bookcase and said, "Let's **hoick** it over here."

Hokum

Pronunciation: Ho-kum   **Type**: Noun

Definition: Nonsense or garbage.

Example: The play I went to see last night was a load of **hokum**. I couldn't understand it at all.

Homogenous

Pronunciation: Hom-oj-in-uss   **Type**: Adjective

Definition: Consisting of parts that are all the same. The opposite of heterogeneous[†].

Example: When they're in uniform, the schoolchildren look **homogeneous**.

Homograph

Pronunciation: Hom-oh-graf   **Type**: Noun

Definition: Two or more words that are spelled the same but which have different meanings or pronunciations.

Example: "Bass" is an example of a **homograph** because it can either refer to a type or fish or a low, deep sound.

Homophone

Pronunciation: Hom-oh-fone   **Type**: Noun

Definition: Two or more words which have the same pronunciation but different meanings or spellings.

Example: "Which" is a **homophone** because it sounds the same as "witch" but has a completely different meaning.

Homunculus

Pronunciation: Ho-munk-yoo-luss   **Type**: Noun

Definition: A very small human or humanoid creature. This noun was initially used to refer to a microscopic human being from which a foetus[†] was believed to develop.

Example: Jenny couldn't sleep at night because she thought there was a **homunculus** in her bed, watching her.

Honcho

Pronunciation: Hon-cho   **Type**: Noun

Definition: A leader, boss or manager; the person who's in charge.

Example: When I asked the builder if he wanted a cup of tea, he said that the **honcho** didn't allow it.

Hooch

Pronunciation: Hooch   **Type**: Noun

Definition: Home-brewed alcohol. Hooch is usually illegal, inferior and of a high alcohol percentage.

Example: The prisoners were caught brewing **hooch** and were punished by the warden.

Hoodoo

Pronunciation: Hoo-doo   **Type**: Noun

Definition: Another word for voodoo; witchcraft.

Example: The old woman used **hoodoo** to seduce her young neighbour.

Hoodwink

Pronunciation: Hood-wink   **Type**: Verb

Definition: To deceive someone with trickery.

Example: I knew I wouldn't be allowed out, so I decided to **hoodwink** my parents into thinking I had a school trip to go to.

Hosiery

Pronunciation: Ho-zee-uh-ree   **Type**: Noun

Definition: Any garment worn on the feet and legs including stockings, socks and tights.

Example: The postman was a fan of **hosiery** because it kept his legs warm on the long winter mornings.

Hospice

Pronunciation: Hoss-piss   **Type**: Noun

Definition: A home providing care for the sick and the dying, particularly those who are terminally ill.

Example: Once Grandpa went into the **hospice**, we knew he was never coming out again.

Hospitalism

Pronunciation: Hoss-pit-al-iz-um   **Type**: Noun

Definition: A diagnosis used to refer to the adverse effects of a prolonged stay in hospital such as a lack of development in children.

Example: My uncle suffered from **hospitalism** as a child and still shows the effects of it today.

Hyperbole

Pronunciation: Hi-purr-bo-lee   **Type**: Noun

Definition: Exaggerated claims or statements that aren't meant to be taken seriously, often used as a literary device to evoke emotion.

Example: The book was almost unreadable because of the large amount of **hyperbole**.

I

Ibex

Pronunciation: I-bex   **Type**: Noun

Definition: A type of wild goat with long, thick horns and a beard, usually found in mountainous areas like the Alps and the Pyrenees.

Example: When Geoffrey was climbing the mountain, he spotted an **ibex** grazing.

Ichthyoid

Pronunciation: Ick-thee-oyd   **Type**: Adjective, Noun

Definition: Of or relating to fish; having fish-like qualities. The noun refers to a dinosaur that possessed fish-like qualities including the ability to breathe underwater. It's thought that this dinosaur might have been a primitive form of the crocodile and the alligator.

Example:
#1: The **ichthyoid** boy was destined for a career as an Olympic swimmer.
#2: The **ichthyoid** chased its food through the water.

Iconoclasm

Pronunciation: I-kon-oh-clazz-um   **Type**: Noun

Definition: The attack, destruction or rejection of established beliefs and institutions, particularly those that are religious.

Example: Harry opted for his own form of **iconoclasm**, burning a cross in the garden.

Ideogram

Pronunciation: Id-ee-oh-gram   **Type**: Noun

Definition: A written character or symbol that's used to indicate the idea or function of something without describing the sounds that are used to say it.

Example: He couldn't speak the language, but the tourist didn't mind because the **ideogram** showed him which toilet to use.

Ideology

Pronunciation: I-dee-ol-oh-jee   **Type**: Noun

Definition: A system of shared ideas and beliefs, particularly one that forms the basis of an economic, religious or political policy.

Example: Gary believed in the communist **ideology** and joined a group of revolutionaries.

Idiosyncrasy

Pronunciation: Id-ee-oh-sin-crass-ee   **Type**: Noun

Definition: A distinctive feature or characteristic that marks something out as individual; a quirk.

Example: Dennis's **idiosyncrasy** was his habit of lighting cigarettes with a blowtorch.

Idyllic

Pronunciation: I-dill-ic   **Type**: Adjective

Definition: Peaceful, happy or picturesque. This adjective is usually used to describe a time or a place.

Example: In his dreams, Dean's life was **idyllic** without the stresses of his daily life.

Ignominy

Pronunciation: Ig-no-min-ee   **Type**: Noun

Definition: Public shame or disgrace.

Example: I couldn't face the **ignominy** of being fired, so I quit my job before they had a chance to dismiss me.

Ignoramus

Pronunciation: Ig-nuh-ray-muss   **Type**: Noun

Definition: A stupid, ignorant person.

Example: When Jessica told me she thought Prince Philip was serving in Iraq, I knew she was an **ignoramus**.

Imam

Pronunciation: Im-am   **Type**: Noun

Definition: A religious leader, particularly one who leads prayers in a mosque.

Example: Whenever he had doubts, Mohammed went to his mosque and asked the **imam** for advice.

Immolate

Pronunciation: Im-oh-late   **Type**: Verb

Definition: To kill something, particularly as a sacrifice, especially by burning.

Example: The shaman ordered his followers to **immolate** the prisoners as an offering to the gods.

Impalpable

Pronunciation: Im-pal-pab-ull   **Type**: Adjective

Definition: Unable to be felt by touch.

Example: An **impalpable** aura of power emanated from the statesman.

Impeach

Pronunciation: Im-peech   **Type**: Verb

Definition: To call into question the integrity of a person or practice, or to charge the holder of a public office with misconduct.

Example: The anarchists wanted to **impeach** the president for crimes against the state.

Impending

Pronunciation: Im-pen-ding   **Type**: Verb

Definition: About to happen.

Example: The soldiers were well aware of their **impending** doom when they began to fight their enemy.

Imperative

Pronunciation: Im-peh-ra-tiv   **Type**: Adjective, Noun

Definition: Of vital importance; crucial. The noun is used to refer to an essential or urgent thing.

Example:
#1: The sergeant said, "It's **imperative** that we take the bridge."
#2: The prime minister claimed that bailing out the banks was an economic **imperative**.

Imperious

Pronunciation: Im-peer-ee-uss   **Type**: Adjective

Definition: Possessing unquestionable authority.

Example: The lieutenant's speech was **imperious**, and we were all prepared to follow him to our deaths.

Implausible

Pronunciation: Im-plaw-zi-bull   **Type**: Adjective

Definition: Unlikely, unconvincing or unbelievable.

Example: Janet's story about a gorilla eating her homework was **implausible**.

Imprimatur

Pronunciation: Im-prim-at-yur   **Type**: Noun

Definition: Official approval or an official license or sanction to publish a book. From the Latin for "let it be printed".

Example: The publisher was given an **imprimatur** and sent the manuscript to the press.

Improbity

Pronunciation: Im-pro-bit-ee   **Type**: Noun

Definition: A lack of integrity or honesty.

Example: We stopped hanging out with Timmy because he was getting a reputation for **improbity**.

Inaniloquent

Pronunciation: In-an-ill-oh-kwunt   **Type**: Adjective

Definition: Full of inane and empty conversation.

Example: Jerry was **inaniloquent** and dull to be around for extended periods of time.

Incarcerate

Pronunciation: In-car-suh-rate   **Type**: Verb

Definition: To put someone in prison.

Example: The policemen realised they needed to **incarcerate** the drunk because his behaviour was a danger to the public.

Incendiary

Pronunciation: In-sen-dee-eh-ree   **Type**: Adjective, Noun

Definition: The adjective is usually used to describe a device or method of attack that's designed to cause fires, while the noun refers to this type of device.

Example:
#1: During the battle, the enemy threw **incendiary** grenades.
#2: The **incendiary** set fire to the trees.

Incestuous

Pronunciation: In-sess-choo-uss   **Type**: Adjective

Definition: Of, involving or guilty of incest – sexual relations between two people or animals that are closely related.

Example: Adam had an **incestuous** relationship with his mother.

Inchoate

Pronunciation: In-co-ate   **Type**: Adjective

Definition: Not fully developed.

Example: Steve's business idea was promising but **inchoate**, and no bank manager would agree to lend him money.

Incognito

Pronunciation: In-cog-neet-oh   **Type**: Adjective

Definition: Possessing a concealed identity. This adjective is usually used to describe a person.

Example: The spy was **incognito** at the military ball.

Incommunicado

Pronunciation: In-com-yoo-nick-arr-doe   **Type**: Adjective

Definition: This adjective is used to describe a situation where communication with outsiders is either impossible or undesirable, either for voluntary or involuntary reasons.

Example: The prisoner of war was held **incommunicado** so he couldn't contact anyone.

Incongruous

Pronunciation: In-con-groo-uss   **Type**: Adjective

Definition: Out of place.

Example: There was something **incongruous** about the black-and-white photos that lined his bedroom wall. It was as if they were from another time.

Incontinent

Pronunciation: In-cont-in-unt   **Type**: Adjective

Definition: Not possessing full control over the bowels or bladder.

Example: Karen's daughter was four years old, but she was still **incontinent**.

Inculpate

Pronunciation: In-cul-pate   **Type**: Noun

Definition: To accuse, blame or incriminate a person or an organisation – to put someone forward as a culprit.

Example: Once he was arrested, Mad Phil had no choice but to **inculpate** his accomplices to avoid jail time.

Incunabulum

Pronunciation: Ink-yoo-nab-yoo-lum   **Type**: Noun

Definition: An image or a piece of text that was printed in Europe before 1501 AD.

Example: The historian held the **incunabulum** carefully as he studied the contents of the manuscript.

Indefatigable

Pronunciation: In-duh-fat-ig-ab-ull   **Type**: Adjective

Definition: This adjective is usually used to describe a person or their efforts when they're never tiring and endlessly persistent.

Example: Joey didn't have a technical knowledge of the game, but the coach gave him the captain's armband because he was **indefatigable** and never gave up.

Indigenous

Pronunciation: In-dij-in-uss   **Type**: Adjective

Definition: Native to or occurring naturally in a particular place.

Example: The explorers couldn't speak the language and struggled to communicate with the **indigenous** people of the island.

Indite

Pronunciation: In-dite   **Type**: Verb

Definition: To produce a piece of literature by writing down or dictating to a scribe.

Example: After the meal, Janet decided to **indite** a letter of love to her boyfriend.

Indoctrinate

Pronunciation: In-dock-trin-ate   **Type**: Verb

Definition: To teach a person or a group of people to accept a fact or a group of (usually religious) beliefs without question or criticism.

Example: The Catholic school wasn't built to educate. It was built to **indoctrinate** students in Catholicism at a young age.

Inducible

Pronunciation: In-jew-sib-ull   **Type**: Adjective

Definition: Able to be induced. Something is induced when it's persuaded, moved or influenced to do something.

Example: The **inducible** beggar would do anything for a penny.

Inebriation

Pronunciation: In-ee-bree-ay-shun   **Type**: Noun

Definition: The state of being inebriated; drunkenness.

Example: Carl was in such an advanced state of **inebriation** that he spent half an hour talking to the dog.

Ineluctable

Pronunciation: In-uh-luck-tib-ull   **Type**: Adjective

Definition: Inescapable or inevitable; unable to be resisted, fought or avoided.

Example: The country's economic breakdown was **ineluctable**.

Ineptitude

Pronunciation: In-ep-ti-chood   **Type**: Noun

Definition: The quality of being inept, which is the awkwardness or unskillfulness that results from a lack of training.

Example: Shaun proved his **ineptitude** when, during his second week as a cashier, he still hadn't mastered the till.

Inertia

Pronunciation: In-ur-sha   **Type**: Noun

Definition: The tendency to do nothing or to stay in the same state.

Example: Janet tried hard to overcome the **inertia** of her career.

Infantile

Pronunciation: In-funt-ile   **Type**: Adjective

Definition: Of, similar to or related to children or infants. It can also mean childish or immature.

Example: Carey's mother shouted at him because of his **infantile** sense of humour.

Infernal

Pronunciation: In-fur-nul   **Type**: Adjective

Definition: Of, relating to or characteristic of hell or the underworld. It can also be used to mean irritating, annoying or tiresome in the same way that hellish is occasionally used.

Example: The conditions on the battlefield were **infernal**.

Infinitesimal

Pronunciation: In-fin-it-ess-im-ul   **Type**: Adjective

Definition: Extremely small – infinitely so.

Example: The mathematician said that the odds of winning the lottery were **infinitesimal**, but I decided to buy a ticket anyway.

Ingot

Pronunciation: Ing-ut   **Type**: Noun

Definition: A (usually oblong) block of metal.

Example: Mr. Jenkins deposited the **ingot** in his safe.

Inguinal

Pronunciation: In-gwin-ul   **Type**: Adjective

Definition: Of, relating to or characteristic of the groin.

Example: I had to go to the doctor after experiencing **inguinal** pain.

Innuendo

Pronunciation: In-yoo-end-oh   **Type**: Noun

Definition: A figure of speech that has two meanings – one literal meaning and one that's implied. Innuendo is often sexual and/or derogatory.

Example: My girlfriend asked me for an **innuendo,** so I gave her one.

Innumerable

Pronunciation: Ih-noom-yuh-ra-bull   **Type**: Adjective

Definition: This adjective is used to describe a collection of things that are too great in number to be counted or calculated.

Example: Gladys loved to stare at the **innumerable** stars in the night sky.

Inscrutable

Pronunciation: In-scroot-a-bull   **Type**: Adjective

Definition: Impossible to read, understand or interpret.

Example: Peter's poker face was **inscrutable.**

Insectivore

Pronunciation: In-sek-tiv-or   **Type**: Noun

Definition: An animal or plant that lives on a diet of insects.

Example: The **insectivore** hunted flies by night and slept by day.

Insidious

Pronunciation: In-sid-ee-uss   **Type**: Adjective

Definition: Progressing slowly but surely with harmful effects.

Example: The effects of global warming are **insidious**.

Insinuate

Pronunciation: In-sin-yoo-ate   **Type**: Verb

Definition: To suggest or hint at something negative in an indirect way.

Example: When Gary said Hilary's boyfriend had crabs, he tried to **insinuate** that she gave them to him.

Insurgent

Pronunciation: In-sur-junt   **Type**: Adjective, Noun

Definition: The adjective describes someone or something that's rising in rebellion against the established regime, while the noun refers to a rebel or revolutionary.

Example:
#1: The **insurgent** groups were armed and dangerous.
#2: The **insurgent** took a pot-shot at the American soldier.

Intense

Pronunciation: In-tense   **Type**: Adjective

Definition: Highly concentrated, forceful or extreme.

Example: When my granddad worked in the boiler room, he had to deal with **intense** heat and physical exertion

Interdisciplinary

Pronunciation: In-tur-diss-ip-lin-eh-ree   **Type**: Adjective

Definition: Of or relating to more than one branch of knowledge or area of study.

Example: Carey's university course was **interdisciplinary**, allowing him to work on his linguistics while learning all about the human body.

Interlard

Pronunciation: In-tur-lard   **Type**: Verb

Definition: To mix different subjects or different types of material together in speech or writing.

Example: Cheri was struggling to meet the word count on her essay so she decided to **interlard** it with opinions and irrelevant quotations.

Interlocutor

Pronunciation: In-tur-lock-yoo-ter   **Type**: Noun

Definition: A person who takes part in a conversation.

Example: The **interlocutor** gesticulated[†] wildly as he delivered the point of his argument.

Interloper

Pronunciation: In-tur-lo-pur   **Type**: Noun

Definition: An intruder.

Example: The **interloper** stole precious secrets from the laboratory.

Interpolate

Pronunciation: In-tur-po-late   **Type**: Verb

Definition: To insert something between fixed points, particularly by adding words to a manuscript to give a false impression of its date of origin.

Example: The editor knew that he needed to **interpolate** the manuscript to modernise it.

Intravenous

Pronunciation: In-tra-vee-nuss   **Type**: Adjective

Definition: Existing inside of or administered into the veins.

Example: The patient was hooked up to an **intravenous** drip to keep him hydrated during the coma.

Introspective

Pronunciation: In-tro-spec-tiv   **Type**: Adjective

Definition: Self-observational and self-examinational; prone to thinking about one's own mental and emotional desires.

Example: The timid youth was **introspective** and used to write about his feelings in his journal.

Invective

Pronunciation: In-veck-tiv   **Type**: Noun

Definition: Language that's highly critical, insulting, offensive or abusive.

Example: Stephen was given a detention for his in-class **invective**.

Inveigh

Pronunciation: In-vay   **Type**: Verb

Definition: To speak or write about something with a passionate hostility.

Example: When the cashier at ASDA refused to give Terry a refund, he decided to **inveigh** against the store on social media.

Invidious

Pronunciation: In-vid-ee-uss   **Type**: Adjective

Definition: Likely to stir up anger, resentment or hatred in others. This adjective is usually used to describe a course of action or a situation. It can also be used to describe a comparison that's unfair or unjust.

Example: The newspaper's **invidious** attack on the up-and-coming starlet angered many of her fans, and they were forced to publish an apology.

Irascible

Pronunciation: Ih-rass-ib-ull   **Type**: Adjective

Definition: Quick to become angry.

Example: We knew that the lecturer was **irascible** after he raged at us for being twelve seconds late to his lesson.

Iridescent

Pronunciation: Ih-rid-ess-unt   **Type**: Adjective

Definition: Showing multiple colours that seem to change when viewed from different angles.

Example: The car's paint job was **iridescent** and made it look spectacular in any weather or clime.

Irradiate

Pronunciation: Ih-ray-dee-ate   **Type**: Verb

Definition: To expose something to radiation. This is often done to food using gamma rays to kill microorganisms.

Example: Before delivering it to the supermarket, the farmer needed to **irradiate** the shipment of fruit and vegetables to make sure it was free of microorganisms.

Irrupt

Pronunciation: Ih-rupt   **Type**: Verb

Definition: To enter somewhere forcibly, suddenly or aggressively. This verb can also be used to refer to the migration of birds or other animals in unusually high numbers.

Example: The burglar opted to **irrupt** into the living room, not realising that the family had returned early from their holiday.

Isinglass

Pronunciation: Ize-in-glass   **Type**: Noun

Definition: A type of gelatine obtained from fish.

Example: Dean was vegan and so he refused to drink wines made with **isinglass**.

J

Jabberwocky

Pronunciation: Jab-ur-wock-ee   **Type**: Noun

Definition: A dragon with four legs and two wings, invented by Lewis Carroll. It can also be used to refer to invented, meaningless or nonsensical language, as that's what Carroll's poem was composed of.

Example: Alice slew a **jabberwocky** with her vorpal sword.

Jabot

Pronunciation: Ja-bo   **Type**: Noun

Definition: An ornamental frill or ruffle on the front of a shirt or blouse.

Example: Rihanna was mortified when she spilled tea on her **jabot**.

Jackanape

Pronunciation: Jack-an-ape   **Type**: Noun

Definition: An impertinent person; someone who's cheeky and presumptuous, despite being unimportant. This noun can also be used to refer to a tame ape or monkey.

Example: The **jackanape** at the photoshoot wouldn't stop talking about her diet.

Jalopy

Pronunciation: Jal-op-ee   **Type**: Noun

Definition: A dilapidated[+] old car.

Example: Dean drove the **jalopy** cross-country to Fresno in spite of it breaking down several times.

Jamboree

Pronunciation: Jam-buh-ree   **Type**: Noun

Definition: A large gathering or party, particularly a lavish and boisterous celebration. Also, a rally of Boy Scouts or Girl Scouts.

Example: Every summer, the youth club hosted a **jamboree**.

Jardinière

Pronunciation: Jar-de-neer   **Type**: Noun

Definition: A large pot or stand used to display plants; also, a garnish of mixed vegetables.

Example: Harold bought a **jardinière** filled with lilies to present to his wife.

Jaundice

Pronunciation: Jorn-diss   **Type**: Noun

Definition: A medical condition characterised by the yellowing of the skin or of the whites of the eyes, usually caused by an obstruction of the bile duct due to a liver disease.

Example: Harry was born yellow thanks to **jaundice,** and the doctors weren't sure if he was going to make it.

Jejune

Pronunciation: Juh-joon   **Type**: Adjective

Definition: Simplistic, dull or superficial.

Example: The **jejune** socialite[†] released a children's novel, but no one was stupid enough to buy it.

Jeremiad

Pronunciation: Jeh-ruh-my-ad   **Type**: Noun

Definition: A long, mournful lamentation.

Example: At the funeral, the **jeremiad** was heartfelt and poignant.

Jerkin

Pronunciation: Jerk-in   **Type**: Noun

Definition: A type of close-fitting men's jacket, usually made from leather and without sleeves.

Example: The earl donned his **jerkin** and prepared to face the day.

Jetsam

Pronunciation: Jet-sum   **Type**: Noun

Definition: A ship's goods or equipment after being purposefully thrown overboard.

Example: The seamen resorted to making **jetsam** in their haste to get away from the pirates.

Jezebel

Pronunciation: Jeh-zuh-bell   **Type**: Noun

Definition: A shameless or immoral woman, usually a prostitute. It's also the name of a biblical princess.

Example: Carl caught crabs from the **jezebel** in the club.

Jocular

Pronunciation: Jock-yoo-la   **Type**: Adjective

Definition: Fond of joking; playful.

Example: The young man was so **jocular** that it was difficult to get a straight answer out of him.

Jodhpurs

Pronunciation: Jod-purrs   **Type**: Noun

Definition: Close-fitting trousers designed for horseback riding. They're tight around the knee and have reinforced patches inside the leg.

Example: Emily climbed into her **jodhpurs** and prepared to take the horse around the paddock.

Journalese

Pronunciation: Jur-nul-eez   **Type**: Noun

Definition: A style of writing that's considered hackneyed[†], characterised by clichés and sensationalism and typical of newspapers and magazines.

Example: I don't understand why anyone reads *The Sun* – it's all **journalese** to me.

Julep

Pronunciation: Jew-lip   **Type**: Noun

Definition: A sweet drink made from a sugary syrup, often containing alcohol or medication.

Example: His mother handed him the **julep** and said, "Drink this. It's good for you."

Juncture

Pronunciation: Junk-cher   **Type**: Noun

Definition: A particular point in time, or a place where two or more things are joined.

Example: Jenny took a deep breath and said, "At this **juncture**, I think it's futile to continue our relationship."

Junta

Pronunciation: Jun-tah   **Type**: Noun

Definition: A political military group that rules a country after seizing power by force.

Example: After the coup d'état[†], the **junta** policed the streets.

Juvenile

Pronunciation: Jew-vuh-nile   **Type**: Adjective, Noun

Definition: Of, for or relating to adolescents. The noun is used to refer to such an adolescent and often contains the implication that the youngster in question causes trouble.

Example:

#1: The theft was **juvenile,** but it made Keith feel like a man.

#2: Jessie became a **juvenile** delinquent after her parents abandoned her.

K

Kafkaesque

Pronunciation: Kaff-ka-esk   **Type**: Adjective

Definition: Characteristic, typical of or reminiscent of the surreal, nightmarish qualities of Franz Kafka's writing.

Example: Tanya's parents banned her from watching television after she started having **Kafkaesque** dreams.

Kaput

Pronunciation: Ka-put   **Type**: Adjective

Definition: Broken or useless.

Example: We couldn't get back home because the car's engine was **kaput**.

Kasbah

Pronunciation: Kaz-bar   **Type**: Noun

Definition: A type of fortress or a formerly fortified complex of buildings, usually where a citadel is found.

Example: Bettie had never been inside the **kasbah**, but she knew that The Clash wanted to rock it.

Kayak

Pronunciation: Kye-yak   **Type**: Noun, Verb

Definition: A type of canoe made from a light frame and a water-tight covering, originally used by the Inuit. The verb describes the act of travelling using this type of transportation.

Example:
#1: Kevin planned to continue his expedition on the water by **kayak**.
#2: They got stuck in the jungle and had to **kayak** downstream.

Kelpie

Pronunciation: Kell-pee   **Type**: Noun

Definition: A water spirit from Scottish folklore[†], taking the form of a supernatural horse that delights in the drowning of travellers. It's also the name of an Australian breed of sheepdog.

Example: Before he drowned, the last thing that Leonard ever saw was the flowing mane of the **kelpie**.

Kenspeckle

Pronunciation: Ken-speck-ul   **Type**: Adjective

Definition: Easy to recognise or conspicuous.

Example: The **kenspeckle** elephant had pink skin.

Kibbutz

Pronunciation: Kih-bootz   **Type**: Noun

Definition: A communal settlement in Israel, usually one that's based on agriculture.

Example: The workers on the **kibbutz** rose early in the morning to tend to the fields before it got too hot.

Kibosh

Pronunciation: Kye-bosh   **Type:** Noun

Definition: To put an end to or dispose of something, or to stop something from happening.

Example: The businessman put the **kibosh** on the deal because it would be too costly to pursue.

Kinaesthesia

Pronunciation: Kin-ass-thee-zee-a   **Type:** Noun

Definition: The sense of the relative position of different parts of the body.

Example: Even though there was zero gravity, the astronaut's **kinaesthesia** told him his head was by his knee.

Kismet

Pronunciation: Kiss-met   **Type:** Noun

Definition: Fate.

Example: It looked like certain death, but **kismet** intervened and saved my life that night.

Kleptomaniac

Pronunciation: Klep-toe-may-nee-ack   **Type:** Noun

Definition: Someone who's addicted to stealing.

Example: The **kleptomaniac** kept the pen that the examiner lent to him.

Knurl

Pronunciation: Nurl   **Type**: Noun

Definition: A small projecting ridge, especially one that's in a series around the edge of something.

Example: Keith cut his finger on the metal **knurl** of the open tin of beans.

Kook

Pronunciation: Kook   **Type**: Noun

Definition: A strange, crazy or eccentric person.

Example: "That old man?" said Owen. "He's nothing but a crazy old **kook**."

Kowtow

Pronunciation: Cow-tow   **Type**: Verb

Definition: To kneel and touch the ground with the forehead or to act in any other subservient[†] manner.

Example: The general refused to **kowtow** to the emperor.

Kryptonite

Pronunciation: Kripp-ton-ite   **Type**: Noun

Definition: A fictional element from the Superman series, created from the radioactive remains of the planet Krypton.

Example: Superman had a mortal fear of **kryptonite**, his only weakness.

Kukri

Pronunciation: Koo-kree   **Type**: Noun

Definition: A curved knife that grows broader and forms a point, often used by Ghurkas.

Example: Jonathan Harker cut off Dracula's head with a **kukri**.

Kumquat

Pronunciation: Kum-kwot   **Type**: Noun

Definition: A type of fruit that's similar to an orange.

Example: Janine's favourite fruit is the **kumquat**.

L

Labyrinthine

Pronunciation: Lab-ih-rin-thine   **Type**: Adjective

Definition: Of or resembling a labyrinth, which is an intricate maze of interconnections.

Example: Death stalked the **labyrinthine** streets in a black cowl.

Lacerate

Pronunciation: Lass-uh-rate   **Type**: Verb

Definition: To tear, rip or cut something, particularly flesh or skin. The verb can also refer to the act of viciously injuring someone's feelings or emotions.

Example: The knife was able to **lacerate** his skin but failed to do permanent damage.

Lachrymose

Pronunciation: Lack-rim-ose   **Type**: Adjective

Definition: Tearful or prone to weeping.

Example: The widower was **lachrymose** after the funeral.

Lackadaisical

Pronunciation: Lack-ah-day-zic-ul   **Type**: Adjective

Definition: Unenthusiastic and lacking determination; lazy, but carelessly so.

Example: Weary from the heat, the traveller dozed to the **lackadaisical** clip-clops of his horse's shoes.

Lackey

Pronunciation: Lack-ee   **Type**: Noun

Definition: A slave or servant.

Example: When Mum asked me to do the dishes, I shouted, "I'm not your **lackey!**"

Laconic

Pronunciation: La-con-ick   **Type**: Adjective

Definition: Using few words; concise. This adjective is usually used to describe a person, their speech or their style of writing.

Example: The old writer was **laconic,** but his stories had a magical quality in spite of their brevity.

Lampoon

Pronunciation: Lam-poon   **Type**: Noun, Verb

Definition: The noun is used to refer to a type of public criticism using sarcasm or ridicule, a technique that's common in speeches, television programmes, books and art. The verb refers to the action of criticising something in this way.

Example:
#1: The politician decided to **lampoon** his opponents in his big speech.
#2: The writer asked his editor, "Did you enjoy my **lampoon** of the middle classes?"

Languid

Pronunciation: Lan-gwid   **Type**: Adjective

Definition: Lazy, lifeless and listless; displaying no desire for physical exertion or effort. This word can also be used to describe a period of time or an event that was lazy and eventless.

Example: Lynval was **languid** in the afternoon because he had to work the night shift.

Lanyard

Pronunciation: Lan-yard   **Type**: Noun

Definition: A cord worn around the neck, shoulder or wrist to hold a whistle, ID card or other small object.

Example: Every visitor to the conference was presented with a **lanyard** that contained a miniature[+] programme.

Larceny

Pronunciation: Lar-suh-nee   **Type**: Noun

Definition: The theft of personal property.

Example: The criminal was sentenced to jail time for **larceny**.

Larrikin

Pronunciation: Lah-rik-in   **Type**: Noun

Definition: A boisterous, badly-behaved young man. Also, someone who ignores convention and does things their own way; a maverick.

Example: The good cop brought me a cup of tea, but I could see that the bad cop was a **larrikin**.

Larva

Pronunciation: Lar-va   **Type**: Noun

Definition: The juvenile[†] or initial form of an insect before it undergoes metamorphosis into adulthood.

Example: The **larva** disappeared into a cocoon and re-emerged as a butterfly.

Lascivious

Pronunciation: La-siv-ee-uss   **Type**: Adjective

Definition: Feeling or revealing a strong sexual desire. This adjective is usually used to describe a person or their actions.

Example: The janitor gave her a **lascivious** wink and told her to meet him in the storage cupboard.

Latent

Pronunciation: La-tunt   **Type**: Adjective

Definition: This adjective is used to describe the state of something when it's in an inactive existence. It can also be used to describe a plant or animal that lies dormant[†] or hidden until the circumstances are right for it to develop.

Example: When she first read the novel, she wasn't aware of the **latent** allegory[†].

Latifundium

Pronunciation: La-ti-fun-dee-um   **Type**: Noun

Definition: A large estate or ranch, typical in ancient Rome and occasionally found in Spain or Latin America. Latifundia are usually staffed by slaves.

Example: The senator returned to his **latifundium**.

Laudable

Pronunciation: Law-da-bull   **Type**: Adjective

Definition: Deserving recognition, praise or commendation. This adjective is usually used to describe an action, ideology[†], goal or idea.

Example: The soldier made the **laudable** decision to sacrifice his life for the greater good.

Layman

Pronunciation: Lay-mun   **Type**: Noun

Definition: A normal person, without professional or specialised knowledge.

Example: The rocket scientist struggled to explain his research to the **layman**.

Lecherous

Pronunciation: Lech-uh-russ   **Type**: Adjective

Definition: Possessing and displaying an excessive level of sexual desire.

Example: The **lecherous** old man pinched the young woman's bottom when she sat down.

Legalese

Pronunciation: Leeg-ul-eez   **Type**: Noun

Definition: The formal and technical language that's typical of legal documents.

Example: Johnny couldn't understand the court papers because they were written in **legalese**.

Leitmotif

Pronunciation: Lite-mo-teef   **Type**: Noun

Definition: A theme that recurs throughout a musical composition or a literary piece.

Example: The main **leitmotif** in Jeremy's short story was his desire for animalistic sex.

Lemming

Pronunciation: Lemm-ing   **Type**: Noun

Definition: A small rodent with a short tail. It's often believed that lemmings commit mass suicide when they migrate, but this is a common misconception. Because of this, the noun can also be used to describe anyone who unthinkingly joins a mass movement.

Example: Gary earned the nickname **Lemming** because he had a pet **lemming** and always wore what the newspapers told him to wear.

Lepidopterist

Pronunciation: Lep-id-op-tuh-rist   **Type**: Noun

Definition: A person who collects or studies butterflies or moths.

Example: The **lepidopterist** was overjoyed to add the Colias Hyale to his collection.

Leprosy

Pronunciation: Lep-russ-ee   **Type**: Noun

Definition: A contagious disease that affects the skin and nerves, causing lumps and discoloration of the skin and occasional disfigurement and loss of limb.

Example: The journalist decided to investigate the treatment options for **leprosy**.

Levee

Pronunciation: Le-vee   **Type**: Noun

Definition: An embankment built to stop a river from overflowing.

Example: The **levee** broke during the heavy rains and the village sank three feet underwater.

Leviathan

Pronunciation: Le-vi-ah-than   **Type**: Noun

Definition: A biblical sea monster.

Example: The **leviathan** crashed into the submarine and damaged the hull.

Levity

Pronunciation: Lev-it-ee   **Type**: Noun

Definition: Frivolity or humour, particularly the treatment of a serious matter with undue humour.

Example: Patrick dealt with the death of his mother with unusual **levity**.

Lewd

Pronunciation: Lood   **Type**: Adjective

Definition: Crude and overtly sexual.

Example: The **lewd** waiter at the restaurant checked the businesswoman out as she sat down.

Lexicologist

Pronunciation: Lec-sic-ol-oh-jist   **Type**: Noun

Definition: A student of language, particularly the components of language such as the nature or meaning of words. Also, a compiler or writer of a dictionary.

Example: The **lexicologist** was overjoyed to discover that lugubrious[†] is a word.

Libertine

Pronunciation: Lib-ur-teen   **Type**: Adjective, Noun

Definition: The adjective describes something that's characterised by a lack of morality, while the noun refers to someone who doesn't have morals.

Example:
#1: The bachelor's parties were **libertine** and often ended in orgies.
#2: The **libertine** refused to be constrained by society, much to the annoyance of his wealthy family.

Libidinous

Pronunciation: Lib-id-in-uss   **Type**: Adjective

Definition: Possessing a strong sexual libido, which is a sexual desire.

Example: The **libidinous** young woman was always picking up guys on the weekends.

Ligature

Pronunciation: Lig-at-yur   **Type**: Noun, Verb

Definition: The noun refers to something that's used to tie or bind something tightly, while the verb refers to the process of tying something with a ligature.

Example:
#1: The assassin decided to use his belt as a **ligature**.
#2: The sadomasochists[†] liked to **ligature** each other.

Lilliputian

Pronunciation: Lil-eep-yoo-tee-un   **Type**: Adjective, Noun

Definition: The adjective is used to describe something small or diminutive, while the noun refers to a creature with these attributes. The word comes from the land of Lilliput from Jonathan Swift's novel, *Gulliver's Travels*.

Example:
#1: The insect was **Lilliputian**, invisible to the naked eye.
#2: The **Lilliputian** lived on food that it stole from the humans.

Linctus

Pronunciation: Link-tuss   **Type**: Noun

Definition: A type of syrupy cough medicine.

Example: "Don't forget to take your **linctus** before bed," his mother shouted.

Lingo

Pronunciation: Lin-go   **Type**: Noun

Definition: The language, dialect and jargon of a particular subset or group of people.

Example: Gary wanted to move to Paris, but he didn't know if he could learn the **lingo**.

Lingua Franca

Pronunciation: Ling-wa Fran-ka   **Type**: Noun

Definition: An artificial language that mixes other languages together to form a composite whole which can be understood by speakers of the component languages.

Example: The settlers spoke to each other in a **lingua franca**.

Lint

Pronunciation: Lint   **Type**: Noun

Definition: The short, fluffy fibres that gather together inside people's pockets.

Example: Peter searched through the **lint** in his pockets to try to find his bus ticket.

Lionise

Pronunciation: Ly-on-ize   **Type**: Verb

Definition: To assign a high amount of social importance to someone or something.

Example: The film studio wanted to **lionise** the ageing filmmaker.

Liquefy

Pronunciation: Lik-wiff-eye   **Type**: Verb

Definition: To turn something into a liquid, typically by using a blender to turn solid food into a liquid or a puree.

Example: I decided to **liquefy** my fruit and to turn it into a smoothie.

Lithosphere

Pronunciation: Lith-oh-sfeer   **Type**: Noun

Definition: The outermost shell of a rocky planet. On Earth, this consists of the crust and the upper mantle.

Example: The scientists couldn't wait to start running tests on the **lithosphere**.

Livery

Pronunciation: Liv-ur-ee   **Type**: Adjective, Noun

Definition: This is an example of a word with two completely different meanings, depending upon whether it's a noun or an adjective. The noun refers to a special type of uniform worn by the servant of an official, while the adjective describes something that resembles liver in colour, taste or consistency.

Example:
#1: The bruise on her cheek had turned a **livery** shade.
#2: The coachman was dressed in his **livery** and waiting at the door by the time that his master rose.

Loanword

Pronunciation: Lone-word   **Type**: Noun

Definition: A word that's been adopted from a foreign language with little to no modification.

Example: Cul-de-sac[†] is my favourite **loanword**.

Locution

Pronunciation: Lo-cue-shun   **Type**: Noun

Definition: A word, phrase or a person's style of speech.

Example: The politician spoke with a curious **locution**.

Logophobia

Pronunciation: Lo-go-fo-bee-ah   **Type**: Noun

Definition: The fear of words or of talking.

Example: The villagers said that the man was a mute, but his doctor knew it was a case of **logophobia** as there was no medical reason behind the man's silence.

Lollygagger

Pronunciation: Lol-ee-gag-ur   **Type**: Noun

Definition: A lazy person or a slacker.

Example: My father always used to call me a **lollygagger** and insisted that I'd never be successful.

Longevity

Pronunciation: Lon-jev-it-ee   **Type**: Noun

Definition: Length.

Example: The politician would always be remembered for the **longevity** of her time in office.

Longueur

Pronunciation: Lon-gurr   **Type**: Noun

Definition: A long, tedious passage in a book or movie, or an extended period of time.

Example: Pam enjoyed *1984*, except for the **longueur** in the middle.

Loquacious

Pronunciation: Lo-kway-shuss   **Type**: Adjective

Definition: Talkative.

Example: My niece is so **loquacious** that the only way to get some peace and quiet is to give her a bowl of ice cream.

Low-Key

Pronunciation: Low-kee   **Type**: Adjective

Definition: Restrained or unobtrusive; trying not to attract attention.

Example: David's stag-do was **low-key**. He was at home in bed by midnight.

Lubricious

Pronunciation: Loo-brish-uss   **Type**: Adjective

Definition: This word usually describes something that's characterised by lust or intended to arouse sexual desire. It can also describe something that's smooth and slippery with oil or a similar lubricant.

Example: Caitlin couldn't keep a straight face in the art gallery because of the **lubricious** statues.

Lucid

Pronunciation: Loo-sid   **Type**: Adjective

Definition: This adjective usually describes something that's expressed clearly or that's easy to understand. It can also be used to describe someone who shows the ability to think clearly, especially in the intervals between periods of confusion. Finally, a lucid dream is a dream in which the sleeper is aware that they're dreaming.

Example: The general took advantage of the **lucid** moment in the war room to announce his imminent retirement.

Lucrative

Pronunciation: Loo-crat-iv   **Type**: Adjective

Definition: Producing or capable of producing a large amount of profit.

Example: The gangster's new business measure was proving to be **lucrative**.

Luddite

Pronunciation: Ludd-ite   **Type**: Noun

Definition: A person who's opposed to or uncomfortable around new technology.

Example: The poet was a **luddite** and only ever wrote in his notebook.

Ludicrous

Pronunciation: Loo-dick-russ   **Type**: Adjective

Definition: This adjective is used to describe something that's so ridiculous or foolish that it's laughable.

Example: Jamie's awkward attempts to seduce the supermodel were **ludicrous**.

Lugubrious

Pronunciation: Loo-goo-bree-uss   **Type**: Adjective

Definition: Looking, sounding or appearing sad or dismal.

Example: The widow was **lugubrious** at her husband's funeral.

Luminescent

Pronunciation: Loo-min-ess-unt   **Type**: Adjective

Definition: Emitting light without emitting heat.

Example: The **luminescent** wallpaper glowed in the dark.

Luncheon

Pronunciation: Lun-chun   **Type**: Noun

Definition: A formal word for lunch, particularly a formal lunch held in connection with a meeting or some other special occasion.

Example: Yesterday morning, we received an invitation in the post to the duchess's charity **luncheon**.

Lupine

Pronunciation: Loo-pine   **Type**: Adjective

Definition: Of, like or relating to wolves.

Example: We suspected that the stranger was a werewolf because of his **lupine** features and his fear of the full moon.

Lurid

Pronunciation: Lurr-id   **Type**: Adjective

Definition: Unattractively bright or vivid in colour.

Example: Kerry hated visiting her grandmother in the retirement home because of the **lurid** orange wallpaper and appalling interior décor[†].

Lutenist

Pronunciation: Loo-tun-ist   **Type**: Noun

Definition: Someone who plays the lute.

Example: The **lutenist** played an impressive solo and earned himself a round of applause.

Lycanthropy

Pronunciation: Ly-can-throp-ee   **Type**: Noun

Definition: The state of being a werewolf.

Example: Harry was convinced that he suffered from **lycanthropy**, but the doctor refused to believe him.

Lymphatic

Pronunciation: Lim-fat-ick   **Type**: Adjective

Definition: Of, similar to or relating to lymph or its secretion. Lymph is a colourless liquid containing white blood cells which bathes the tissue inside the body.

Example: The open sore was **lymphatic** and needed cleaning.

Lynch

Pronunciation: Linch   **Type**: Verb

Definition: This verb refers to the action of killing someone as a large group. In particular, it refers to the process of hanging someone without an official trial.

Example: When they found out about the sex offender, the locals decided to **lynch** him as quickly as possible.

M

Macabre

Pronunciation: Mah-car-bre   **Type**: Adjective

Definition: Disturbing or horrifying because of an association with or a depiction[+] of death, gore or injury.

Example: Harold took his fiancée out to see the latest **macabre** horror film.

Macerate

Pronunciation: Mass-ur-ate   **Type**: Verb

Definition: To soften something or to cause it to disintegrate by soaking it in water.

Example: The chef decided to **macerate** the dessert with custard.

Machiavellian

Pronunciation: Mack-ee-av-ell-ee-an   **Type**: Adjective

Definition: Cunning, scheming and unscrupulous.

Example: The politician used **Machiavellian** tactics to climb to the top of his profession.

Machismo

Pronunciation: Ma-cheez-mo   **Type**: Noun

Definition: An overly aggressive form of masculine pride with characteristics including fierceness, bravado and chauvinism.

Example: The woman fell in love with the wrestler because of his enduring **machismo**.

Maelstrom

Pronunciation: Male-strom   **Type**: Noun

Definition: A powerful whirlpool either in the sea or in a river.

Example: The ship was tragically lost during the **maelstrom**, along with all hands.

Mafioso

Pronunciation: Maff-ee-oh-so   **Type**: Noun

Definition: A member of the Mafia.

Example: The **mafioso** was a dangerous man to mess with.

Magma

Pronunciation: Mag-mah   **Type**: Noun

Definition: Molten rock found underneath the surface of the Earth. Magma becomes lava once it reaches the surface.

Example: The **magma** spewed out of the volcano.

Magnanimous

Pronunciation: Mag-nan-im-uss   **Type**: Adjective

Definition: Generous or forgiving, particularly towards a rival or a losing opponent.

Example: The general was **magnanimous** in victory. He always said that a subservient[†] enemy was better than a dead one.

Magnum Opus

Pronunciation: Mag-num Oh-pus   **Type**: Noun

Definition: An important piece of literature, music or art. The phrase means "great work" in Latin.

Example: The painter bowed with a flourish as he added the final touch to his **magnum opus**.

Maharishi

Pronunciation: Ma-ha-rish-ee   **Type**: Noun

Definition: A sage or spiritual leader.

Example: The musicians flew to Tibet to visit the **maharishi** to ask for guidance.

Malaise

Pronunciation: Mal-aze   **Type**: Noun

Definition: A vague feeling of discomfort, illness or uneasiness without an apparent cause.

Example: There was nothing medically wrong with Joey, so the doctors diagnosed him with **malaise**.

Malevolent

Pronunciation: Mal-ev-oh-lunt   **Type**: Adjective

Definition: Possessing or demonstrating a wish to do evil or harm to others.

Example: Gary was haunted by a **malevolent** spirit in his dreams.

Malinger

Pronunciation: Mal-ing-ur   **Type**: Verb

Definition: To feign⁺ illness to escape from doing work.

Example: We knew that morale was low when the troops began to **malinger** and rebel.

Manifesto

Pronunciation: Man-if-ess-toe   **Type**: Noun

Definition: A public declaration of one's policy, aims and method, particularly when issued before a political election or a vote. Manifestoes are usually either written or spoken.

Example: Harold wasn't impressed when he read the **manifesto** as he disagreed with the policies it described.

Manifold

Pronunciation: Man-if-old   **Type**: Adjective

Definition: Having many different forms, types, parts or possibilities.

Example: Upon graduating college, Emma's job opportunities were **manifold** as she had five offers to choose from.

Manky

Pronunciation: Man-kee   **Type**: Adjective

Definition: Disgusting due to dirtiness or griminess.

Example: The floor was so **manky** that we couldn't tell if we were stepping in dust or excrement.

Manqué

Pronunciation: Mon-kay   **Type**: Adjective

Definition: Frustrated and unfulfilled in achieving one's ambition.

Example: The **manqué** author was jealous of his successful friend.

Maquette

Pronunciation: Mak-et   **Type**: Noun

Definition: A preliminary model or a sketch, particularly an early draft of an architectural work or a sculpture.

Example: The artist sold his **maquette** to pay for the completion of the final piece.

Maraud

Pronunciation: Mah-rord   **Type**: Verb

Definition: To roam freely in search of things to steal, people to attack or women to rape.

Example: The Vikings were known to **maraud** along the coast, and people feared them.

Marmoreal

Pronunciation: Mar-mor-ee-al   **Type**: Adjective

Definition: Made of, resembling or having similar properties to marble.

Example: The **marmoreal** statues glimmered in the sunlight.

Martyr

Pronunciation: Mar-tur   **Type**: Noun, Verb

Definition: A person who's killed because of their beliefs. The verb means to kill someone because of their beliefs, thus turning them into a martyr.

Example:
#1: The church built a statue to the **martyr** in honour of his sacrifice.
#2: The sergeant refused to execute the prisoners because he didn't want to **martyr** them.

Masochism

Pronunciation: Mass-oh-kiz-um   **Type**: Noun

Definition: The tendency to feel pleasure from your own pain or humiliation.

Example: The priest was a firm practitioner of **masochism** and flogged himself twice daily.

Mastectomy

Pronunciation: Mass-tekt-oh-mee   **Type**: Noun

Definition: An operation to surgically remove one or both breasts, typically to treat breast cancer.

Example: Harry's wife looked glum after she booked the date for her **mastectomy**.

Masticate

Pronunciation: Mass-tick-ate   **Type**: Verb

Definition: To chew.

Example: The farmer watched his cows **masticate** grass in the sun.

Matriarch

Pronunciation: May-tree-ark   **Type**: Noun

Definition: An important older woman at the head of a family, tribe or organisation.

Example: Queen Victoria was the **matriarch** of both the country and her family.

Maturation

Pronunciation: Mat-yor-ay-shun   **Type**: Noun

Definition: The process of maturing.

Example: The barrel of whiskey was stored in the sheds while it underwent **maturation**.

Matutinal

Pronunciation: Mat-yoo-tin-ul   **Type**: Adjective

Definition: Of, related to or occurring in the morning.

Example: The **matutinal** fog slowly disappeared as the sun came out in the afternoon.

Maudlin

Pronunciation: Mord-lin   **Type**: Adjective

Definition: Extremely sentimental – tearfully or self-pityingly so.

Example: "I know that it's useless and **maudlin**," sang Simon. "When you live in the past, you're an orphan."

Mawkish

Pronunciation: Mor-kish   **Type**: Adjective

Definition: Excessively or overwhelmingly sentimental.

Example: The war veterans' conversations were **mawkish**, but they did the other patients no harm.

Maxim

Pronunciation: Max-im   **Type**: Noun

Definition: A short statement expressing a general truth, rule or saying.

Example: The old woman had lived her life by her favourite **maxim**: 'Work hard, play hard.'

Meander

Pronunciation: Me-an-dur   **Type**: Verb

Definition: To wander at random or to follow a winding course.

Example: Grandma decided to go for a **meander** in the countryside and didn't get back until midnight.

Megadeath

Pronunciation: Meh-gah-deth   **Type**: Noun

Definition: A unit created to describe the casualties of nuclear war, equivalent to the deaths of a million people.

Example: The terrorist planned to detonate the warhead from afar and cause the world's first **megadeath**.

Meh

Pronunciation: Meh   **Type**: Exclamation

Definition: An interjection equivalent to a verbal shrug; an expression of apathy, indifference or boredom.

Example: When Alice asked if I preferred tea or coffee, I shrugged my shoulders and said "**Meh**".

Melancholia

Pronunciation: Mel-an-coll-ee-ah   **Type**: Noun

Definition: A deep sense of sadness, gloom or depression.

Example: The salesman quit his job and sought professional help for his **melancholia**.

Melee

Pronunciation: Mel-ay   **Type**: Noun

Definition: A confused fight, scuffle or skirmish[†].

Example: The soldier lost his firearm in the **melee** and couldn't find it with all the fighting around him.

Menarche

Pronunciation: Men-arr-kee   **Type**: Noun

Definition: A woman's first period, when menstruation begins for the first time.

Example: The youngster was confused when she went through **menarche** as she'd never talked to her mother about her changing body.

Mendacious

Pronunciation: Men-day-shuss   **Type**: Adjective

Definition: Untruthful.

Example: During the war, the enemy tried to lower morale by spreading **mendacious** propaganda[†].

Mensch

Pronunciation: Mensh   **Type**: Noun

Definition: A person of integrity and honour.

Example: Gabe thought Joram was a real **mensch** because he could always count on him to do the right thing.

Menses

Pronunciation: Men-sees   **Type**: Noun

Definition: The blood and other matter that's discharged from the uterus during menstruation.

Example: Josie went to the toilet to clean the **menses** from her gusset[†].

Meretricious

Pronunciation: Meh-ruh-trish-uss   **Type**: Adjective

Definition: Appearing attractive despite having no redeemable qualities, value or integrity.

Example: Paris Hilton's abilities as an actress are **meretricious** at best.

Meritorious

Pronunciation: Meh-rit-or-ee-uss   **Type**: Adjective

Definition: Worthy of merit; deserving reward or praise.

Example: Bobbie won employee of the month because of her **meritorious** work on the boss' favourite client.

Metalanguage

Pronunciation: Met-a-lang-wij   **Type**: Noun

Definition: A type of language that's used when language itself is being discussed or examined.

Example: Syntax[†], adverb and iambic pentameter are all examples of **metalanguage**.

Micturition

Pronunciation: Mick-chur-ish-un   **Type**: Noun

Definition: Urination.

Example: The patient had difficulty initiating **micturition**, as well as a poor stream rate.

Milieu

Pronunciation: Mi-loo   **Type**: Noun

Definition: A person's social environment.

Example: After the sergeant's retirement, he began to miss the military **milieu**.

Milt

Pronunciation: Milt   **Type**: Noun

Definition: The semen of a male fish.

Example: Kevin refused to go swimming in the sea because of all the **milt**.

Minatory

Pronunciation: Min-at-or-ee   **Type**: Adjective

Definition: Expressing or conveying menace; threatening.

Example: The hooligan raised a **minatory** fist and told me to get lost.

Miniature

Pronunciation: Min-ee-atch-ur   **Type**: Adjective, Noun

Definition: The adjective is used to describe something that's extremely small. The noun is used to refer to such an item, typically one that's part of a collection – small bottles of spirits, for example.

Example:
#1: The new smartphone was fitted with a dozen **miniature** computer chips.
#2: Carol decided to drink Kevin's prized **miniature** to help her get through the divorce.

Mire

Pronunciation: Mire   **Type**: Noun

Definition: An area of swampy, muddy or boggy ground.

Example: The horses met their demise in the **mire** after getting stuck in the mud.

Misanthropy

Pronunciation: Miss-an-throw-pee   **Type**: Noun

Definition: A dislike of humanity and humankind.

Example: The old man used to be friendly and polite, but since his illness he's turned into an advocate of **misanthropy**.

Mise-En-Scène

Pronunciation: Meez On Sen   **Type**: Noun

Definition: The arrangement of scenery and props during a theatrical or cinematic production that represents the place where the action is taking place. The phrase literally means "placing on stage".

Example: A good editor is always aware of the **mise-en-scène** of the film that he's working on.

Misnomer

Pronunciation: Miz-no-mer   **Type**: Noun

Definition: A wrong or inaccurate name or designation, or an inaccurate use of a name or other word.

Example: When Christopher Columbus arrived in America, he thought he was in the West Indies. Naming Native Americans Indians was a **misnomer** because they're not from the West Indies.

Misogyny

Pronunciation: Miss-oj-in-ee   **Type**: Noun

Definition: The hatred of women and girls, particularly by men.

Example: Because of her boss's **misogyny**, Sadie was passed up for the promotion once again.

Misprision

Pronunciation: Miss-priz-yun   **Type**: Noun

Definition: The deliberate concealment of the knowledge of a criminal act.

Example: Mr. Phillips was facing jail time after it was revealed that he'd committed **misprision** by not revealing that he knew about the missing funds.

Mnemonic

Pronunciation: Nuh-mon-ick   **Type**: Noun

Definition: A way of remembering things that uses associations or patterns of letters to spark the memory.

Example: "Every Good Boy Deserves Football" is a **mnemonic** designed to help people to read sheet music.

Modicum

Pronunciation: Mod-ick-um   **Type**: Noun

Definition: A small quantity of something, especially something that's considered valuable or important.

Example: The old man's lies contained a **modicum** of truth.

Mojo

Pronunciation: Mo-jo   **Type**: Noun

Definition: This word was originally used to refer to a magic charm, talisman or spell. However, it's taken on a new meaning and is now a slang word for self-confidence and sexual charm.

Example: Josh has lost his **mojo** and hasn't had sex for years.

Molecular

Pronunciation: Moll-eck-yoo-lar   **Type**: Adjective

Definition: Of, relating to or consisting of molecules.

Example: Peter's father was an award-winning **molecular** biologist.

Moiety

Pronunciation: Moy-ut-ee   **Type**: Noun

Definition: Each of the parts into which a thing can be divided.

Example: They couldn't understand the message because of the **moiety** of parts it was delivered in.

Monandry

Pronunciation: Mo-nan-dree   **Type**: Noun

Definition: The practice and custom of having one husband at a time.

Example: The Mormons were unpopular with the advocates of **monandry**.

Monoglot

Pronunciation: Mon-oh-glot   **Type**: Noun

Definition: A person who can only speak one language.

Example: Peter was a **monoglot** who only ever holidayed in England.

Monotonous

Pronunciation: Mon-ot-un-uss   **Type**: Adjective

Definition: Boring and repetitive; lacking in variety. As well as being used to describe tasks and chores, this word can also be used to describe someone's voice when it doesn't vary in tone, pitch or volume.

Example: The students refused to sit through another **monotonous** lecture. They wanted the class to do something different.

Moonstruck

Pronunciation: Moon-struck   **Type**: Adjective

Definition: Unable to think or act correctly, particularly as a result of being in love.

Example: Johnny was so **moonstruck** over Katie that he failed the exam.

Moribund

Pronunciation: Moh-rib-und   **Type**: Adjective

Definition: At the bottom of a decline.

Example: Under Ottoman rule, Egypt became the neglected corner of a large and **moribund** empire.

Mortify

Pronunciation: Mor-tif-eye   **Type**: Verb

Definition: To cause somebody to feel ashamed, embarrassed or humiliated.

Example: Karen managed to **mortify** her boyfriend when she got her tits out at the festival.

Motley

Pronunciation: Mot-lee   **Type**: Adjective

Definition: Varied in appearance and/or character; incongruous†.

Example: The friends were a **motley** bunch, and everyone stared when they went out in public.

Mountebank

Pronunciation: Mount-uh-bank   **Type**: Noun

Definition: A person who deceives other people, particularly to cheat them out of their money.

Example: My grandparents lost all their money to a **mountebank** who claimed to be selling timeshares.

Mucus

Pronunciation: Mew-kus   **Type**: Noun

Definition: A slimy substance that's secreted from the **mucus** membranes for a variety of reasons including lubrication and protection.

Example: The monster was covered with **mucus,** and it terrified all who gazed upon it.

Mulch

Pronunciation: Mulch   **Type**: Noun

Definition: A material, typically compost or decaying[†] leaves, that's spread over a plant to enrich or insulate the soil.

Example: The gardener spread the **mulch** over the flowerbeds with a shovel.

Mulct

Pronunciation: Mulkt   **Type**: Noun

Definition: A fine or a compulsory payment.

Example: The debt collector took his **mulct** and headed back to headquarters.

Multifarious

Pronunciation: Mul-tee-fare-ee-uss   **Type**: Adjective

Definition: Possessing many parts or aspects.

Example: The actor's **multifarious** talents allowed him to write, star in and direct the award-winning production.

Multitudinous

Pronunciation: Mul-tee-choo-din-uss   **Type**: Adjective

Definition: Highly numerous; consisting of or containing many individuals or elements.

Example: The choice of games for the Xbox 360 is **multitudinous**.

Mummer

Pronunciation: Mum-mur   **Type**: Noun

Definition: An actor, particularly one who communicates with gestures and facial expressions.

Example: The Hollywood starlet started out as a **mummer**.

Mundane

Pronunciation: Mun-dane   **Type**: Adjective

Definition: Lacking interest, excitement, life or vitality. This adjective can also be used to describe earthly matters, particularly when opposed to the spiritual or the heavenly.

Example: Ian was bored of his job and didn't know how much longer he could stand his **mundane** lifestyle.

Munificent

Pronunciation: Mew-niff-iss-unt   **Type**: Adjective

Definition: Larger or more generous than is strictly necessary.

Example: The diplomats brought a **munificent** gift of diamonds and gold.

Muppet

Pronunciation: Mupp-it   **Type**: Noun

Definition: This noun was originally used by Jim Henson to refer to his puppet creations. Since its introduction in the 1950s, it's taken on various new meanings in different parts of the world. In general, it's now used to refer to an incompetent, stupid or foolish person.

Example: Kevin's dad didn't like my joke – he called me a **muppet** and left the room.

Muscovite

Pronunciation: Muss-co-vite   **Type**: Adjective, Noun

Definition: The adjective describes something that's related to Moscow, while the noun can be used to refer to a citizen of the city. The noun is also another name for 'isinglass'[†].

Example:
#1: The **muscovite** streets were paved with snow and ice.
#2: The old **muscovite** wore a tall hat and made a fortune on the stock market.

Mycology

Pronunciation: My-coll-oh-gee   **Type**: Noun

Definition: The scientific study of fungi and mushrooms.

Example: The hippie claimed to be a professor of **mycology,** citing his experience with magic mushrooms.

Myopia

Pronunciation: My-oh-pee-ah   **Type**: Noun

Definition: Bad eyesight.

Example: Benny has **myopia** and has to wear strong glasses with thick lenses.

Myriad

Pronunciation: Mih-ree-ad   **Type**: Adjective

Definition: Countless or great in number.

Example: The internet consists of **myriad** computers that are all connected together.

Myropolist

Pronunciation: My-rop-oh-list   **Type**: Noun

Definition: A perfume dealer.

Example: My sister and I went to the **myropolist** to get something special for Mum's birthday.

N

Nadir

Pronunciation: Nad-eer   **Type**: Noun

Definition: A low point in the fortunes of a person or organisation. This noun is opposite in meaning to 'zenith.'[†]

Example: Carlos's career hit a **nadir** when he was fired for misconduct.

Napalm

Pronunciation: Nay-parm   **Type**: Noun

Definition: An extremely flammable jelly used during warfare. It can be used to create incendiary[†] bombs and flamethrowers and was popular during the Vietnam War.

Example: The military dropped **napalm** from an attack plane to lower the enemy's morale.

Nascent

Pronunciation: Nay-sunt   **Type**: Adjective

Definition: Not yet fully developed. This adjective is often used to describe a business, a process or a movement.

Example: Juliette's **nascent** singing career had taken her to the Royal Albert Hall, but she still had to work two other jobs to pay her bills.

Nebulous

Pronunciation: Neb-yoo-luss   **Type**: Adjective

Definition: Hazy, unclear, vague or ill-defined.

Example: The concept† of fairness is **nebulous** and subjective.

Necromancy

Pronunciation: Neck-ro-man-see   **Type**: Noun

Definition: The art, theory and practice of communication with the dead, particularly to resurrect them in the form of animated skeletons and zombies or to predict the future. The noun can also be used to refer to the practice of witchcraft, sorcery or black magic as a whole.

Example: The **necromancy** student was caught stealing from graves in the middle of the night.

Necrophilia

Pronunciation: Neck-ro-fee-lee-ah   **Type**: Noun

Definition: An erotic fascination with or attraction towards corpses, or the act of having sexual intercourse with a corpse.

Example: She was sexually adventurous, but she drew the line at **necrophilia**.

Nefarious

Pronunciation: Nuh-fare-ee-uss   **Type**: Adjective

Definition: Wicked, immoral or criminal.

Example: Ronald's mother wasn't happy about his **nefarious** friends, but she couldn't ask him to stop seeing them.

Neologism

Pronunciation: Nee-ol-oh-jiz-um   **Type**: Noun

Definition: A new word or expression, or the creation and usage of new words and expressions.

Example: My favourite **neologism** is 'Googlewhack'[†].

Nepotism

Pronunciation: Nep-oh-tiz-um   **Type**: Noun

Definition: The phenomenon that occurs when people in power favour their relatives and friends, particularly when giving people jobs.

Example: Kevin only got that job through **nepotism** because his father is the boss.

Newfangled

Pronunciation: New-fang-uld   **Type**: Adjective

Definition: New-fashioned, modern or high-tech.

Example: I bought my granddad a Kindle for Christmas, but he can't figure out how to use it. He says it's too **newfangled** and that he prefers to feel the pages in his hands.

Newspeak

Pronunciation: New-speek   **Type**: Noun

Definition: A fictional language from George Orwell's *1984*. In general use, the noun is used to describe an ambiguous language used mainly for political propaganda[†]. In Orwell's novel, newspeak was a deliberately weakened form of English that was used by the state and intended to make any antiestablishment thought or speech impossible.

Example: "Cancel stop unproceed constructionwise antegetting plusfull estimates machinery overheads stop end message" is an example of Orwellian[†] **newspeak**.

Nexus

Pronunciation: Nex-uss   **Type**: Noun

Definition: A connected group or a series of connections that link two or more things together.

Example: The writer's head was a **nexus** of ideas for many different stories.

Nicety

Pronunciation: Ni-suh-tee   **Type**: Noun

Definition: A fine detail or distinction, particularly one that's intricate and fussy. This noun is also a byword[†] for accuracy and precision.

Example: The visitor wasn't constrained by the usual rules of diplomatic **nicety** and was able to speak freely.

Nictitate

Pronunciation: Nic-ti-tate   **Type**: Verb

Definition: To blink or close the eyes for a short period of time.

Example: I was so terrified that I could barely **nictitate**.

Niggardly

Pronunciation: Nig-ud-lee   **Type**: Adjective

Definition: Stingy, particularly when it comes to financial matters.

Example: The company was too **niggardly** to grant its employees their traditional Christmas bonuses.

Nihilism

Pronunciation: Nye-ill-iz-um   **Type**: Noun

Definition: A viewpoint that's occasionally described as 'extreme scepticism,' including a rejection of all religious and moral principles. Nihilism is often associated with the belief that life is meaningless and that nothing in the world has a real existence.

Example: Richard's atheism eventually paved the way for a foray into **nihilism**.

Noctambulist

Pronunciation: Noc-tamb-yoo-list   **Type**: Noun

Definition: A sleepwalker.

Example: My dad, the **noctambulist**, used to scare me when I was younger by walking into my room in the middle of the night.

Nomenclature

Pronunciation: No-men-clay-chur   **Type**: Noun

Definition: The art and science of choosing names for things. The noun can also be used to refer to the collection of names assigned to a particular topic or subject.

Example: Jane's sister studied scientific **nomenclature** during her time at university.

Nomophobia

Pronunciation: Nome-oh-fo-be-ah   **Type**: Noun

Definition: A shortened form of 'no mobile phobia' – the fear of being left without your phone.

Example: John has **nomophobia** and keeps patting his pockets to check that he still has his phone.

Nonagenarian

Pronunciation: Non-a-jun-air-ee-un   **Type**: Noun

Definition: Someone who's between the ages of ninety and ninety-nine.

Example: For a **nonagenarian**, Great Aunt Brenda could play a damn good game of table tennis.

Nonconformist

Pronunciation: Non-con-form-ist   **Type**: Noun

Definition: A person whose behaviour, attitude, style or opinions don't conform to the established norm.

Example: The writer was a **nonconformist** who didn't own a computer or a mobile phone.

Nouniness

Pronunciation: Now-nee-niss   **Type**: Adjective

Definition: The state or quality of being a noun. The term is also used to describe the quality of a piece of writing with an excessive number of nouns.

Example: It's always a good policy to choose baby names based upon their **nouniness**.

Novitiate

Pronunciation: No-vish-ee-ate   **Type**: Noun

Definition: The state of being a novice, particularly in a religious order or institution. The noun can also be used to refer to the person themselves.

Example: The **novitiate** arrived at the church, excited to finally fulfil her calling of being a nun.

Nuance

Pronunciation: Noo-arnts   **Type**: Noun

Definition: A subtle, fine detail.

Example: The show just isn't the same if you don't understand the **nuance** behind the production.

Nudiustertian

Pronunciation: Noo-di-uss-tur-shee-un   **Type**: Adjective

Definition: Of, associated with or typical of the day before yesterday.

Example: Still nursing a sore head, Phillip began to regret his **nudiustertian** adventure.

Numismatics

Pronunciation: Noo-miz-mat-icks   **Type**: Noun

Definition: The study or collection of coins, currency, bank notes and medals.

Example: The pawn shop owner's one weakness was his interest in **numismatics**.

Nutation

Pronunciation: Noo-tay-shun   **Type**: Noun

Definition: A rocking or swaying in the tilt of the axis of or the rotation of an object.

Example: The lecturer told his students that the earth's **nutation** was due to the gravitational tug of the moon.

Nyctalopia

Pronunciation: Nick-ta-lo-pee-ah   **Type**: Noun

Definition: A medical condition that's characterised by difficulties in seeing in the dark or in areas with bad lighting.

Example: James's **nyctalopia** prevented him from being able to drive at night.

O

Oakum

Pronunciation: Oh-kum   **Type**: Noun

Definition: Loose fibres from untwisted ropes.

Example: The prisoners were forced to pick **oakum** so that the wardens could keep them busy.

Obeah

Pronunciation: Oh-bee-ah   **Type**: Noun

Definition: A kind of folk magic, sorcery or religion that's practiced in the Caribbean.

Example: The villagers distrusted the old practitioner of **Obeah**.

Obeisance

Pronunciation: Oh-bay-sunse   **Type**: Noun

Definition: Respect, or a gesture which shows such respect.

Example: During the queen's visit, the prime minister bowed in **obeisance**.

Obelisk

Pronunciation: Ob-ul-isk   **Type**: Noun

Definition: A tall stone pillar, usually in the shape of a cuboid[†] with a pyramid at the top, set up as a landmark or a monument.

Example: The ancients left no trace behind except for an **obelisk** in praise of the sun god.

Obelus

Pronunciation: Ob-ul-uss   **Type**: Noun

Definition: A dagger-like symbol used as a reference mark, often to show that a person is deceased[†].

Example: In this book, an **obelus** indicates a word that appears as an entry elsewhere.

Obfuscate

Pronunciation: Ob-fuss-cate   **Type**: Verb

Definition: To render something obscure, unclear or unintelligible.

Example: The soldier hoped to **obfuscate** his superior with his indecipherable map of the mountains.

Objurgate

Pronunciation: Ob-jur-gate   **Type**: Verb

Definition: To scold someone or to tell them off severely.

Example: My mum used to **objurgate** me every time I came home after curfew.

Obloquy

Pronunciation: Ob-lo-kee   **Type**: Noun

Definition: A strong level of public criticism or verbal abuse. Also, a public disgrace that's been brought about by this sort of criticism.

Example: Because of the **obloquy** thrown at her by the press, the politician reconsidered her run for office.

Obsequiously

Pronunciation: Ob-see-kwee-uss-lee   **Type**: Adverb

Definition: In an obsequious manner; overly obedient or attentive.

Example: The butler bowed **obsequiously** and went to fetch the tea.

Obsolescent

Pronunciation: Ob-so-less-unt   **Type**: Adjective

Definition: Becoming or growing obsolete. Something is obsolete when it's outdated, unsupported or no longer used.

Example: The **obsolescent** typewriters in the senator's office needed to be replaced.

Obstetric

Pronunciation: Ob-stet-rick   **Type**: Noun

Definition: Of or relating to the practice of obstetrics, the branch of medicine dealing with childbirth and the care of the mother during childbirth.

Example: During her pregnancy, my wife called the **obstetric** hospital every other day.

Obstinance

Pronunciation: Ob-stin-unce   **Type**: Noun

Definition: The trait or quality of stubbornness.

Example: The other children called Kevin "the Mule" because of his unending **obstinance**.

Obstreperous

Pronunciation: Ob-strep-uh-russ   **Type**: Adjective

Definition: Noisy or difficult to control.

Example: The crowd was too **obstreperous** for the bouncers to handle, so they had to call the police.

Obviate

Pronunciation: Ob-vee-ate   **Type**: Verb

Definition: To remove an obstacle or difficulty, or to do something that prevents such an obstacle from occurring.

Example: The housewife put up Venetian blinds to **obviate** the need for curtains.

Occiput

Pronunciation: Ocks-ip-ut   **Type**: Noun

Definition: The back of the head or the skull.

Example: Jeremy ran his hand over his head and stroked his **occiput**, then stared into the distance, thoughtfully.

Odalisque

Pronunciation: Oh-dal-isk   **Type**: Noun

Definition: A female slave or concubine[†] in a harem[†].

Example: The slave-driver bellowed orders that the **odalisque** couldn't refuse.

Odium

Pronunciation: Oh-dee-um   **Type**: Noun

Definition: A general or widespread hatred that's directed at someone or something in particular.

Example: The pop star risked the **odium** of the public when she voiced her homophobic opinions.

Offal

Pronunciation: Off-ul   **Type**: Noun

Definition: The blood and entrails[†] from inside an animal.

Example: Carl went to the butchers and bought a pound of **offal**.

Ogle

Pronunciation: Og-ull   **Type**: Verb

Definition: To stare at someone in a lecherous[†] or debauched manner.

Example: The young woman always felt uncomfortable at the folk club because the old men liked to **ogle** her.

Oleaginous

Pronunciation: Oh-lee-aj-in-uss   **Type**: Adjective

Definition: Rich in or covered with oil and grease. By extension, this adjective can also be used to describe someone who's unpleasantly complimentary.

Example: The first thing that the mechanic noticed after popping the hood was how **oleaginous** the engine was.

Olfaction

Pronunciation: Ol-fack-shun   **Type**: Noun

Definition: The sense of smell.

Example: Aaron had a weaker sense of **olfaction** than most because of a half-forgotten childhood accident with a chemistry set.

Oligarch

Pronunciation: Ol-ig-ark   **Type**: Noun

Definition: A rich businessman with a great deal of influence in politics and law.

Example: The wife of the **oligarch** was used to the best things in life.

Ombudsman

Pronunciation: Om-buds-man   **Type**: Noun

Definition: A person who carries out a third-party investigation into individual complaints against aspects of the state and its administration.

Example: The political **ombudsman** was drafted in to investigate claims that

MPs were making false claims on their expenses.

Omniphobia

Pronunciation: Om-ni-fo-bee-ah   **Type**: Noun

Definition: A medical condition also known as 'non-specific fear'. Omniphobes have a vague but persistent feeling of dread.

Example: Carol refused to leave the house because her **omniphobia** made it impossible for her to deal with day-to-day situations.

Onanism

Pronunciation: Oh-nan-iz-um   **Type**: Noun

Definition: Ejaculation outside of the vagina during intercourse. The term can also be used to refer to the act of masturbation.

Example: Despite being a firm believer in **onanism**, Chelsea still managed to get pregnant.

Onerous

Pronunciation: On-uh-russ   **Type**: Adjective

Definition: Involving or requiring a large amount of effort. This adjective is usually used to describe a task or a duty.

Example: The farmer's apprentice hoped that ploughing the fields wouldn't be too **onerous**.

Onomatopoeia

Pronunciation: On-oh-mat-oh-pee-ah   **Type**: Noun

Definition: A linguistic phenomenon that occurs when a word sounds like what it describes.

Example: 'Sizzle' and 'bang' are my favourite examples of **onomatopoeia**.

Ophthalmic

Pronunciation: Op-thal-mick   **Type**: Noun

Definition: Of, similar to or relating to the eye and its diseases.

Example: Clarissa booked an appointment with an **ophthalmic** specialist because her sight was getting worse.

Oracy

Pronunciation: Oh-rass-ee   **Type**: Noun

Definition: The ability to express oneself fluently and articulately through speech.

Example: The politician knew he needed to improve his **oracy** skills before participating in the debate.

Ordure

Pronunciation: Or-jure   **Type**: Noun

Definition: Excrement. By extension, it can also be used to refer to something vile, dirty or worthless.

Example: Martin's day went steadily downhill after he stepped in the **ordure**.

Orgiastic

Pronunciation: Or-jee-ass-tick   **Type**: Adjective

Definition: Of, characteristic of or resembling an orgy.

Example: Critics panned the play for being **orgiastic** and hedonistic[†].

Orrery

Pronunciation: Oh-ruh-ree   **Type**: Noun

Definition: A mechanical model of the solar system that's used to represent the planets' relative positions and motions.

Example: The scientist was proud of his **orrery** and refused to let visitors leave until they'd seen it.

Orthography

Pronunciation: Orth-og-raff-ee   **Type**: Noun

Definition: The study of spelling and the way that letters combine to represent sounds and form words. This noun can also be used to refer to the spelling system of a particular language.

Example: Words had always fascinated the professor, which is why he studied **orthography** as an undergraduate.

Orwellian

Pronunciation: Or-well-ee-un   **Type**: Adjective

Definition: Of, similar to or relating to the works of George Orwell. This adjective is most frequently used to describe something that resembles his depiction[†] of a totalitarian[†], dystopian police state.

Example: Kevin's nightmares were **Orwellian** and frighteningly realistic.

Oscillate

Pronunciation: Oss-ill-ate   **Type**: Verb

Definition: To move backwards and forwards at a regular speed.

Example: Harold's grandson liked to watch the pendulum of the old clock **oscillate** in the evenings.

Ostensibly

Pronunciation: Oss-ten-sib-lee   **Type**: Adverb

Definition: Apparently; taken on appearance alone.

Example: Melissa went to college to study mechanics, **ostensibly** to forge a career.

Ostler

Pronunciation: Oss-la   **Type**: Noun

Definition: A stable boy.

Example: The traveller handed the reins to the **ostler** and asked the innkeeper to fetch him a pint of ale.

Ostracise

Pronunciation: Oss-tra-size   **Type**: Verb

Definition: To expel someone from a group.

Example: The hipsters were quick to **ostracise** the pop fans on the discussion forum.

Otiose

Pronunciation: Oh-she-ose **Type**: Adjective

Definition: Useless, lazy or indolent.

Example: Mr. Robertson didn't allow his children to read fiction because he thought that anything untrue was **otiose** and not worthy of their attention.

Oubliette

Pronunciation: Ooh-blee-ett **Type**: Noun

Definition: A secret dungeon with access only through the ceiling. Historically, prisoners would fall into an oubliette and be left there to die in the darkness. The word literally means "forgotten place" in French.

Example: The emperor ordered his men to throw the prisoners into the **oubliette**.

Overture

Pronunciation: Oh-vur-ture **Type**: Noun

Definition: An introduction to something more substantial. This word is often used to refer to an instrumental introduction to an opera.

Example: Carl and Bianca arrived late to the opera hall and missed most of the **overture**.

Oxymoron

Pronunciation: Ox-ee-more-on   **Type**: Noun

Definition: A figure of speech where two contradictory terms are presented side-by-side.

Example: 'Same difference' is my favourite **oxymoron.**

P

Pachyderm

Pronunciation: Pack-id-urm   **Type**: Noun

Definition: Any large mammal with thick skin, particularly an elephant, rhinoceros or hippopotamus.

Example: The soldier moved aside to dodge the charging **pachyderm**.

Paean

Pronunciation: Pee-un   **Type**: Noun

Definition: Something that expresses praise or thanks, particularly a song or a poem.

Example: The lyricist spent six months perfecting his **paean**, praising his mother for her constant support.

Paginate

Pronunciation: Paj-in-ate   **Type**: Verb

Definition: To split a manuscript into separate pages or to number each of the pages.

Example: Dane had to **paginate** *The Lexicologist's Handbook* before sending it off to print.

Palaver

Pronunciation: Pah-larv-urr   **Type**: Noun

Definition: This noun refers to a state of confused and noisy disturbance.

Example: The teacher pushed between the fighting boys and demanded to know the cause of the **palaver**.

Palaeography

Pronunciation: Pay-lee-og-raff-ee   **Type**: Noun

Definition: The study of old writing.

Example: The professor of **palaeography** delivered a seminar on Ancient Egyptian hieroglyphics.

Palimpsest

Pronunciation: Pal-imp-sest   **Type**: Noun

Definition: A manuscript or canvas on which the original piece of work has been erased or covered to make room for something else. By association, this noun can also refer to anything that's been re-used or otherwise altered but which still retains visible traces of its original form.

Example: The archaeologists quickly realised that the clay tablet was a **palimpsest** when they saw traces of a second layer of writing.

Palindromic

Pronunciation: Pal-in-drom-ick   **Type**: Adjective

Definition: This adjective is used to describe a word or phrase that reads the same from left to right as it does from right to left.

Example: The phrase "Madam, I'm Adam" is **palindromic**.

Palisade

Pronunciation: Pal-iss-ade   **Type**: Noun, Verb

Definition: A fence made out of wooden or iron railings that are hammered into the ground to form an enclosure. The verb refers to the act of creating such a fence.

Example:
#1: The invading armies were kept at bay by the **palisade**.
#2: The soldiers needed to **palisade** the keep if they wanted to stay alive.

Palladium

Pronunciation: Pal-lay-dee-um   **Type**: Noun

Definition: A silvery-white metal element that resembles platinum.

Example: Connie asked her husband to buy her a ring made of **palladium**.

Palliative

Pronunciation: Pal-ee-at-iv   **Type**: Adjective, Noun

Definition: The adjective is used to describe something that possesses the ability to remove pain or to alleviate the symptoms of a problem without dealing with the actual cause. The noun refers to a remedy, a drug or a medicine that possesses these properties.

Example:
#1: The drug was **palliative** and helped Tanya to deal with her chemotherapy.
#2: The doctor prescribed a **palliative**.

Palter

Pronunciation: Pall-ter   **Type**: Verb

Definition: To be deliberately ambiguous or unclear to avoid revealing information.

Example: The students quickly learned how to **palter** with their teachers in the hopes that their noncommittal answers would be scored as correct.

Panacea

Pronunciation: Pah-nay-see-ah   **Type**: Noun

Definition: A universal cure.

Example: The scientist thought that the search for a cure for cancer would uncover a **panacea**.

Panache

Pronunciation: Pan-ash   **Type**: Noun

Definition: Flamboyant[†] confidence.

Example: He had all the **panache** of a movie star.

Pander

Pronunciation: Pan-dur   **Type**: Verb

Definition: To fulfil or indulge someone's needs and desires, particularly when those needs and desires are immoral.

Example: "I'm not going to **pander** to your every whim," shouted the bride.

Panegyric

Pronunciation: Noun   **Type**: Pan-eh-jeer-ick

Definition: A public speech or a piece of prose in praise of someone or something.

Example: The statesman hoped to jump ahead in the opinion polls with his **panegyric** for the dead princess.

Panjandrum

Pronunciation: Pan-jan-drum   **Type**: Noun

Definition: The belief that one has a huge amount of influence, power and authority.

Example: The gentleman's club was famed for its members' **panjandrum**. They had connections across the globe.

Pantheon

Pronunciation: Pan-thee-on   **Type**: Noun

Definition: All of the gods of a religion. Alternatively, a temple that's dedicated to the gods.

Example: The explorer took his first steps into the **pantheon** and admired the sculptures around him.

Papilla

Pronunciation: Pap-ill-ah   **Type**: Noun

Definition: A nipple-like protuberance[†].

Example: Harold was found dead with a **papilla**-like growth on his skull.

Parabolic

Pronunciation: Pah-rab-ol-ick   **Type**: Adjective

Definition: Of or relating to parables, simple stories that are designed to illustrate moral or spiritual lessons. The same word can also be used to describe something that has the form of a parabola, which is a mirror-symmetrical, U-shaped curve.

Example: The wisdom of Harry's grandmother was often **parabolic**.

Paradigm

Pronunciation: Pah-rad-ime   **Type**: Noun

Definition: A model or typical example of something.

Example: The artist's seminal[†] work was considered to be a new **paradigm** for public art.

Paragram

Pronunciation: Pah-rag-ram   **Type**: Noun

Definition: A pun made by changing the letters of a word.

Example: The speaker presented the audience with a **paragram** and walked offstage to polite applause.

Paramour

Pronunciation: Pah-ram-or   **Type**: Noun

Definition: A lover, particularly the secret lover of a married man.

Example: Mr. Pilton was obsessed with his latest **paramour** and hoped his wife wouldn't find out.

Paregmenon

Pronunciation: Pah-reg-muh-non   **Type**: Noun

Definition: A literary phenomenon that occurs when similar words are placed close together or side by side.

Example: 'Sense and sensibility' is Jeremiah's favourite **paregmenon**, but I prefer 'curvaceous curves.'

Pariah

Pronunciation: Pah-ry-ah   **Type**: Noun

Definition: An outcast.

Example: Getting pregnant at fourteen was enough to make Charlotte a **pariah** in the eyes of her family and friends.

Parotid

Pronunciation: Pa-rot-id   **Type**: Adjective

Definition: Of or relating to the parotid gland, the largest of the salivary glands.

Example: Mumps commonly causes inflammation of the **parotid** glands.

Paroxysm

Pronunciation: Pah-rox-iz-um   **Type**: Noun

Definition: An unexpected attack or a sudden violent expression of activity or emotion.

Example: At the mere sight of his daughter, the old man flew into a **paroxysm** of rage.

Parsimonious

Pronunciation: Par-sim-oh-nee-uss   **Type**: Adjective

Definition: Stingy or frugal[†] – unwilling to spend money or resources unnecessarily.

Example: The **parsimonious** priest only owned two shirts.

Parturient

Pronunciation: Par-chorr-ee-unt   **Type**: Adjective, Noun

Definition: The adjective is used to describe a woman or a female mammal that's about to give birth. The noun is occasionally used to refer to such a female.

Example:
#1: The pregnant refugee was **parturient,** and they rushed her to the hospital.
#2: The **parturient** in the waiting room sobbed as her baby thrashed inside her.

Pastiche

Pronunciation: Pass-teesh   **Type**: Noun, Verb

Definition: The noun refers to a piece of artistic work that imitates another work. The verb refers to the process of such imitation.

Example:
#1: Although it was the most popular piece in the gallery, the curator hated the **pastiche**.
#2: The student decided to **pastiche** his hero's distinct style.

Pathos

Pronunciation: Pay-thoss   **Type**: Noun

Definition: A quality or trait that conjures up feelings of sadness or pity.

Example: The playwright decided to reel the audience in with **pathos** before delivering the climactic scene.

Patricide

Pronunciation: Pat-riss-ide   **Type**: Noun

Definition: The act of killing one's father.

Example: The twenty-four-year-old was found guilty of **patricide** and sentenced to life imprisonment.

Patronymic

Pronunciation: Pat-ron-im-ick   **Type**: Noun

Definition: A name that's derived from the name of a father or an ancestor, often by the addition of a prefix or a suffix.

Example: 'Davidson' is a **patronymic**, as is 'Johnson' and 'O'Brien.'

Paucity

Pronunciation: Pore-sit-ee   **Type**: Noun

Definition: The existence of something in small or insufficient amounts.

Example: Thomas wanted to water the garden, but he couldn't because of the hosepipe ban brought on by the **paucity** of rainfall.

Paunch

Pronunciation: Pornch   **Type**: Noun

Definition: A fat or protruding stomach or abdomen.

Example: The sumo wrestler surveyed his **paunch** in the mirror.

Payola

Pronunciation: Pay-oh-la   **Type**: Noun

Definition: The practice of using bribery to force someone to use their influence, position or power to promote a particular body or interest.

Example: The music aficionados[†] protested against the **payola** they saw when the radio presenters were 'gifted' thousands of pounds by the rapper.

Peccadillo

Pronunciation: Peck-ad-ill-oh   **Type**: Noun

Definition: A minor or insignificant offence or sin.

Example: Although he only told white lies, Peter was ashamed of his secret **peccadillo**.

Peccant

Pronunciation: Peck-ant   **Type**: Adjective

Definition: This adjective is used to describe someone sinful. It can also be used to describe something that's diseased or that has the ability to cause disease.

Example: The archbishop despised the **peccant** masses but still tried to get them to repent for their sins.

Pecksniffian

Pronunciation: Peck-sniff-ee-an   **Type**: Adjective

Definition: Possessing a manner of benevolence, particularly in a hypocritical or sanctimonious[†] manner.

Example: The **pecksniffian** nobleman tossed a dirty coin at the feet of the beggar boy.

Pedagogy

Pronunciation: Ped-ag-og-ee   **Type**: Noun

Definition: The practice of teaching.

Example: The student wrote her dissertation on the subject of feminist **pedagogy**.

Pedant

Pronunciation: Ped-ant   **Type**: Noun

Definition: A person who obsesses over minor details.

Example: The **pedant** was so focused on his spelling and grammar that he never finished writing his masterpiece.

Pederasty

Pronunciation: Ped-ur-ass-tee   **Type**: Noun

Definition: Sexual or erotic[†] activity between an older man and an adolescent boy.

Example: The Catholic priest was arrested when several boys from his congregation accused him of **pederasty**.

Penchant

Pronunciation: Pon-shant   **Type**: Noun

Definition: A strong, habitual liking or fondness for something.

Example: The old woman had a **penchant** for breeding cats.

Penetralium

Pronunciation: Pen-uh-tray-lee-um   **Type**: Noun

Definition: The most secret or innermost part of a building or fortification.

Example: "Quick," shouted the cook. "To the **penetralium**. They'll never find us there!"

Perambulate

Pronunciation: Puh-ramb-yoo-late   **Type**: Verb

Definition: To walk around in a leisurely way, purely for the pursuit of pleasure.

Example: Every evening after dinner, the baron would **perambulate** around the grounds.

Perineum

Pronunciation: Peh-rin-ee-um   **Type**: Noun

Definition: The area of the body between the anus and either the scrotum or the vulva, depending upon gender.

Example: The builder scratched his **perineum** and sniffed his finger.

Permeability

Pronunciation: Purr-me-ab-il-it-ee   **Type**: Noun

Definition: The state or quality of a material or membrane that enables it to allow liquids or gases to pass through it.

Example: The water passed through the filter but the oil was siphoned off, thanks to the **permeability** of the material.

Pernicious

Pronunciation: Purr-nish-uss   **Type**: Adjective

Definition: Resulting in negative or harmful effects, particularly in a subtle, gradual or sneaky way.

Example: The **pernicious** storm tore through the seaside town.

Perquisite

Pronunciation: Perk-wiz-it   **Type**: Noun

Definition: A special right or privilege that's enjoyed as a result of one's job or position. The word 'perk' is a shortened form of 'perquisite.'

Example: Dave received a company car as a **perquisite**.

Persiflage

Pronunciation: Purr-sif-larj   **Type**: Noun

Definition: Light mockery or banter†, in speech or in writing.

Example: The boys in the pub were no strangers to **persiflage**. They made fun of each other all the time.

Pernickety

Pronunciation: Purr-nick-ut-ee   **Type**: Adjective

Definition: Too focused on minor or trivial details. This adjective can also be used to describe something that requires this type of approach.

Example: The **pernickety** pensioner hated it when he missed *Countdown* because it formed the start of his evening ritual.

Perspicacious

Pronunciation: Purr-spic-kay-shuss   **Type**: Adjective

Definition: Possessing a quick insight and a keen understanding of the workings of things.

Example: The student was **perspicacious** and could equal or better his teacher after only two years of training.

Pertinacious

Pronunciation: Purr-tin-ay-shuss   **Type**: Adjective

Definition: Sticking rigidly to an opinion, a viewpoint or a plan of action.

Example: The captain remained **pertinacious**, despite the dissent amongst his men.

Perversion

Pronunciation: Purr-vurs-yun   **Type**: Noun

Definition: The alteration of something from its original state into a corruption that's nearly unrecognisable when compared to the original version. This noun is also used to refer to sexual behaviour or desire that's considered abnormal, immoral or unacceptable.

Example: Sandra's **perversion** of choice was her collection of whips and chains.

Pessary

Pronunciation: Pess-uh-ree   **Type**: Noun

Definition: A device or treatment that's inserted into the vagina to act as a contraceptive, to treat infection or to support the uterus.

Example: Charlotte booked an appointment with her GP to discuss the advantages of a **pessary** as birth control.

Pestilential

Pronunciation: Pest-ill-en-shul   **Type**: Adjective

Definition: Possessing the quality of pestilence, being harmful, destructive or lethal to crops or livestock.

Example: A **pestilential** wind blew in from the north and many of the animals grew sick.

Petrification

Pronunciation: Pet-riff-ick-ay-shun   **Type**: Noun

Definition: The process by which organic matter turns into a stony substance. This noun is often used in a mythical context. It can also refer to a state of extreme fear in which the person experiencing the fear is frozen and metaphorically turned to stone.

Example: In classical mythology, Medusa's gaze was believed to have the power of **petrification**.

Pettifogger

Pronunciation: Pet-ee-fog-gur   **Type**: Noun

Definition: An inferior lawyer, particularly one who uses unscrupulous or morally dubious† practices to win in court or who deals with petty cases.

Example: The criminal had made plans for his arrest – his **pettifogger** was ready to argue until the police had no choice but to release him.

Petulant

Pronunciation: Pet-yoo-lunt   **Type**: Adjective

Definition: This adjective is used to describe a person or their behaviour when they're sulky or childishly ill-tempered.

Example: The **petulant** teenager told her parents that she wished they were dead.

Phalanx

Pronunciation: Fal-anks   **Type**: Noun

Definition: A group of people or objects that are packed closely together to form a compact body or a close formation. The noun is often used to describe a group of soldiers or police officers that are standing or moving in close formation.

Example: The Roman 'tortoise' formation is a type of **phalanx**.

Phantasmagorical

Pronunciation: Fan-taz-mah-goh-rick-al   **Type**: Adjective

Definition: Characterised by fantastic or deceptive imagery or appearances.

Example: After eating the mushrooms, Janet had a **phantasmagorical** experience.

Phenakism

Pronunciation: Fen-ack-iz-um   **Type**: Noun

Definition: Trickery or deception.

Example: Harold was punished by his parents for his **phenakism** when he snuck out to go to a party.

Phenomena

Pronunciation: Fuh-nom-in-ah   **Type**: Noun

Definition: The plural of 'phenomenon', a noun which is used to refer to a fact or a situation that can be observed to exist or to happen. Phenomena are remarkable because their causes are often unknown, questionable or seemingly impossible.

Example: The scientist led a team to investigate the **phenomena**.

Phial

Pronunciation: Fye-ul   **Type**: Noun

Definition: A small glass tube or bottle that's used to contain a liquid.

Example: The scientist uncorked the **phial** and examined the contents.

Philander

Pronunciation: Fill-and-ur   **Type**: Verb

Definition: To quickly or frequently enter casual sexual relationships. This verb is most commonly used to refer to the actions of heterosexual men.

Example: The footballer liked to **philander** with the women at the nightclub.

Philanthropist

Pronunciation: Fill-ann-thro-pist   **Type**: Noun

Definition: A person who tries to protect and promote the welfare of other people or animals. Many philanthropists are wealthy individuals who donate large sums of money to multiple good causes.

Example: Bill Gates is a well-known **philanthropist**.

Philophobia

Pronunciation: Fill-oh-fo-bee-ah   **Type**: Noun

Definition: The irrational fear of love and intimacy.

Example: Adam has had a bad case of **philophobia** since his wife left him.

Philtre

Pronunciation: Fill-tur   **Type**: Noun

Definition: A drink with magical powers which causes the drinker to fall in love with the person who gave it to them.

Example: The alchemist knew he could never have seduced the supermodel without his **philtre**.

Phlebotomist

Pronunciation: Fleb-ot-oh-mist   **Type**: Noun

Definition: A person who practices phlebotomy, the act of drawing blood.

Example: The **phlebotomist** made an incision, and the operation began.

Phlegm

Pronunciation: Flem   **Type**: Noun

Definition: The thick liquid that's secreted by the mucus[†] membranes of the respiratory system, particularly if it's secreted when coughing.

Example: Geoffrey coughed up some **phlegm** and tried to hide it by wiping it on his jeans.

Phlegmatic

Pronunciation: Fleg-mat-ic   **Type**: Adjective

Definition: Unemotional, calm or apathetic.

Example: The old farmer was practical and **phlegmatic**, important qualities in his line of work.

Phrenology

Pronunciation: Fren-ol-oh-gee   **Type**: Noun

Definition: The study of the shape and size of the cranium as an indicator of character, intelligence and personality.

Example: The professor of **phrenology** took an instant dislike to me because of my big head.

Picador

Pronunciation: Pick-a-door   **Type**: Noun

Definition: A bullfighter who rides a horse and uses a lance to weaken and enrage the bull.

Example: The crowd applauded ferociously as the bull charged at the **picador** on his horse.

Picaresque

Pronunciation: Pick-a-resk   **Type**: Adjective

Definition: Of, similar to or relating to a style of fiction which deals with the adventures of a rough, dishonest or rascally hero who still appeals and endears himself to his audience.

Example: Peter went to the book shop and bought a **picaresque** novel from the 1920s.

Pillion

Pronunciation: Pill-ee-un   **Type**: Noun

Definition: A seat for a passenger behind a jockey on a horse or the driver of a motorbike.

Example: Juliet climbed on to the **pillion** on the motorcycle and held on for dear life.

Pince-nez

Pronunciation: Pince-nez   **Type**: Noun

Definition: Glasses which clip on to the nose with a spring instead of being supported by arms over the ears.

Example: The professor put on his **pince-nez** and settled down in his favourite armchair to read the newspaper.

Pinchpenny

Pronunciation: Pinch-pen-ee   **Type**: Noun

Definition: A miser; someone who's unwilling to give or spend money.

Example: The **pinchpenny** was outraged when the government raised the price of stamps.

Pinion

Pronunciation: Pin-yun   **Type**: Noun, Verb

Definition: The outer part of a bird's wing, including the feathers, that's used for flight. The verb refers to the action of tying, holding or otherwise restricting someone's arms

Example:
#1: The birdwatcher admired the eagle's **pinion**.
#2: The jailors had to **pinion** the prisoner to march him to his cell.

Piscatorial

Pronunciation: Piss-cat-or-ee-ul   **Type**: Adjective

Definition: Of, similar to or related to fishermen or fishing.

Example: Dennis decided to join the **piscatorial** society so he could spend his retirement fishing.

Pizzicato

Pronunciation: Pits-ick-ar-toe   **Type**: Adverb, Adjective, Noun

Definition: The adverb is often used as a musical direction and describes a type of performance where a stringed instrument is played by plucking the strings with a finger. The adjective is used to describe a piece of music or a musical instrument that's performed in this way, and the noun refers to this technique of playing.

Example:
#1: John played his cello **pizzicato** to impress the ladies.
#2: The conductor wanted to play the **pizzicato** operetta, but he was overruled by the musicians.
#3: Harold struggled to master **pizzicato**.

Platonic

Pronunciation: Plat-on-ick   **Type**: Adjective

Definition: This adjective is most commonly used to describe a type of love or friendship that's close, intimate and affectionate without being sexual. It can also refer to something that's associated with the Ancient Greek philosopher Plato or his ideas.

Example:
Tom thought Jenny was going to sleep with him, but it turned out their relationship was **platonic**.

Plenipotentiary

Pronunciation: Plen-ee-po-ten-she-eh-ree   **Type**: Adjective, Noun

Definition: The noun refers to a person who's been granted full power of independent action on behalf of their government, while the adjective describes the possession of this power.

Example:
#1: The diplomat was **plenipotentiary** and knew he had the power to cause a major incident.
#2: The **plenipotentiary** promised the prime minister that his country would come to their aid if a conflict broke out.

Pleonasm

Pronunciation: Plee-oh-naz-um   **Type**: Noun

Definition: The use of more words than necessary to convey a meaning. It usually occurs as a stylistic fault due to a lack of skill as a writer, but it can also be used for emphasis.

Example: Steve told Kevin off for his **pleonasm** when he said he couldn't see through the pitch-black darkness.

Plethora

Pronunciation: Pleth-uh-rah   **Type**: Noun

Definition: An excess of something.

Example: Joey found it hard to make a decision about his future because of the **plethora** of advice from his family.

Plutocracy

Pronunciation: Ploo-tock-rass-ee   **Type**: Noun

Definition: A type of government where the wealthy have all the power. The word can also refer to a country or a society that's governed in this manner.

Example: The left-wing groups accused the Tory government of perpetrating a **plutocracy**.

Poetaster

Pronunciation: Po-it-ast-ur   **Type**: Noun

Definition: A person who writes bad or inferior poetry.

Example: John's father said, "That rapper is nothing but a **poetaster**."

Pogrom

Pronunciation: Po-grom   **Type**: Noun

Definition: A planned massacre, riot or mob attack that's directed at a particular minority or ethnic group.

Example: Mr. Spiegelman was the first to die in the **pogrom** in the Jewish village.

Pointillism

Pronunciation: Pwant-ill-iz-um   **Type**: Noun

Definition: An artistic technique where an overall work is created by tiny dots that become blended in the eye of the beholder. It evolved from impressionism in the 1880s.

Example: Vincent Van Gogh's *Self Portrait of 1887* is an example of **pointillism**.

Poltroon

Pronunciation: Pol-troon   **Type**: Noun

Definition: A coward.

Example: Ever the **poltroon**, Darren ran away from the bar-room brawl and left Tyler to deal with it alone.

Polychromatic

Pronunciation: Pol-ee-chro-mat-ick   **Type**: Adjective

Definition: Multi-coloured; the opposite of 'monochromatic'.

Example: Alex paused to appreciate the colours on his **polychromatic** scarf in the mirror.

Polygamous

Pronunciation: Pol-ig-am-uss   **Type**: Adjective

Definition: Practicing, relating to or involving polygamy, the act of having more than one spouse or sexual partner at a time.

Example: Mormons are famously **polygamous**.

Polyglot

Pronunciation: Pol-ee-glot   **Type**: Noun

Definition: A person who can read or speak more than one language.

Example: The **polyglot** made a living by translating manuscripts between English, Russian and Japanese.

Polysyllabic

Pronunciation: Pol-ee-sil-ab-ick   **Type**: Adjective

Definition: Possessing more than one syllable.

Example: Most of the words in *The Lexicologist's Handbook* are **polysyllabic**.

Polytheism

Pronunciation: Pol-ee-thee-iz-um   **Type**: Noun

Definition: The belief in or the worship of multiple gods.

Example: Hinduism is a large religion based on **polytheism**.

Pontificate

Pronunciation: Pon-tiff-ick-ate   **Type**: Noun, Verb

Definition: The verb traditionally means to act in the capacity of a bishop of the Roman Catholic Church, particularly at Mass. However, it's been bastardised in popular speech and can now refer to the act of speaking pompously in an attempt to convince someone else of your own point of view. The noun refers to the office or position of a Catholic bishop.

Example:
#1: Upon ascending to the **pontificate**, the bishop gave away all of his worldly possessions.
#2: At the pub, Dave decided to **pontificate** about his favourite football club.

Populace

Pronunciation: Pop-yoo-liss   **Type**: Noun

Definition: The inhabitants of a particular country, region or geographical area.

Example: The government's actions angered the **populace** and prompted a civil uprising.

Portentous

Pronunciation: Porr-ten-shuss   **Type**: Adjective

Definition: This adjective is used to describe a sign or a warning that something momentous or important is likely to happen. It's similar in meaning to 'ominous.'

Example: The dark sky and thunderclaps were **portentous**, and the villagers refused to leave their houses.

Portmanteau

Pronunciation: Port-man-tow   **Type**: Noun

Definition: A word that's created by combining two or more pre-existing words into a new, composite whole, often combining both sounds and meanings.

Example: 'Smog' is a **portmanteau**, a combination of 'smoke' and 'fog.'

Post-coital

Pronunciation: Post-coy-tull   **Type**: Adjective

Definition: Occurring immediately after the act of sexual intercourse.

Example: After they had sex, Harry put his boxer shorts back on and lit a **post-coital** cigarette.

Posterior

Pronunciation: Poss-teer-ee-ur   **Type**: Adjective, Noun

Definition: The adjective describes something that's backwards in position or near the rear end of something. The noun is used to refer to a person's buttocks.

Example:
#1: The security guard was on duty at the **posterior** entrance.
#2: Joe said to Kate, "You have a fantastic **posterior**."

Postern

Pronunciation: Poss-turn   **Type**: Noun

Definition: An entrance at the back or the side of a building or fortification.

Example: The attackers knew that their only chance to take the keep lay in capturing the **postern**.

Postulate

Pronunciation: Poss-choo-late   **Type**: Verb

Definition: To suggest that something that can't currently be proven is true as a basis for further reasoning or discussion.

Example: The scientist had to **postulate** that if the universe was expanding, there was something for it to expand into.

Potation

Pronunciation: Po-tay-shun   **Type**: Noun

Definition: A drink or the act of drinking.

Example: The managing director left strict instructions not to be disturbed during his evening **potation**.

Pragmatic

Pronunciation: Prag-mat-ick   **Type**: Adjective

Definition: Practical.

Example: Ever **pragmatic**, the ex-policeman was the first person to react after the bomb went off.

Precarious

Pronunciation: Prick-air-ee-uss   **Type**: Adjective

Definition: This adjective is used to describe something that's dependent upon circumstances beyond one's own control. It's often used to describe something that's at risk of falling or collapsing.

Example: The newspapers claimed that relations between the Russians and the Americans were **precarious**.

Prehensile

Pronunciation: Pre-hen-sile   **Type**: Adjective

Definition: Capable of grasping or holding things. This adjective is usually used to describe an animal's feet, hands or tail.

Example: The scientists couldn't learn much from the fossil, but they did know that the creature's hands were **prehensile**.

Presentiment

Pronunciation: Pre-sent-im-unt   **Type**: Noun

Definition: An intuitive feeling or knowledge of the future, particularly a bad feeling or a feeling of foreboding.

Example: The night before the battle, the king had a **presentiment** of his own untimely death.

Prestidigitator

Pronunciation: Press-tid-ij-it-ate-ur   **Type**: Noun

Definition: A magician who practices tricks that rely on sleight-of-hand.

Example: For Benji's sixth birthday party, his parents hired a **prestidigitator** to amaze the children with his magic.

Preternatural

Pronunciation: Pre-tur-nat-yur-ul   **Type**: Adjective

Definition: This adjective is used to describe something which appears to be outside or beyond whatever's considered normal or natural. In contrast to supernatural phenomena[†], things that are preternatural are presumed to have a rational explanation that's currently unknown.

Example: Dave was a self-taught businessman and had a **preternatural** understanding of financial and corporate matters.

Prevaricate

Pronunciation: Pre-vah-rick-ate   **Type**: Verb

Definition: To speak or act evasively.

Example: The politician chose to **prevaricate** when the journalists asked him about his expenses so that he wouldn't have to answer.

Primal

Pronunciation: Pry-mull   **Type**: Adjective

Definition: Primitive or basic.

Example: When the soldier charged at the enemy lines, his **primal** battle cry could be heard half a mile away.

Primogeniture

Pronunciation: Pry-mo-jen-it-yur   **Type**: Noun

Definition: Either the state of being a firstborn child or the right to succession that comes with it, particularly the inheritance of the father's title or land.

Example: Christopher felt content in his **primogeniture** and resolved to kill his father at the earliest opportunity.

Privation

Pronunciation: Pry-vay-shun   **Type**: Noun

Definition: The lack of one or more of the basic necessities or comforts in life, such as food, warmth or shelter.

Example: The hermit returned to society after a six-year **privation** on the mountainside.

Procrastination

Pronunciation: Pro-crast-in-ay-shun   **Type**: Noun

Definition: The act of postponing something to a later date, typically by using something trivial as an excuse to avoid doing something important.

Example: The students failed their exams because their revision time was overtaken by **procrastination**.

Procreate

Pronunciation: Pro-cree-ate   **Type**: Verb
Definition: To reproduce via sexual intercourse.

Example: The farmer encouraged his best cows to **procreate** in the hope that their young would grow to be just as lean and strong.

Prodigious

Pronunciation: Pro-dij-uss   **Type**: Adjective

Definition: Remarkably or impressively large in size or extent.

Example: The author's library was **prodigious**; all the walls were covered in tall bookcases.

Profanity

Pronunciation: Pro-fan-it-ee   **Type**: Noun

Definition: Obscene or blasphemous language.

Example: Little Johnny received a slap on the wrist from his mother when he uttered a **profanity**.

Profligacy

Pronunciation: Prof-lig-ass-ee   **Type**: Noun

Definition: Extravagance or indulgence in sensual pleasure, particularly when it involves spending a large amount of money.

Example: Harold's friends accused him of **profligacy** when he showed up to the nightclub in a limousine.

Prolegomenon

Pronunciation: Pro-leg-om-un-on   **Type**: Noun

Definition: A preliminary discussion, particularly a critical essay in a book.

Example: Janice never bothered to read *The Iliad* because the **prolegomenon** was sixty pages long.

Proletariat

Pronunciation: Pro-lut-air-ee-at   **Type**: Noun

Definition: The masses; working-class people as a whole.

Example: The **proletariat** rose up against the oppressive regime.

Prolix

Pronunciation: Pro-licks   **Type**: Adjective

Definition: This adjective is used to describe a speech or a piece of writing that contains too many words.

Example: The author's style was repetitive and boring and so the publishers rejected his **prolix** manuscript.

Promulgate

Pronunciation: Prom-ul-gate   **Type**: Verb

Definition: To promote an idea or a cause. This verb can also be used to refer to the action of putting a law into effect by making an official proclamation.

Example: The scientist decided to **promulgate** his research to increase his chances of funding.

Propaganda

Pronunciation: Prop-ag-and-ah   **Type**: Noun

Definition: Dubious[†] information of a biased or misleading nature that's produced and distributed to support a particular political party or point of view.

Example: During the Second World War, the air force dropped leaflets full of **propaganda** over enemy cities to promote their cause.

Prostrate

Pronunciation: Pross-trate   **Type**: Adjective

Definition: Lying flat on the ground, stretched out and facing the floor.

Example: The policeman took one look at the **prostrate** bodies and decided to call for back-up.

Protagonist

Pronunciation: Pro-tag-an-ist   **Type**: Noun

Definition: The main character in a work of film, theatre or literature.

Example: Frodo Baggins is the **protagonist** of the *Lord of the Rings* trilogy.

Protuberance

Pronunciation: Pro-choob-uh-runce   **Type**: Noun

Definition: Something that sticks out from something else, particularly on the body.

Example: "You should get that **protuberance** checked out," said Harold, eyeing Stephen's swollen knee.

Provost

Pronunciation: Pro-vost   **Type**: Noun

Definition: A senior officer at a college or university.

Example: The **provost** was an imposing figure who terrified the students whenever he left his office and walked amongst them.

Prurient

Pronunciation: Proo-ree-unt   **Type**: Adjective

Definition: Possessing, showing or encouraging an excessive amount of interest in sexual matters.

Example: The **prurient** businessman returned from his twice-weekly visit to the brothel.

Psychobabble

Pronunciation: Sy-co-bab-ull   **Type**: Noun

Definition: The jargon that's used by the general public when discussing the popular or mainstream aspects of psychology.

Example: The professor's least-favourite **psychobabble** terms are 'codependent' and 'narcissistic.'

Psychopomp

Pronunciation: Sike-oh-pomp   **Type**: Noun

Definition: A person or creature that guides or conducts the souls of the newly dead to the afterlife.

Example: When Barry saw the **psychopomp,** he regretted not taking out life insurance.

Psychosomatic

Pronunciation: Sy-co-sum-at-ick   **Type**: Adjective

Definition: This adjective describes an illness that's aggravated by a mental factor such as stress or exhaustion. It can also describe something that's typical of or characterised by the connection between the body and the brain.

Example: Jessica's red rash was a **psychosomatic** reaction to the stress of her exams.

Puerile

Pronunciation: Pure-ile   **Type**: Adjective

Definition: Childish or immature. This adjective is often used to describe someone's sense of humour.

Example: When Lance picked his nose and flicked it at his sister, their mother scolded him for being so **puerile.**

Pugilist

Pronunciation: Pew-jil-ist   **Type**: Noun

Definition: A boxer.

Example: The **pugilist** came out of the ring with a broken nose and bruised knuckles.

Pulveratricious

Pronunciation: Pull-veh-rat-rish-uss   **Type**: Adjective

Definition: This adjective can mean dusty or it can be used to describe a bird that nests on the ground.

Example: The **pulveratricious** children were told to shower off by their mother.

Purloin

Pronunciation: Purr-loyn   **Type**: Verb

Definition: To steal something.

Example: The intruder tried to **purloin** the legal documents but couldn't break into the safe.

Purulent

Pronunciation: Pure-uh-lunt   **Type**: Adjective

Definition: Consisting of, containing or discharging pus.

Example: Lars's teenage acne was **purulent**, and he disliked going out in public because of it.

Purveyor

Pronunciation: Purr-vay-ur   **Type**: Noun

Definition: A person or organisation that supplies, sells or deals in a particular type of goods.

Example: Leroy's Delicatessen was well known as the city's leading **purveyor** of salami.

Pusillanimous

Pronunciation: Puh -sill-an-im-uss   **Type**: Adjective

Definition: Scared or cowardly; showing a lack of courage or determination.

Example: David's attempts to get even with the school bully were **pusillanimous** at best. He never could stand up to him.

Putrescent

Pronunciation: Pew-tress-unt   **Type**: Adjective

Definition: Filthy or putrid; undergoing the effects of decomposition.

Example: Hilary shuddered as she saw the **putrescent** mouse that her cat had caught.

Q

Quandary

Pronunciation: Kwan-da-ree   **Type**: Noun

Definition: Uncertainty over what should be done in a particular situation. The noun can refer to the uncertainty or the situation itself.

Example: Gerald was in a **quandary.** Should he tell his fiancée about the affair?

Quango

Pronunciation: Kwan-go   **Type**: Noun

Definition: An acronym meaning 'quasi-autonomous non-governmental organisation'. Essentially, it refers to an organisation that's funded by the government but is outside of governmental control.

Example: The wily drug dealer managed to establish a **quango** to provide a legitimate face for his smuggling business.

Quinquennium

Pronunciation: Kwin-kwen-ee-um   **Type**: Noun

Definition: A period of five years.

Example: Gerry and Phillipa spent a **quinquennium** travelling Eastern Europe.

Quisling

Pronunciation: Quiz-ling   **Type**: Noun

Definition: A person who betrays his country to collaborate with or act as an informant to an enemy power that's occupying the country.

Example: During the Second World War, Jean-Pierre acted as a **quisling** and provided the enemy with information.

Quixotic

Pronunciation: Kwik-sot-ick   **Type**: Adjective

Definition: Resembling Don Quixote, particularly by being romantically idealistic, unrealistic or impractical.

Example: As an author, Peter found that his style was influenced by the **quixotic** love stories he read as a child.

Quorum

Pronunciation: Kwor-um   **Type**: Noun

Definition: The minimum number of people that need to be present at a meeting to make the proceedings and any decisions that are made valid.

Example: The club's **quorum** met on Sunday night to discuss the new proposal.

Quoit

Pronunciation: Kwoyt   **Type**: Noun

Definition: A ring made from rope, iron or rubber that's thrown to land around a peg. The word can also refer to a game that involves throwing such a ring.

Example: The little girls played **quoit** happily, landing rings on the peg for hours.

Quoth

Pronunciation: Kwoth   **Type**: Verb

Definition: An archaic[†] word meaning "said". It's used only in the first and third person singular[†] and always goes before the subject.

Example: "I see an iceberg," quoth the sailor.

R

Rabbinical

Pronunciation: Rab-in-ick-ul   **Type**: Adjective

Definition: Of, related to or typical of a rabbi or his teachings.

Example: Upon graduating high school, Allen decided to go to the seminary to pursue his rabbinical studies.

Raconteur

Pronunciation: Rack-on-turr   **Type**: Noun

Definition: A storyteller, particularly one who's adept at the art of telling anecdotes in an interesting and amusing way.

Example: Gyles Brandreth is a celebrated **raconteur**, holding the world record for the longest ever after-dinner speech.

Rachmanism

Pronunciation: Rack-man-iz-um   **Type**: Noun

Definition: The unscrupulous mistreatment, exploitation[†] and intimidation of tenants by a landlord. The word is named after Peter Rachman, notorious for the mistreatment of his tenants during the 1950s and the 1960s.

Example: The students accused their landlord of **Rachmanism** when he tried to bill them for damage caused by the previous tenants.

Radiophonic

Pronunciation: Ray-dee-oh-fon-ick   **Type**: Adjective

Definition: Of, relating to or typical of sound that's produced electronically.

Example: It took George seven years to perfect his **radiophonic** symphony.

Raffish

Pronunciation: Raff-ish   **Type**: Adjective

Definition: Unconventional or slightly disreputable, but in a manner that members of the opposite sex find attractive.

Example: Harry had always been cocky and **raffish**, yet the ladies seemed to prefer him to Kevin, his more sensible friend.

Raiment

Pronunciation: Ray-munt   **Type**: Noun

Definition: Clothing.

Example: Joey was a connoisseur of fine **raiment** and insisted on only wearing clothes by high-end designers

Rakish

Pronunciation: Ray-kish   **Type**: Adjective

Definition: Dashing or jaunty in appearance and personality.

Example: The **rakish** gentleman invited the women from the pool hall to follow him back to his apartment.

Rambunctious

Pronunciation: Ram-bunk-shuss   **Type**: Adjective

Definition: Boisterous and exuberant.

Example: The **rambunctious** teenager woke his neighbours when he returned from the pub.

Rancid

Pronunciation: Ran-sid   **Type**: Adjective

Definition: This adjective was originally used to describe foods that smelled or tasted unpleasant. In common usage, it's now used to refer to anything dirty or repulsive.

Example: Jennifer could never understand how the doctors on *Embarrassing Bodies* could stand to look at so many **rancid** body parts.

Rancour

Pronunciation: Rank-ur   **Type**: Noun

Definition: Long-standing bitterness, jealousy or resentment.

Example: When Elisabeth told her mother that she hated her stepfather, she put it down to **rancour** and refused to act upon it.

Rankle

Pronunciation: Rank-ul   **Type**: Verb

Definition: To cause pain or annoyance to someone. This verb is often used to refer to a wound that's beginning to fester.

Example: The gash on Darren's leg was beginning to **rankle** in the humidity.

Rapport

Pronunciation: Rap-or   **Type**: Noun

Definition: A close connection or relationship where the individuals or groups involved are able to understand each other easily and communicate clearly.

Example: The PR company developed a strong **rapport** with the advertising agency.

Rapprochement

Pronunciation: Rap-roash-marn   **Type**: Noun

Definition: This noun is primarily used in diplomatic circles to refer to the establishment or resumption of a friendly relationship between two or more countries.

Example: After the war, the two enemies sought **rapprochement** to broker peace.

Rapscallion

Pronunciation: Rap-skall-ee-un   **Type**: Noun

Definition: A mischievous person. The noun started out as an alteration of 'rascallion', which has its roots in the word 'rascal.'

Example: The shopkeeper ejected the young **rapscallion** from his premises before he could cause trouble.

Rastafarian

Pronunciation: Rass-taf-air-ee-un   **Type**: Adjective, Noun

Definition: The adjective describes something that's of or related to the

Rastafarian movement, a religious movement originating in Jamaica. Rastafarianism is commonly associated with reggae music and the spiritual use of cannabis. The noun refers to a member of or believer in the Rastafarian movement or doctrine.

Example:
#1: Jamaica is often believed to be a **Rastafarian** country, despite the fact that less than 1% of its inhabitants identify themselves as **Rastafarian**.
#2: The **Rastafarian** was constantly harassed by the local police.

Ratify

Pronunciation: Rat-if-eye   **Type**: Verb

Definition: To sign a document or to give formal consent to something, making it officially valid and legal.

Example: The businessman agreed to **ratify** the deal if it could be witnessed by his lawyer.

Raunchy

Pronunciation: Rawn-chhe   **Type**: Adjective

Definition: Sexually explicit or suggestive.

Example: The model's show-reel was **raunchy** and had been shot during her glamour days.

Rave

Pronunciation: Rayve   **Type**: Noun, Verb

Definition: Both the noun and the verb have multiple meanings. Originally, the noun referred to an enthusiastic recommendation or review, while the verb referred to the action of talking quickly or incoherently, as if suffering from delirium or insanity. In colloquial terms, a rave is a type of party that features fast-paced electronic music and light shows. The verb can refer to the act of dancing in a style that's associated with these parties, as well as the act of attending one.

Example:
#1: Philip met a pretty blonde woman at the **rave**.
#2: The journalist knew he had to **rave** about the play because it had been written by his sister-in-law.

Ravenous

Pronunciation: Rav-un-uss   **Type**: Adjective

Definition: Extremely hungry; starving.

Example: Luke was **ravenous** and ate all the snacks in his cupboard.

Razzmatazz

Pronunciation: Razz-mat-azz   **Type**: Noun

Definition: Anything flashy and showy with no real content, particularly something that's created with the aim of confusing or impressing an opponent.

Example: The stage play relied on a bunch of **razzmatazz** to win the approval of the audience.

Rebuttal

Pronunciation: Rib-ut-ul   **Type**: Noun

Definition: A statement or a piece of evidence that contradicts or rejects a theory or argument.

Example: Keith claimed that he had the most friends, but Harry showed him his Facebook page as a **rebuttal**.

Recalcitrant

Pronunciation: Reek-al-sit-rant   **Type**: Adjective, Noun

Definition: The adjective describes someone with an uncooperative attitude or outlook towards authority. The noun is used to refer to such a person.

Example:
#1: The **recalcitrant** fifteen-year-old refused to go to school.
#2: At the launch of the new nightclub, a **recalcitrant** was arrested for supplying cocaine.

Receptacle

Pronunciation: Riss-ep-tick-ul   **Type**: Noun

Definition: An object or area that is designed to receive something, often for storage purposes.

Example: The supervisor asked the staff members to throw their rubbish into the nearest **receptacle**.

Reciprocity

Pronunciation: Ress-ip-ross-it-ee   **Type**: Noun

Definition: The practice of reciprocating (exchanging things with others for a mutual benefit).

Example: Because of their established **reciprocity**, Ben drove Peter to college every day and Peter did Ben's homework.

Recidivist

Pronunciation: Riss-id-iv-ist   **Type**: Noun

Definition: A person who repeatedly relapses into criminal behaviour.

Example: The judge gave the accused three years because he was a **recidivist**.

Recompense

Pronunciation: Reck-om-ponce   **Type**: Noun, Verb

Definition: The noun refers to an object or service that's offered as a reward or compensation. The verb refers to the process of making amends or of offering such compensation.

Example:
#1: The insurance company gave the injured builder £6,000 in **recompense**.
#2: After the accident, the company was forced to **recompense** the team members.

Reconnaissance

Pronunciation: Ree-con-iss-arnts   **Type**: Noun

Definition: Preliminary research or observation, particularly into the lay of the land or the spread of enemy troops ahead of a military attack.

Example: The grunts carried out **reconnaissance** ahead of the big mission to find out how many troops their enemy had.

Recto

Pronunciation: Rec-toe   **Type**: Noun

Definition: The right-hand page of the two-page spread of an open book.

Example: Angelica ran her fingers down Percy's yellowed **recto** and read the foreword.

Recusant

Pronunciation: Reck-yoo-sarnt   **Type**: Adjective, Noun

Definition: The adjective is used to describe someone who refuses to submit to an authority or to obey rules and regulations, while the noun refers directly to such a person.

Example:
#1: The **recusant** student refused to attend classes.
#2: The father of the **recusant** faced jail because his child never went to school.

Redound

Pronunciation: Ree-downd   **Type**: Verb

Definition: To have an effect or a consequence.

Example: The politician was surprised to watch his promises **redound** to his discredit.

Reflexology

Pronunciation: Ree-flex-ol-oh-gee   **Type**: Noun

Definition: This noun can refer to one of two things. The first is a type of massage that aims to relieve muscle tension and treat illness, based on the notion of reflex points on certain body parts. It can also refer to the scientific study of how reflexes affect behaviour in people or animals.

Example: The esteemed professor of **reflexology** prepared to lecture on how massaging the hands and feet can benefit other body parts.

Reformatory

Pronunciation: Ree-form-at-or-ee   **Type**: Adjective, Noun

Definition: The adjective describes something that causes or is intended to cause reform, which is a change in the character of a person or a thing for the better. The noun refers to a type of institution where young offenders are taken as an alternative to prison, ostensibly[†] with the goal of improving them and guiding them away from crime.

Example:
#1 The teenager was sent to a **reformatory** school as punishment for his constant truancy.
#2: The young man's delight at avoiding prison was short-lived, as he was ordered to spend six months at a **reformatory**.

Refrangible

Pronunciation: Ree-fran-jib-ull   **Type**: Adjective

Definition: Capable of being refracted, which is when a wave of some sort changes direction because of a change in speed.

Example: The scientists observed the **refrangible** rays of light.

Refulgent

Pronunciation: Riff-ull-junt   **Type**: Adjective

Definition: Shining brightly; radiant.

Example: The lone star was **refulgent** in the night sky.

Regicide

Pronunciation: Rej-iss-ide   **Type**: Noun

Definition: The act of killing a king.

Example: The anarchist attempted **regicide** but was unsuccessful, and he wound up getting killed himself.

Regress

Pronunciation: Ree-gress   **Type**: Verb

Definition: To return to an earlier or less developed state.

Example: The psychiatrist watched his patient **regress** into childhood.

Regurgitate

Pronunciation: Re-gurj-it-ate   **Type**: Verb

Definition: To bring food that's already been swallowed back into the mouth. By association, it can also mean to repeat something learned or overheard without thinking about its meaning.

Example: Catherine stood in the park and watched the bird **regurgitate** a mulch[†]-covered worm into its baby's mouth.

Rehash

Pronunciation: Ree-hash   **Type**: Noun, Verb

Definition: The noun refers to something that was created by using old ideas or objects in a new way, while the verb refers to the act of using this technique.

Example:
#1: The critic thought that the new comedy show was nothing but a tired **rehash** of a Monty Python sketch.
#2: The artist decided to **rehash** his masterpiece to create something new that the public would adore.

Remand

Pronunciation: Rim-and   **Type**: Noun, Verb

Definition: The noun refers to the state of being in custody, while the verb is used to refer to the action of placing someone on bail or taking them into custody, particularly following a preliminary trial or after a trial has been adjourned. The noun refers to the state of being in custody.

Example:
#1: The criminal was placed on **remand** after the trial.
#2: The judge had no choice but to **remand** the suspect.

Remission

Pronunciation: Re-mish-un   **Type**: Noun

Definition: The cancellation or reduction of a debt, penalty or charge. This noun can also refer to the easing of the symptoms or causes of an illness.

Example: The cancer patient was in **remission** and had a new outlook on life.

Renegade

Pronunciation: Ren-uh-gayd   **Type**: Adjective, Noun

Definition: The adjective is used to describe anything that's typical of or associated with a renegade, which is a person who deserts, abandons or betrays his country or principles.

Example:
#1: The **renegade** messages gave away important military secrets.
#2: As a **renegade**, the corporal was executed by his country's soldiers as soon as they tracked him down.

Renege

Pronunciation: Ren-ayg   **Type**: Verb

Definition: To go back on or to break a promise, deal or agreement.

Example: Keith didn't want to miss the party, but he couldn't **renege** on his date with Katie and so he prepared to take her dancing instead.

Repartee

Pronunciation: Rep-art-ee   **Type**: Noun

Definition: The skill of carrying out conversations or discussions that are characterised by a level of intelligence and quick, witty responses.

Example: The duchess enjoyed the earl's witty **repartee** at the tea party.

Repertoire

Pronunciation: Rep-ur-twar   **Type**: Noun

Definition: The collection of items that are regularly performed by an artist or a group. An actor's repertoire might include the list of plays that he's appeared in.

Example: The band wanted to go on tour but knew that their slim **repertoire** would need to be expanded before they could put on a full show.

Reprehensible

Pronunciation: Rep-ree-hen-sib-ull   **Type**: Adjective

Definition: Deserving blame or criticism.

Example: Stephen's crime was minor but **reprehensible**, drawing the criticism of his family and friends alike.

Reprobate

Pronunciation: Rep-ro-bate   **Type**: Noun

Definition: A person without morals or principles.

Example: The **reprobate** attempted to leave the bar without settling his tab.

Reprography

Pronunciation: Re-prog-raff-ee   **Type**: Noun

Definition: The science and practice of copying or reproducing art, images or documents.

Example: The photocopier was enough to satisfy Pierre's passion for **reprography**.

Resplendent

Pronunciation: Riss-plen-dunt   **Type**: Adjective

Definition: Extremely attractive, beautiful or impressive; possessing great beauty or splendour.

Example: The duchess looked **resplendent** in a bright blue dress, and the earl couldn't look away.

Restaurateur

Pronunciation: Ress-tuh-rat-urr   **Type**: Noun

Definition: A person who owns or manages a restaurant.

Example: The **restaurateur** planned to open new venues in Barnsley and Liverpool in the summer.

Resurgent

Pronunciation: Re-sur-junt   **Type**: Adjective

Definition: This adjective is used to describe something that's increasing in popularity after a period of inactivity.

Example: The Labour Party was **resurgent** during the great recession.

Reticent

Pronunciation: Ret-iss-unt   **Type**: Adjective

Definition: Closed or withdrawn; not quick to reveal one's thoughts, feelings or opinions.

Example: The doctor was **reticent** to offer his opinion on his patient's chances of long-term survival.

Retro

Pronunciation: Ret-ro   **Type**: Adjective

Definition: Either imitative of or belonging to a style, fashion, trend or movement from the past.

Example: Kevin's **retro** flares are from the 1960s.

Retronym

Pronunciation: Ret-ro-nim   **Type**: Noun

Definition: A word that's created to provide a new name for an object or a concept[†] to differentiate its original form from a more recent form. The original word is often given an extra adjective to create the retronym. Retronyms are typically required due to advances in technology.

Example: "Acoustic guitar" is a **retronym** because they were only ever called "guitars" until the development of the electric guitar.

Reveille

Pronunciation: Re-val-ee   **Type**: Noun

Definition: A signal, particularly the sound of a bugle, a drum or another military instrument, that's used to wake soldiers and other personnel in the armed forces.

Example: The new recruits quickly began to dread the **reveille** each morning.

Revenant

Pronunciation: Rev-un-ant   **Type**: Noun

Definition: A person who's returned from the dead; a ghost or an animated corpse.

Example: Every night, Pieter was visited by his estranged father, a **revenant** sent back to haunt his dreams.

Revile

Pronunciation: Riv-ile   **Type**: Verb

Definition: To criticise something in an abusive, angry or insulting manner.

Example: The villagers were quick to **revile** outsiders.

Revulsion

Pronunciation: Riv-ul-shun   **Type**: Noun

Definition: A sense of disgust or hatred.

Example: As soon as she saw the monster, Katharine was filled with fear and **revulsion**.

Rhapsody

Pronunciation: Rap-sud-ee   **Type**: Noun

Definition: An expression of enthusiasm or ecstasy, or a type of instrumental composition.

Example: The reveller flew into a **rhapsody** of praise and thankfulness when the sun rose.

Rhetoric

Pronunciation: Reh-toh-rick   **Type**: Noun

Definition: The art, study and practice of effective, clear or persuasive speech or writing. In some circumstances, this noun can also refer to the deliberate use of language which is intended to persuade, impress or influence the reader or audience but which often lacks integrity or sincerity.

Example: The audience found it easy to get lost in the speaker's **rhetoric**.

Rhetorical

Pronunciation: Ruh-toh-rick-ul   **Type**: Adjective

Definition: Of, relating to or typical of the art of rhetoric. In everyday usage, this adjective is primarily used to describe a type of question which is asked to make a point, rather than in expectation of a reply.

Example: When my father said, "Do you think I'm made of money?", I knew it was a **rhetorical** question.

Rheumatism

Pronunciation: Roo-mat-iz-um   **Type**: Noun

Definition: A disease or illness that's characterised by inflammation and pain in the joints or muscles. Common rheumatoid illnesses include arthritis, lupus and fibromyalgia.

Example: Gladys doesn't get out much these days because her **rheumatism** makes it difficult to walk.

Ribaldry

Pronunciation: Rib-all-dree   **Type**: Noun

Definition: A type of humorous entertainment, talk or behaviour that borders on indecency and which typically includes the breaking of taboos and vulgarity.

Example: When her parents returned home early, they kicked me out and scolded Peggy for allowing such **ribaldry** in their house.

Ricochet

Pronunciation: Rick-oh-shay   **Type**: Noun, Verb

Definition: The noun refers to a shot or a moving object that bounces off a surface. The verb is used to describe the action of a bullet, shell or other projectile weapon that bounces off a surface in this way.

Example:
#1: The soldier was killed by a **ricochet**.
#2: Little Johnny laughed after he watched the spit-ball **ricochet** off his father's forehead.

Rigidify

Pronunciation: Rij-id-if-eye   **Type**: Verb

Definition: To become stiff, unmovable or unbendable.

Example: The scientists tried to force their subject to **rigidify** by pumping an electric current through his body.

Rigmarole

Pronunciation: Rig-ma-role   **Type**: Noun

Definition: A long, dull and rambling statement, story or procedure.

Example: The police considered taking the homeless man back to the station, but they couldn't be bothered to deal with the **rigmarole**.

Rimy

Pronunciation: Rye-me   **Type**: Adjective

Definition: Covered with frost.

Example: The ground was **rimy** after the snowstorm, and a shrill wind whistled through the eaves of the old houses.

Rivulet

Pronunciation: Riv-yoo-lit   **Type**: Noun

Definition: A small stream.

Example: The perspiration formed a **rivulet** on his brow.

Rollick

Pronunciation: Rol-ick   **Type**: Verb

Definition: To act, to behave or to move in a carefree, jovial or exuberant manner.

Example: Peter watched the children **rollick** in the playground over the top of his newspaper.

Rosarium

Pronunciation: Ro-zair-ee-um   **Type**: Noun

Definition: A rose garden.

Example: Terence strolled through the **rosarium** and inhaled the pleasant scent of the flowers.

Roundelay

Pronunciation: Round-uh-lay   **Type**: Noun

Definition: A simple poem or song with a recurring refrain.

Example: The songwriter won an award for his catchy **roundelay**.

Roustabout

Pronunciation: Roust-ab-owt   **Type**: Noun

Definition: A labourer, typically one who performs temporary work that requires little-to-no skill, often on an oil rig.

Example: The **roustabout** smoked cheap cigarettes and had a habit of spitting on the floor.

Rowdy

Pronunciation: Rowd-ee   **Type**: Adjective

Definition: Noisy, boisterous and disorderly, often with an undertone of aggression.

Example: On match day, the pub was usually packed with **rowdy** punters.

Rubbernecker

Pronunciation: Rub-ur-neck-ur   **Type**: Noun

Definition: An inquisitive person who often stares.

Example: The **rubbernecker** had a minor car accident when he drove into a lamppost because he was looking the other way.

Rubicon

Pronunciation: Roo-bick-on   **Type**: Noun

Definition: A point of no return. It's named after the river that Julius Caesar crossed in January of 49 BC, which led directly to the Roman Civil War.

Example: As he prepared to jump out of the aeroplane, the skydiver knew he was approaching a **Rubicon**.

Rubicund

Pronunciation: Roo-bick-und   **Type**: Adjective

Definition: Ruddy-coloured or of a healthy red complexion. This adjective is usually used to describe the colour of someone's face.

Example: The **rubicund** sailor turned his head to face away from the wind.

Rudimentary

Pronunciation: Roo-dim-ent-eh-ree   **Type**: Adjective

Definition: Simple or undeveloped; basic.

Example: Jessica had a **rudimentary** knowledge of HTML.

Rufous

Pronunciation: Roo-fuss   **Type**: Adjective

Definition: A reddish-brown colour.

Example: The **rufous** sun set slowly over the horizon.

Ruination

Pronunciation: Roo-in-ay-shun   **Type**: Noun

Definition: The action of ruining something or the state of being ruined.

Example: The abandoned house was in a state of **ruination** and the estate agent knew that no-one would ever want to buy it.

Rumbustious

Pronunciation: Rum-bus-tee-uss   **Type**: Adjective

Definition: Uncontrollably boisterous or unruly.

Example: Phillipa's son was so **rumbustious** that he was constantly in trouble at school.

Ruminant

Pronunciation: Room-in-unt   **Type**: Adjective, Noun

Definition: The adjective is used to describe something that's of, related to or belonging to cud-chewing mammals. The noun can be used to refer to these mammals, as well as to a contemplative person or someone who enjoys thinking and meditation.

Example:
#1: The **ruminant** waitress was always in her own world and lost her job for not paying enough attention to the customers.
#2: The **ruminant** was unswayed by the rain and continued to chew at the grass.

Runt

Pronunciation: Runt   **Type**: Noun

Definition: A small, weak or undersized person or animal, particularly the smallest in a litter.

Example: When we went to look at Jessica's new kitten, it was so small that we wondered if it was the **runt** of the litter.

S

Sabbatical

Pronunciation: Sab-at-ick-ul   **Type**: Adjective, Noun

Definition: The adjective describes something that's typical of or related to a sabbatical, a period of paid leave that's granted to a teacher or a lecturer for them to spend studying or travelling. The noun refers to the leave itself.

Example:
#1: Jeff was looking forward to his **sabbatical** holiday.
#2: When the pressure of work grew too much for him, Peter asked for a **sabbatical**.

Saboteur

Pronunciation: Sab-ut-urr   **Type**: Noun

Definition: A person who deliberately destroys, damages or otherwise obstructs something, particularly something belonging to an opponent in a war, skirmish[†] or conflict.

Example: When everything went wrong at the presentation, Caleb suspected that a **saboteur** might have been responsible.

Sadomasochism

Pronunciation: Sade-oh-mass-oh-kiz-um   **Type**: Noun

Definition: A psychological tendency to derive sexual pleasure from giving and receiving pain, or the practice of committing acts that are sadomasochistic in nature.

Example: Kevin and Deirdre were keen advocates of **sadomasochism** and got their whips out at every opportunity.

Sagacity

Pronunciation: Sag-ass-it-ee   **Type**: Noun

Definition: The quality of being wise, insightful and shrewd of judgement.

Example: **Sagacity** is an important trait if you want to be a politician.

Salacious

Pronunciation: Sal-ay-shuss   **Type**: Adjective

Definition: Indecently sexual, lustful or lecherous[†].

Example: The old man gave the waitress a **salacious** wink as she delivered his coffee.

Salarium

Pronunciation: Sal-air-ee-um   **Type**: Noun

Definition: A form of payment where the worker is paid in goods instead of money. This word comes from Latin and originally referred to payment in salt.

Example: Keith was sick of working for his parents at the diner and wanted a job that gave him something more than a **salarium**.

Salient

Pronunciation: Say-lee-unt   **Type**: Adjective

Definition: This adjective is used to describe something that's prominent, conspicuous, or important.

Example: The private detective was quick to discover the **salient** point of the mystery to solve the case.

Salubrious

Pronunciation: Sal-ooh-bree-uss   **Type**: Adjective

Definition: Healthy, wholesome or pleasant.

Example: The summer weather was **salubrious**, and the invalid quickly began to feel better.

Salutations

Pronunciation: Sal-yoo-tay-shuns   **Type**: Noun

Definition: Gestures or expressions that are made as a greeting or as an acknowledgement of the arrival, presence or departure of another person.

Example: The visitor waved his hand and said "hello," but nobody returned his **salutations**.

Salvo

Pronunciation: Sal-vo   **Type**: Noun

Definition: A simultaneous release of a number of ranged weapons, particularly artillery or other guns during a battle.

Example: The enemy fired a **salvo** at our fortifications when we were supposed to be observing a ceasefire, so the general ordered an immediate retaliation.

Samizdat

Pronunciation: Sam-is-dat   **Type**: Noun

Definition: The copying and distribution of literature or publications that are banned by the government, particularly in communist countries.

Example: The rebels had to resort to **samizdat** to spread the word about the cause.

Sanctimonious

Pronunciation: Sank-tim-oh-nee-uss   **Type**: Adjective

Definition: A derogatory term used to describe someone who acts as though they're morally superior to other people.

Example: I can't stand the old priest. He's a **sanctimonious** bastard.

Sanguinary

Pronunciation: San-gwin-eh-ree   **Type**: Adjective

Definition: Involving, accompanied by or causing bloodshed.

Example: Keith liked the idea of being a soldier, but he was terrified by the prospect of a **sanguinary** battlefield.

Sanskrit

Pronunciation: San-skrit   **Type**: Adjective, Noun

Definition: The adjective describes anything that's of, characterised by or otherwise related to the Sanskrit language. The noun refers to the language itself, an ancient Indian language which was used to write Hindu scriptures and classical works of Indian poetry.

Example:
#1: The **Sanskrit** papers were difficult to translate and the professor had to call in a specialist.
#2: The temple was engraved with **Sanskrit** and the villagers visited regularly to receive a blessing.

Saprophyte

Pronunciation: Sap-ro-fite   **Type**: Noun

Definition: Any plant, fungus, insect or other organism that lives on dead, rotting or decaying[†] organic matter.

Example: The **saprophyte** began the slow process of digesting the remains of the corpse.

Sapient

Pronunciation: Say-pee-unt   **Type**: Adjective

Definition: Possessing the ability to think or to act with judgement. This adjective is usually used to describe plant or animal life.

Example: Keith refused to eat a **sapient** creature, but he ate fish because he believed they were too simple to know what was happening.

Sardonic

Pronunciation: Sar-don-ick   **Type**: Adjective

Definition: Cruelly sarcastic or cynical.

Example: The **sardonic** schoolboy gave his teacher hell.

Satori

Pronunciation: Sat-or-ee   **Type**: Noun

Definition: Sudden enlightenment; the spiritual goal of Zen Buddhism.

Example: David's road to **satori** was long and treacherous.

Saturnine

Pronunciation: Sat-urn-ine   **Type**: Adjective

Definition: Slow, gloomy, dark or mysterious. This adjective is usually used to describe a person, their manner or their features. The word developed because of the supposed astrological influence of Saturn.

Example: The young man was **saturnine** and unresponsive to the questioning stares of the other punters.

Satyr

Pronunciation: Sat-ur   **Type**: Noun

Definition: This noun was originally used to refer to a type of drunken, lustful god that lived in the woods. The Greeks portrayed them as men with horses' ears and tails, while the Romans believed they were men with a goat's ears, tail, legs and horns. By association, the same noun can now be used to refer to any man with strong, lecherous† desires.

Example: The **satyr** was caught looking up the young women's skirts.

Saurian

Pronunciation: Sow-ree-un   **Type**: Adjective, Noun

Definition: The adjective describes something that resembles a lizard, while the noun can be used to refer to any large reptile, particularly one that's extinct or fictional.

Example:
#1: Nobody trusted Nigella because of her **saurian** eyes.
#2: My favourite part of the film was when the heroine was running from the **saurian**.

Savant

Pronunciation: Sav-ont   **Type**: Noun

Definition: A scholar or learned person.

Example: The **savant** studied hard and was awarded a PhD for her troubles.

Savvy

Pronunciation: Sav-ee   **Type**: Adjective, Noun, Verb

Definition: The adjective describes a shrewd level of knowledge and understanding, while the noun refers to this type of knowledge. The verb refers to the process of knowing or understanding something.

Example:
#1: He has a **savvy** understanding of the way that computers work.
#2: The youngster had his fair share of **savvy** and knew who he was going to vote for.
#3: He could never **savvy** what his girlfriend wanted him to do.

Scabbard

Pronunciation: Scab-erd   **Type**: Noun

Definition: A sheath for a large bladed weapon, typically a sword but also occasionally for a knife or a dagger.

Example: After the battle, the soldier cleaned the blade of his sword and returned it to his **scabbard**.

Scallywag

Pronunciation: Skall-ee-wag   **Type**: Noun

Definition: A deceitful and unreliable rogue or scoundrel.

Example: I can never trust Callum to do what he promises to. He's such a **scallywag**.

Scandalmonger

Pronunciation: Scan-dul-mung-ur   **Type**: Noun

Definition: A person who stirs up outrage and dislike towards someone by spreading rumours, gossip and lies.

Example: Jeremy's marriage was brought to an end by the **scandalmonger** who lived opposite him and who couldn't resist telling his wife about the affair.

Scaramouche

Pronunciation: Scah-rah-moosh   **Type**: Noun

Definition: A roguish, clown-like character, found in theatre and literature, who's often depicted[†] as a boastful coward wearing a black mask and glasses.

Example: The **Scaramouche** danced the fandango every night for the pleasure of the theatregoers.

Scarify

Pronunciation: Scar-if-eye   **Type**: Verb

Definition: The act of making cuts or scratches into something, particularly flesh or skin, in an attempt to leave a mark or scar behind.

Example: The punk rocker walked into the tattoo parlour and asked if they could **scarify** a swastika on to his forearm.

Scatology

Pronunciation: Scat-ol-oh-gee   **Type**: Noun

Definition: An interest, obsession or preoccupation with excrement and excretion, as well as the scientific study of faeces. The noun can also refer to an obscene form of photography, film and literature which deals with these matters.

Example: The art gallery had a **scatology** showcase that was poorly attended.

Schadenfreude

Pronunciation: Shard-un-froy-duh   **Type**: Noun

Definition: Similar to sadism, schadenfreude is a form of malicious pleasure or enjoyment that's derived from observing another person's misfortune.

Example: The footballer felt **schadenfreude** when he watched his rival score an own goal.

Schism

Pronunciation: Skiz-um   **Type**: Noun

Definition: A rift, split or division between two opposing things or groups of people, often caused by a conflict of religious beliefs. The noun can also refer to the formal separation of a church into two separate entities.

Example: The company was rapidly heading towards a **schism**, and the CEO knew that it could destroy them and lead to bankruptcy.

Schlemiel

Pronunciation: Schlum-eel   **Type**: Noun

Definition: A stupid, awkward, bungling person.

Example: Karen, the **schlemiel**, would forget her head if it wasn't bolted on.

Schlep

Pronunciation: Shlep   **Type**: Noun, Verb

Definition: The noun refers to a long, arduous journey, while the verb refers to the action of dragging or carrying something heavy or awkward on such a journey.

Example:
#1: Courtney couldn't be bothered with the **schlep** he faced every morning, so she called in sick and took the day off.
#2: Josephine had to **schlep** to the junkyard with a trolley full of rubbish and household detritus[†].

Schooner

Pronunciation: Skoon-er   **Type**: Noun

Definition: A type of sailing ship with a minimum of two masts, characterised by a forward mast that's equal to or smaller in height than the rear masts.

Example: The sailor boarded the **schooner** and prepared to spend time at sea.

Scintillating

Pronunciation: Sin-till-ate-ing   **Type**: Adjective

Definition: Depending upon the context, this adjective can either describe an object that's sparkling, bright or shiny, or a person that's animated and full of life, especially conversationally.

Example: The speaker delivered a **scintillating** presentation and exited to thunderous applause.

Scopperloit

Pronunciation: Scop-ur-loit   **Type**: Noun

Definition: A time of idleness or play.

Example: The children went outside for **scopperloit**.

Scourge

Pronunciation: Skurj   **Type**: Noun, Verb

Definition: Originally, the noun was a name for a whip and the verb meant to whip someone as a punishment. Nowadays, the word has evolved and the noun can refer to anything that causes a huge amount of suffering, while the verb means to cause such suffering.

Example:
#1: The slave driver beat the boy with a **scourge**.
#2: The genocidal tyrant knew he'd have to **scourge** the population if he wanted them to obey him.

Scraggy

Pronunciation: Skrag-ee   **Type**: Adjective

Definition: Very thin or skinny.

Example: The dinner lady hated the way that the **scraggy** children always pushed their way to the front of the line.

Screed

Pronunciation: Skreed   **Type**: Noun

Definition: A long, tedious speech or piece of writing.

Example: The conference attendees were forced to sit through sixty-five minutes of **screed**.

Scrivener

Pronunciation: Skriv-un-er   **Type**: Noun

Definition: Someone who writes things down.

Example: The **scrivener** went home with blisters on his fingers after his first day at the new job.

Scruples

Pronunciation: Skroo-pulls   **Type**: Noun

Definition: Feelings of doubt, hesitation or uncertainty regarding the morality of an action.

Example: The politician had no **scruples** about taking money from the local schools and using it to refurbish the town hall.

Scurrilous

Pronunciation: Scur-ill-uss   **Type**: Adjective

Definition: Given to, consisting of or prone to verbal abuse.

Example: Jessica was on the receiving end of a **scurrilous** accusation.

Sebaceous

Pronunciation: Seb-ay-shuss   **Type**: Adjective

Definition: Consisting of, typical of or similar to oil, grease or fat.

Example: The skin on Jeffrey's face was **sebaceous** and pocked with acne.

Sedentary

Pronunciation: Sed-unt-eh-ree   **Type**: Adjective

Definition: Characterised by inactivity or prone to spending too much time sitting down. This adjective can be used to describe a person, a job or a way of life.

Example: Joe's **sedentary** lifestyle wasn't healthy, and he needed to exercise more.

Sedulous

Pronunciation: Sed-yoo-luss   **Type**: Adjective

Definition: Showing a level of dedication, diligence and devotion.

Example: The **sedulous** student worked hard to get into law school.

Semantic

Pronunciation: Sem-an-tick   **Type**: Adjective

Definition: Of or relating to the study of meaning in language.

Example: The professor of languages carried out a **semantic** analysis of the Elizabethan text.

Semaphore

Pronunciation: Sem-aff-or   **Type**: Noun, Verb

Definition: The noun is the name of a system of communication by which messages are sent by positioning the arms or by holding two flags in certain positions, according to a pre-determined alphabetic code. The verb refers to the action of sending a message using semaphore.

Example:
#1: On the cover of The Beatles's *Help* album, the four band members signal in **semaphore**.
#2: The soldiers were cut off from most forms of communication and had to **semaphore** for reinforcements.

Semblance

Pronunciation: Sem-blunce   **Type**: Noun

Definition: The outward appearance of something, particularly when the reality or the inside is different to how it appears. The same noun can also mean a similarity or resemblance.

Example: The stunned young woman tried to compose her mind and to force her thoughts back into some **semblance** of normality.

Seminal

Pronunciation: Sem-in-ul   **Type**: Adjective

Definition: There are two different meanings to this word. It's usually used to describe an event, a movement or a piece of literary or artistic work that has an influence on later developments. It can also be used to describe something that's of, related to or similar to semen.

Example: The Beatles's *Sgt. Pepper's Lonely Hearts Club Band* album is often described as a **seminal** rock 'n' roll record.

Seminary

Pronunciation: Sem-in-eh-ree   **Type**: Noun

Definition: A type of college or university that prepares its students to become priests, ministers or rabbis.

Example: The young man gained admission to a **seminary** and found his faith was restored.

Semiotics

Pronunciation: Sem-ee-ot-icks   **Type**: Noun

Definition: The art and study of signs and symbols and their usage, interpretation or meaning.

Example: The professor of **semiotics** found hieroglyphs fascinating.

Senesce

Pronunciation: Sen-ess   **Type**: Verb

Definition: To age or grow older, or to deteriorate because of age.

Example: As he grew older, the footballer worried he'd **senesce** and have to retire from the game.

Seneschal

Pronunciation: Sen-ush-al   **Type**: Noun

Definition: An officer or a governor; the person in charge of a large household or body of people.

Example: The **seneschal** said that all visitors should be introduced to him personally.

Sentience

Pronunciation: Sen-tee-unce   **Type**: Noun

Definition: The ability to feel and to be conscious of things that are happening around oneself.

Example: The hippie refused to eat anything capable of **sentience** and survived predominantly on a vegan diet.

Seppuku

Pronunciation: Sep-ook-ooh   **Type**: Noun

Definition: A type of Japanese ritual suicide in which the person disembowels themselves on a sword. **Seppuku** was originally practiced by Samurai.

Example: It was a tragic case: the victim committed **seppuku** because he couldn't keep up with his mortgage repayments.

Sepulchre

Pronunciation: Sep-ulk-er   **Type**: Noun

Definition: A burial chamber.

Example: The children were too scared to go near the **sepulchre** because of generations of ghost stories.

Seraglio

Pronunciation: Suh-ral-ee-oh   **Type**: Noun

Definition: Apartments inside a Muslim household or palace that are designed to keep the wives and concubines[†] separated from the rest of the population.

Example: The women lived a sheltered life inside the **seraglio**.

Seraphim

Pronunciation: Seh-raff-eem   **Type**: Noun

Definition: Angels or angelic beings, usually of the highest order.

Example: Joseph prayed for **seraphim** to save his soul.

Serendipity

Pronunciation: Seh-ren-dip-it-ee   **Type**: Noun

Definition: A beneficial occurrence or a sequence of beneficial events that develop by chance.

Example: The discovery of penicillin by Alexander Fleming is a classic example of **serendipity**. It happened completely by accident.

Serotonin

Pronunciation: Seh-ruh-toe-nin   **Type**: Noun

Definition: A chemical compound in the body that's thought to contribute to feelings of happiness and well-being.

Example: Sunlight helps to regulate **serotonin** and can be used to treat mild depression.

Serpentine

Pronunciation: Sur-pen-tine   **Type**: Adjective

Definition: This adjective is used to describe something snake-like.

Example: The **serpentine** roads meandered† through the countryside.

Sesquicentenary

Pronunciation: Sess-kwi-sen-ten-uh-ree   **Type**: Adjective, Noun

Definition: The adjective is used to describe something that's of or related to the noun, which is an anniversary of one hundred and fifty years.

Example:
#1: Marjory was kept busy by the **sesquicentenary** preparations.
#2: The country prepared to celebrate its **sesquicentenary**.

Sesquipedalian

Pronunciation: Sess-kwi-ped-ale-ee-un   **Type**: Adjective

Definition: This adjective is used to describe a long word or to describe something that's characterised by being long-winded.

Example: The word **sesquipedalian** is **sesquipedalian**.

Shackles

Pronunciation: Shack-ulls   **Type**: Noun

Definition: A pair of metal bracelets that are used to restrain people and are worn around the wrists or ankles and held together with a chain.

Example: The guard shouted, "Get me the **shackles**. I'll take no more trouble from this one."

Shamateur

Pronunciation: Sham-atch-yer   **Type**: Noun

Definition: Someone who plays sports and makes money from doing so, though still classed as an amateur.

Example: Terry, the pool player and part-time **shamateur**, won £250 at the pool hall.

Shank

Pronunciation: Shank   **Type**: Noun, Verb

Definition: The noun refers to a rudimentary† home-made knife, usually found in a prison. Shanks are often made from scrap metal or fashioned from the bones of food. The verb refers to the action of stabbing someone with such a knife.

Example:
#1: The prisoner lashed out with a **shank** and the guard dropped to the floor.
#2: The warden heard a rumour that MacGyver was threatening to **shank** his cell-mate.

Shareware

Pronunciation: Share-ware   **Type**: Noun

Definition: Computer software that's released for free on a trial basis, after which users are asked to pay a fee to continue using it.

Example: Adrian bought a video camera and downloaded some **shareware**.

Shebang

Pronunciation: Shub-ang   **Type**: Noun

Definition: An event or operation.

Example: "Take me to your supervisor," the inspector demanded. "I'd like to see who's behind this **shebang**."

Shemozzle

Pronunciation: Shum-oz-ul   **Type**: Noun

Definition: A Yiddish word that describes a state of confusion, chaos or disorder.

Example: Seth knocked an old woman over and vanished during the **shemozzle**.

Shenanigans

Pronunciation: Shun-an-ig-gans   **Type**: Noun

Definition: Tomfoolery, mischief or other secretive or slightly dishonest activity.

Example: Young Joey was grounded for a week because of his **shenanigans**.

Sherpa

Pronunciation: Shur-pa   **Type**: Noun

Definition: One or more members of a race of Himalayan people that live on the borders of Nepal and Tibet and are well known for their mountaineering skills. Because of this, the noun is often used to refer to any mountain guide.

Example: The mountaineer would never have reached the summit without his **Sherpa**.

Shibboleth

Pronunciation: Shib-ull-eth   **Type**: Noun

Definition: A custom or a belief that distinguishes one class, group or race of people from another.

Example: The old **shibboleth** about women maintaining their virginity until their wedding night no longer applies.

Shillelagh

Pronunciation: Shill-lay-la   **Type**: Noun

Definition: A wooden club or cosh, often made from oak, that's wielded as a weapon. The word and the object are both associated with and originally from Ireland.

Example: The thugs cracked the shopkeeper on the head with a **shillelagh**, and he quickly lost consciousness.

Shinto

Pronunciation: Shin-toe   **Type**: Noun

Definition: A Japanese religion that includes the worship of one's ancestors and a belief in spirits of nature and a sacred power that permeates both animate and inanimate objects.

Example: The student of **Shinto** was an old man with a hooked nose and sharp, aquiline[†] features.

Shrive

Pronunciation: Shrive   **Type**: Verb

Definition: This verb has two meanings, depending upon the context. It can refer to the act of listening to a confession and assigning penance or absolution[†] to someone, or it can refer to the action of presenting oneself to a priest for the purposes of confession, penance or absolution[†].

Example: The soldier went to see the pastor to **shrive** and to ask for guidance.

Shyster

Pronunciation: Shy-sta   **Type**: Noun

Definition: A professional person, often a lawyer, who uses immoral, unscrupulous, deceptive or fraudulent methods when going about his business.

Example: Lottie lost £24,000 to a **shyster**.

Sibilance

Pronunciation: Sib-il-unce   **Type**: Noun

Definition: This noun can either refer to a sibilant sound or the state of being sibilant. Sibilance is a linguistic quality where a string of one or more consonants is characterised by a hissing sound.

Example: "Sheryl's soft snake slithered slowly south" is an example of sibilance.

Simian

Pronunciation: Sim-ee-un   **Type**: Adjective, Noun

Definition: The adjective describes something that's typical of, related to or that resembles an ape or a monkey, while the noun refers to any such animal.

Example:
#1: The boy's **simian** intelligence held him back from a career in medicine.
#2: The **simian** foraged for fruit in the undergrowth.

Similitude

Pronunciation: Sim-ill-it-yood   **Type**: Noun

Definition: The quality or state of being similar to something.

Example: The identical twins were proud of their **similitude**.

Simony

Pronunciation: Sye-mo-nee   **Type**: Noun

Definition: The trading of religious privileges, such as titles, positions and favours.

Example: The merchant was afraid of eternal damnation and resorted to **simony** to try to clear his name.

Simulacrum

Pronunciation: Sim-yoo-lay-crum   **Type**: Noun

Definition: An identical copy or representation of something.

Example: The artist created a good **simulacrum** of the painting, but the curator still knew it was a forgery.

Simulcast

Pronunciation: Sye-mul-cast   **Type**: Noun, Verb

Definition: The noun refers to the simultaneous transmission of a radio or television show on two or more channels, while the verb refers to the process of broadcasting or transmitting something in this way.

Example:
#1: John couldn't stand the **simulcast** of *Antiques Roadshow* and considered writing a letter of complaint.
#2: The football was **simulcast** on BBC One and ITV.

Sinecure

Pronunciation: Sin-ick-yor   **Type**: Noun

Definition: A position of employment or a political office which doesn't require much work but which grants status, financial benefit or power.

Example: The politician hoped to be given a **sinecure** but was disappointed.

Singular

Pronunciation: Sing-yoo-la   **Type**: Adjective, Noun

Definition: The adjective is used to describe something that's a one-off, that's exceptional or that's otherwise unique. The noun refers to a singular word, which is a word that refers to just one thing, as opposed to a plural, which refers to multiple.

Example:
#1: The **singular** events that led up to my sudden marriage seem almost as if they came out of a romantic novel.

#2: The word "cow" is a **singular**, while "cows" is a plural.

Sinology

Pronunciation: Si-nol-oh-gee   **Type**: Noun

Definition: The study of China and the Chinese, particularly the language, the customs, the history or the politics.

Example: Dean was fascinated by **sinology** and couldn't wait to book his first oriental holiday.

Skald

Pronunciation: Scold   **Type**: Noun

Definition: A composer, reciter or performer of poetry that celebrates mythical or real heroes and their stories.

Example: The villagers were enthralled by the visiting **skald**.

Skedaddle

Pronunciation: Skid-ad-ul   **Type**: Verb

Definition: An informal word meaning to leave quickly or to run away.

Example: The miscreants decided to **skedaddle** when they heard the distant howl of police sirens.

Skeuomorphs

Pronunciation: Skew-oh-morfs   **Type**: Noun

Definition: Design elements that mimic something that was functionally necessary in an earlier design but that's now purely ornamental.

Example: Camera shutter sound effects on mobile phone cameras are **skeuomorphs**.

Skimpy

Pronunciation: Skim-pee   **Type**: Adjective

Definition: This adjective is used to describe clothes that are short and revealing.

Example: "Jessica," shouted her father. "I'm not allowing you to leave the house in that **skimpy** outfit."

Skint

Pronunciation: Skint   **Type**: Adjective

Definition: Poor or penniless.

Example: "I can't come to the pub tonight," I said. "I'm too **skint**."

Skirl

Pronunciation: Skurl   **Type**: Noun, Verb

Definition: The shrill sound that bagpipes make. The verb refers to the act of making such a sound.

Example:
#1: The children put their hands over their ears when they heard the **skirl**.
#2: The musician decided to **skirl** his way through "Auld Lang Syne."

Skirmish

Pronunciation: Skur-mish   **Type**: Noun, Verb

Definition: A short and unplanned bout of fighting, particularly between small sections of armies. The verb refers to the action of engaging an enemy in a skirmish.

Example:
#1: The soldier was court-martialled for fleeing from the **skirmish**.
#2: The general decided that the best course of action was to **skirmish** on the borders.

Skit

Pronunciation: Skit   **Type**: Noun

Definition: A humorous sketch or a short piece of comedy.

Example: The actors waited nervously to be called to the stage for their **skit**.

Skulduggery

Pronunciation: Skull-dug-ur-ee   **Type**: Noun

Definition: A piece of crafty or deceptive trickery.

Example: It wasn't until her mother's death that Alice realised the full extent of the lawyer's **skulduggery**. All their valuables were gone.

Slattern

Pronunciation: Slat-urn   **Type**: Noun

Definition: A dirty, untidy and sexually promiscuous woman, particularly a prostitute who attracts customers by walking the streets.

Example: Robert advised Charles to avoid the **slattern** on Baker Street unless he wanted an STD.

Sleuth

Pronunciation: Slooth **Type**: Noun, Verb

Definition: The noun refers to a detective, while the verb refers to the action of carrying out a search, an investigation or an enquiry.

Example:
#1: The **sleuth** peered at the fingerprints through his magnifying glass.
#2: When my neighbours told the landlord that I'd killed their cat, he decided to **sleuth** for evidence.

Slipshod

Pronunciation: Slip-shod **Type**: Adjective

Definition: Characterised by a lack of care, planning, thought or organisation. The word can also be used to describe something that's worn down, shabby or untidy.

Example: The company hired the graduate for his brains and not for his **slipshod** appearance.

Slovenly

Pronunciation: Slov-un-lee **Type**: Adjective

Definition: Messy or careless in personal appearance or in work.

Example: The sailor was drunken and **slovenly**.

Slugabed

Pronunciation: Slug-ab-ed   **Type**: Noun

Definition: A lazy person who stays in bed late.

Example: The student was a renowned **slugabed** who never made it to his lectures.

Smarmy

Pronunciation: Smar-mee   **Type**: Adjective

Definition: Excessively or irritatingly ingratiating; full of false charm or insincerity.

Example: Beatrice couldn't stand her **smarmy** superior and threatened to resign unless she was moved to a different department.

Smoko

Pronunciation: Smo-ko   **Type**: Noun

Definition: Originally a dialect word from Australia and New Zealand, a smoko is a short (and often unauthorised) break from work to smoke a cigarette.

Example: "Quick," said Johnny. "Let's have a **smoko** before the boss gets back."

Smörgåsbord

Pronunciation: Smore-gus-bord   **Type**: Noun

Definition: A type of Scandinavian meal that's served in the style of a buffet with a variety of dishes including both hot and cold foods. By association, the noun can now be used to refer to anything that comes in a wide range or variety.

Example: The visitors were taken aback by the **smörgåsbord** of entertainment on offer.

Snafu

Pronunciation: Snaff-oo   **Type**: Noun

Definition: A state of chaos or confusion. The word evolved from the military acronym SNAFU, which means "situation normal – all fucked up".

Example: Jessica's daughter disappeared during the **snafu**, and she struggled to find her in the crowd.

Snicker

Pronunciation: Snick-ur   **Type**: Noun, Verb

Definition: A half-suppressed laugh or giggle. The verb refers to the action of laughing in such a way.

Example:
#1: The student emitted a **snicker** during the exam and was punished by being forced to re-take the paper.
#2: Gerald's ridiculous outfit made us **snicker**.

Snook

Pronunciation: Snook   **Type**: Noun

Definition: A breed of fish that's native to the Caribbean.

Example: Jerome wanted to taste local food while visiting the Caribbean, so he ordered **snook** for dinner.

Snub

Pronunciation: Snub   **Type**: Adjective, Noun, Verb

Definition: The adjective has a completely different meaning to the noun and the verb and describes something that's unusually short and stumpy. The noun refers to an act of disdain or rebuttal[†], while the verb refers to the action of spurning someone or refusing to acknowledge them.

Example:
#1: The animal was **snub**-nosed and secretive.
#2: When his date didn't turn up for dinner, Gary took it as a **snub**.
#3: She called Gary the next day and said, "I'm so sorry. I didn't mean to **snub** you."

Snuff

Pronunciation: Snuff   **Type**: Adjective, Noun, Verb

Definition: This is another example of a word with multiple different meanings, depending upon the context. The adjective is usually used to describe a film that shows the taking of a life, and the noun refers to a type of powdered tobacco that's inhaled, rather than smoked. The verb usually means to extinguish a candle, but by extension it can also mean to bring an end to something, often a life. It can also refer to the act of inhaling or sniffing.

Example:
#1: Peter bought a **snuff** film on the black market to satisfy his fantasies of death and murder.
#2: George went to the tobacconists to buy half an ounce of **snuff**.
#3: "Don't forget to **snuff** the candle before you leave," warned Peter.

Sobriquet

Pronunciation: So-brick-kay   **Type**: Noun

Definition: A nickname or an alias.

Example: Robert Zimmerman's **sobriquet** is "Bob Dylan."

Socialite

Pronunciation: So-shull-ite   **Type**: Noun

Definition: A person who's well-known in society for their love of socialising and social activities.

Example: Paris Hilton is a well-known **socialite**.

Sojourn

Pronunciation: So-jurn   **Type**: Noun, Verb

Definition: The noun refers to a temporary visit or stay, while the verb refers to the action of taking such a stay.

Example:
#1: Gladys seemed to be in much higher spirits after her **sojourn**.
#2: When she was made redundant, Jennifer decided to **sojourn** in the countryside.

Solarium

Pronunciation: So-lare-ee-um   **Type**: Noun

Definition: A room that's built mainly from glass to allow sunlight to enter, or a room that's equipped with tanning beds and sun lamps for the purpose of acquiring an artificial tan.

Example: The retired professor spent most of his retirement in the **solarium**, convinced that the serotonin[†] would prolong his life.

Solecism

Pronunciation: Sol-uh-siz-um   **Type**: Noun

Definition: A nonstandard usage of grammar in speech or writing. By extension, it can now refer to any breach of good manners or etiquette.

Example: Dane never forgave himself for his **solecism**.

Soliloquy

Pronunciation: So-lill-oh-kwee   **Type**: Noun

Definition: When someone speaks their thoughts aloud, whether whilst alone or within earshot of other people. Soliloquies are often found in plays, and the word can also refer to a play that involves or is largely based on such a speech.

Example: The actress practiced her lines over and over again before her big **soliloquy**.

Solipsism

Pronunciation: Soll-ip-siz-um   **Type**: Noun

Definition: The view, theory or belief that the self is the only thing that can be known or proven to exist.

Example: Kevin's belief in **solipsism** was just one of many factors that turned him in to a womaniser.

Solmisation

Pronunciation: Sol-my-zay-shun   **Type**: Noun

Definition: A naming system by which the notes of the musical scale are represented by sounds or syllables, instead of by numbers.

Example: David practiced **solmisation** by singing "do re mi fa so la ti do."

Solstice

Pronunciation: Sol-stiss   **Type**: Noun

Definition: An astronomical event occurring twice a year (once in the summer and once in the winter) when the sun reaches its highest or lowest point in the sky at noon, causing the longest day of the year in the summer and the shortest day of the year in winter.

Example: The druids were excited to celebrate the **solstice**.

Somatic

Pronunciation: Suh-mat-ick   **Type**: Adjective

Definition: Of, belonging to or related to the body, especially in contrast to the mind.

Example: The patient had a previously unknown **somatic** disorder and the doctors were unsure how to treat her.

Somnambulism

Pronunciation: Sum-namb-yoo-liz-um   **Type**: Noun

Definition: The practice of sleepwalking or the medical condition of being a sleepwalker.

Example: David's studies in **somnambulism** began when, at an early age, his father walked into his room in the middle of the night.

Sonorous

Pronunciation: Son-uh-russ   **Type**: Adjective

Definition: Having or capable of producing a rich, full and deep sound. This adjective is often used to describe a person's voice.

Example: Barry's **sonorous** voice silenced the babble of the audience and brought the proceedings to order.

Soothsayer

Pronunciation: Sooth-say-ur   **Type**: Noun

Definition: A person who has the supposed ability to see into and predict the future.

Example: The king went to see a **soothsayer** to find out how long his reign would last.

Sophism

Pronunciation: So-fizz-um   **Type**: Noun

Definition: An argument that appears to be correct but that's actually fallacious or untrue, particularly one that's used with the intention of deceiving someone.

Example: The politician was elected upon the strength of a **sophism** and by the time that the voters realised it, it was too late.

Soporific

Pronunciation: So-por-if-ick   **Type**: Adjective, Noun

Definition: The adjective is used to describe something that has the ability to induce drowsiness or sleep, while the noun refers to a drug that possesses this ability.

Example:
#1: The play was **soporific** and the children's parents paid little attention to what was happening on stage.
#2: The doctor prescribed Mr. Jamieson with a **soporific** to help him sleep through the pain.

Soubrette

Pronunciation: Soo-bret   **Type**: Noun

Definition: A minor dramatic role as a saucy or flirtatious young woman, often in a comedy. The word has taken on new life outside of dramatic circles and can be used to describe any pert, mischievous or flirtatious young woman.

Example: The teenager went home from the play with an empty wallet and a minor crush on the **soubrette** from the second act.

Sough

Pronunciation: Soff   **Type**: Noun, Verb

Definition: The noun refers to a moaning or whistling sound like the wind in the trees or the sea, while the verb refers to the action of making such a sound.

Example:
#1: The **sough** woke Percy from his light slumber.
#2: Katherine listened to the wind **sough** through the trees in the garden.

Southpaw

Pronunciation: South-por   **Type**: Noun

Definition: A left-handed person. The term is often used within sporting circles.

Example: The coach hired the **southpaw** because the rest of his pitchers were right-handed.

Spasmodic

Pronunciation: Spaz-mod-ick   **Type**: Adjective

Definition: Occurring in brief, irregular bursts, like a spasm. This adjective can also be used to describe something that's caused by, subject to or suffering from one or more spasms.

Example: Mr. Jenkins booked an appointment with his doctor to discuss his recurring **spasmodic** cough.

Speakeasy

Pronunciation: Speek-ee-zee   **Type**: Noun

Definition: An illegal liquor store, public house or nightclub during an era of prohibition.

Example: Carey needed a drink, and so he stopped off for some moonshine at the **speakeasy**.

Speleology

Pronunciation: Spee-lee-ol-oh-gee   **Type**: Noun

Definition: The study, charting or exploration of caves.

Example: Peter beat claustrophobia to pursue a successful career in **speleology**.

Speleothem

Pronunciation: Spee-lee-oath-em   **Type**: Noun

Definition: A structure that's formed inside a cave by mineral deposits that are left behind by water.

Example: Stalactites[†] and stalagmites[†] are both examples of a **speleothem**.

Spelunker

Pronunciation: Spuh-lunk-ur   **Type**: Noun

Definition: A person who explores caves, usually as a pastime.

Example: Peter gasped in horror as he read about the **spelunker** who died in a tragic accident.

Sphincter

Pronunciation: Ss-fink-ter   **Type**: Noun

Definition: A ring of muscle that surrounds an opening or a tube and closes it when necessary, particularly the ring of muscle around the anus.

Example: Juliet refused to go down on her boyfriend until he sorted out his smelly **sphincter**.

Spindrift

Pronunciation: Spin-drift   **Type**: Noun

Definition: This noun usually refers to the spray that's blown from the crests of waves by the wind during gales and storms.

Example: The first mate brushed the **spindrift** from his forehead and bellowed orders at the other sailors.

Spiv

Pronunciation: Spiv   **Type**: Noun

Definition: A person who appears flashy or smartly dressed despite being technically unemployed, making money from illicit, immoral or questionable dealings.

Example: Karen bought a new TV from the local **spiv** and ended up having it confiscated by the police as evidence for the prosecution.

Splenetic

Pronunciation: Splen-et-ick   **Type**: Adjective

Definition: Bad-tempered, mean or spiteful. This adjective can also be used to describe something that's related to the spleen as it was traditionally believed that anger originated there.

Example: The old drunkard was unprepared for the **splenetic** operation.

Spondulicks

Pronunciation: Spond-yoo-lix   **Type**: Noun

Definition: A slang term for money, originating in America but also popular in Britain and Australia, among other places.

Example: "I can't go out tonight," Dave said. "I don't have any **spondulicks**."

Spoonerism

Pronunciation: Spoo-nur-iz-um   **Type**: Noun

Definition: A verbal mistake or an error in pronunciation where the speaker accidentally confuses the initial sounds of two or more words and swaps them with each other, often with a humorous result.

Example: Stephen said he was fighting a liar instead of lighting a fire, and his parents laughed at his inadvertent **spoonerism**.

Sporadic

Pronunciation: Spuh-rad-ick   **Type**: Adjective

Definition: Occurring at or happening between seemingly random intervals or at an irregular or scattered pace.

Example: The Germans were coming under **sporadic** fire from the allied trenches.

Spumous

Pronunciation: Spyoo-muss   **Type**: Adjective

Definition: Foamy or frothy, like the sea.

Example: The pond was **spumous** and home to unknown amounts of wildlife.

Spurious

Pronunciation: Spyor-ee-uss   **Type**: Adjective

Definition: Fake/not genuine.

Example: The diamond was found to be **spurious** and the tradesman was arrested by the police.

Squalor

Pronunciation: Skwal-ur   **Type**: Noun

Definition: A state of filth, dirtiness and poverty.

Example: The beggar boy lived in **squalor** in a small shed that showed signs of a rat infestation.

Squiffy

Pronunciation: Skwiff-ee   **Type**: Adjective

Definition: Slightly intoxicated.

Example: Granddad was **squiffy** after a few beers at the family meal and didn't make much sense.

Stalactite

Pronunciation: Stal-ack-tite   **Type**: Noun

Definition: A structure that's formed by the calcium salts in dripping water, usually found hanging from the ceilings of caves.

Example: The caver banged his head against a **stalactite**.

Stalagmite

Pronunciation: Stal-ag-mite   **Type**: Noun

Definition: The opposite of a stalactite[†]. A similar structure of calcium salts that grows upwards from the floor of a cave.

Example: The caver banged his toe against a **stalagmite**.

Stalwart

Pronunciation: Stall-wart   **Type**: Adjective, Noun

Definition: The adjective describes someone who's a loyal or hard-working supporter, while the noun refers to an individual of this type.

Example:
#1: Steve was a **stalwart** supporter of Arsenal and celebrated for weeks when they won the premiership.
#2: James was a **stalwart** at the company, and nobody could imagine how life would continue without him.

Statutory

Pronunciation: Stat-yoot-or-ee   **Type**: Adjective

Definition: Required by formal and written law.

Example: Percy's crime came with a **statutory** minimum sentence of six years of penal servitude.

Staunch

Pronunciation: Stornch   **Type**: Adjective

Definition: Loyal, dedicated or committed; unmovable.

Example: Timothy was a **staunch** Christian and didn't believe anything that Richard Dawkins said.

Stellate

Pronunciation: Stell-ate   **Type**: Adjective

Definition: Arranged in a pattern that bears a resemblance to the shape of a star.

Example: The pebble was **stellate**, and Peter immediately added it to his collection.

Stenography

Pronunciation: Sten-og-raff-ee   **Type**: Noun

Definition: The process or art of writing in shorthand or of receiving dictation.

Example: The **stenography** assistant transcribed the trial as it was happening.

Stentor

Pronunciation: Stent-or   **Type**: Noun

Definition: A person with a strong, powerful voice.

Example: The **stentor** called for attention and the congregation fell silent.

Stentorious

Pronunciation: Sten-tor-ee-uss   **Type**: Adjective

Definition: Possessing the qualities of a stentor[†].

Example: The **stentorious** young man was destined for a career as a town crier.

Stevedore

Pronunciation: Stee-vuh-dor   **Type**: Noun

Definition: A person or a company that works at a dock, loading and unloading cargo from ships.

Example: The **stevedore** could usually be found in the bar when he wasn't on the ship.

Stigmata

Pronunciation: Stig-mar-ta   **Type**: Noun

Definition: The plural of stigma; marks of disgrace or shame that are associated with a particular circumstance or illness. In Christian tradition, it refers to marks which appear on a person's body and resemble the entry points that were allegedly left on Jesus's body after the crucifixion, particularly in location and appearance.

Example: "Kevin, come quick!" shouted Olivia. "Our boy has **stigmata**!"

Stimuli

Pronunciation: Stim-yoo-lie   **Type**: Noun

Definition: The plural of stimulus; things or events that evoke a specific response or reaction.

Example: Catrina was overwhelmed during the movie because of the abundance of visual **stimuli**.

Stipend

Pronunciation: Sty-pend   **Type**: Noun

Definition: A regular sum that's paid as a salary or an allowance.

Example: The farmer's wife always claimed that she struggled to survive on the modest **stipend** that he gave to her.

Stoicism

Pronunciation: Stoe-iss-iz-um   **Type**: Noun

Definition: The endurance of pain, unpleasantness or hardship in the face of adversity, without any display of unhappiness or complaint.

Example: The British populace[†] was renowned for its **stoicism** during the war.

Stolid

Pronunciation: Stol-id   **Type**: Adjective

Definition: Calm, practical and dependable, with little emotion or animation.

Example: Kevin was **stolid** when confronted with an unhappy customer.

Strabismus

Pronunciation: Strab-iz-muss   **Type**: Noun

Definition: The condition of having a squint.

Example: Josef paid a visit to the ophthalmologist about his **strabismus**, but there was nothing the doctor could do.

Straphanger

Pronunciation: Strap-hang-ur   **Type**: Noun

Definition: A passenger that's standing up on a bus or train. The term comes from the dangling straps that are provided for passengers to hold on to.

Example: I hate going on buses because I always get stuck next to a **straphanger** with body odour problems.

Streamline

Pronunciation: Streem-line   **Type**: Verb

Definition: The act of designing something in such a form that it presents little resistance, usually to the flow of air or water. It can also refer to any action that makes lengthy processes easier and faster.

Example: The scientists knew that if they wanted to break the sound barrier, they'd have to **streamline** the aeroplane.

Strident

Pronunciation: Stry-dunt   **Type**: Adjective

Definition: Loud and harsh, particularly when presenting a controversial point of view in an unpleasant and forceful way.

Example: The **strident** young man was quick to provoke the anger of his peers.

Stringent

Pronunciation: Strin-junt   **Type**: Adjective

Definition: Strict and precise. This adjective is most commonly used to describe laws, regulations or requirements.

Example: Alex wanted to join the army but failed the **stringent** medical test.

Stripling

Pronunciation: Strip-ling   **Type**: Noun

Definition: A young man.

Example: The **stripling** could often be found in the library studying for his classes.

Stultify

Pronunciation: Stul-tiff-eye   **Type**: Verb

Definition: To cause someone to lose enthusiasm or to make them appear foolish or ridiculous, especially as a direct result of the tedium of a restrictive routine.

Example: It only took Smith two months to **stultify** after joining the big PR company.

Stygian

Pronunciation: Stij-ee-un   **Type**: Adjective

Definition: Typical of or relating to the river Styx. As an extension of this, it can also be used to mean "very dark."

Example: By day, the vampire slept in a **stygian** crypt.

Sublime

Pronunciation: Sub-lime   **Type**: Adjective, Verb

Definition: The adjective is used to describe something that's so beautiful that it inspires admiration or awe in the beholder. The verb refers to the process by which a solid substance changes directly into vapour when heated, usually forming a solid deposit again once it cools.

Example:
#1: The Sistine Chapel was **sublime**; I barely spoke for hours.
#2: The scientists watched the crystals **sublime** inside the vacuum.

Submersible

Pronunciation: Sub-mur-sib-ul   **Type**: Adjective, Noun

Definition: The adjective describes something that's designed to function fully while submerged under water. The noun usually refers to a small boat or submarine, particularly one that's been created for the purposes of scientific research and exploration.

Example:
#1: The **submersible** watch operated at depths of up to five hundred feet and was popular with police divers.
#2: The researchers boarded the **submersible** and prepared to begin their investigation.

Subnormal

Pronunciation: Sub-norm-ul   **Type**: Adjective

Definition: Below standard or failing to reach a level that's regarded as average, particularly in reference to intelligence, growth or development.

Example: The child was judged to be of **subnormal** intellect and was sent to a special school where his needs could be catered to.

Suborn

Pronunciation: Sub-orn   **Type**: Verb

Definition: To convince or induce someone to commit an illegal act, often through bribery or blackmail.

Example: The gangster tried to **suborn** the shopkeeper to make him act as a front for their money laundering operation.

Subservient

Pronunciation: Sub-sur-vee-unt　　　**Type**: Adjective

Definition: Quick to obey commands or instructions without question.

Example: The **subservient** butler responded to every request in a quick and thorough manner.

Subsume

Pronunciation: Sub-shoom　　　**Type**: Verb

Definition: To include or to absorb something into something else.

Example: The new office manager had to **subsume** some of the tasks of the cleaners.

Subterfuge

Pronunciation: Sub-turf-yooj　　　**Type**: Noun

Definition: Deliberate deception that's carried out in order to achieve a specific goal.

Example: The diplomats resorted to **subterfuge** to escape the country with the secret plans.

Succedaneum

Pronunciation: Suck-ad-ane-ee-um　　　**Type**: Noun

Definition: A substitute, usually a medicine, that's taken in place of another medicine to achieve the same effect.

Example: David took ibuprofen as a **succedaneum** for aspirin.

Succinct

Pronunciation: Suck-sinkt   **Type**: Adjective

Definition: Briefly and clearly explained or expressed in either written or spoken language.

Example: The lecturer was celebrated for his **succinct** speech at the annual convention.

Sudorific

Pronunciation: Soo-dur-if-ick   **Type**: Adjective, Noun

Definition: The adjective describes something that causes sweating, while the noun refers to a drug that causes this effect.

Example:
#1: The weather was **sudorific** and made it difficult to concentrate.
#2: The doctor injected his patient with a **sudorific** to help him to sweat out the illness.

Sumptuary

Pronunciation: Sump-choo-eh-ree   **Type**: Adjective

Definition: This adjective describes something that relates to laws that limit expenditure on foods, drinks and personal items.

Example: The inspection caught the prisoners with a number of items that flouted the **sumptuary** regulations.

Superannuate

Pronunciation: Soo-purr-an-yoo-ate   **Type**: Verb

Definition: To retire an employee, giving them a pension in the process.

Example: Because of his decades of long, hard work, the post office decided to **superannuate** Postman Pat.

Superate

Pronunciation: Soo-purr-ate   **Type**: Verb

Definition: To outdo, outperform or to otherwise exceed.

Example: The athlete managed to **superate** all prior expectations when he took to the track.

Supercilious

Pronunciation: Soo-purr-sill-ee-uss   **Type**: Adjective

Definition: Acting or behaving as though you think you're superior to other people.

Example: The waitress was **supercilious** and was quickly dismissed by the restaurant because of customer complaints.

Supererogation

Pronunciation: Soo-purr-eh-ro-gay-shun   **Type**: Noun

Definition: The act of performing more work than one's duty requires.

Example: Dane realised that he was guilty of **supererogation**, particularly when he checked his bank account and realised how much the company was paying him.

Supine

Pronunciation: Soo-pine   **Type**: Adjective

Definition: Lying down, facing upwards. This adjective is normally only used to describe a person.

Example: The lovers slept **supine** and side-by-side.

Suppositious

Pronunciation: Sup-oh-sish-uss   **Type**: Adjective

Definition: Based on assumptions rather than on fact.

Example: The scientist's theory was **suppositious** and didn't hold up to a full investigation.

Surfeit

Pronunciation: Surf-it   **Type**: Noun

Definition: An excess of something.

Example: The school used the **surfeit** of funds to build a new library.

Surreptitious

Pronunciation: Suh-rep-tish-uss   **Type**: Adjective

Definition: This adjective describes something that's done in secret because to make it public or obvious would be frowned upon.

Example: Harold kept a **surreptitious** allotment. His wife thought it was a waste of time.

Susurrus

Pronunciation: Suh-suh-russ   **Type**: Noun

Definition: A whispering, murmuring or rustling sound, like the sound made by the wind in the leaves of the trees.

Example: The stream rolled on in a gentle **susurrus**.

Sutler

Pronunciation: Sut-ler   **Type**: Noun

Definition: A person who follows an army around, selling food and other supplies.

Example: The **sutler** made a fortune selling his wares during the invasion.

Suttee

Pronunciation: Soot-ee   **Type**: Noun

Definition: A former Hindu practice in which a widow committed suicide by burning herself to death on her husband's funeral pyre. The noun can also refer to a woman who carries out such an act.

Example: The family went into mourning after Aditya became a **suttee**.

Svelte

Pronunciation: Svelt   **Type**: Adjective

Definition: Slender or elegant.

Example: The bachelor was **svelte** and eligible in the eyes of the local women.

Swarthy

Pronunciation: Swore-thee   **Type**: Adjective

Definition: Dark-skinned.

Example: Laura's father was **swarthy** and often discriminated against by the police force.

Swashbuckler

Pronunciation: Swosh-buck-la   **Type**: Noun

Definition: A rough, noisy and boastful swordsman. The noun has evolved and can now also be used to describe anyone who's reckless or impetuous.

Example: The **swashbuckler** was killed in a bar-room brawl.

Swinge

Pronunciation: Swinj   **Type**: Verb

Definition: To hit something hard or to beat something.

Example: The boxer had a plan for the fight. All he had to do was to **swinge** his opponent until he couldn't stand up any more.

Sybarite

Pronunciation: Sib-ah-rite   **Type**: Noun

Definition: A self-indulgent person with an addiction to luxury and the pleasuring of the senses.

Example: The wealthy **sybarite** lived a life of ease and debauchery[†].

Sycophant

Pronunciation: Sick-oh-fant   **Type**: Noun

Definition: A person who attempts to win favour by behaving obsequiously[†] or by flattering influential people.

Example: Everybody hated the **sycophant**, even the prince who employed him.

Syllepsis

Pronunciation: Sill-ep-sis   **Type**: Noun

Definition: A figure of speech or a linguistic phenomenon by which one word is applied to two other words in two different senses.

Example: The phrase "he caught the train and a cold" is an example of **syllepsis**.

Syllogism

Pronunciation: Sil-oh-jizz-um   **Type**: Noun

Definition: A form of reasoning in which a conclusion is drawn from two premises, each of which shares something in common with the conclusion and something in common that isn't present in the conclusion.

Example: A famous **syllogism** is that all dogs are animals, all animals have four legs and, therefore, all dogs have four legs.

Sylvan

Pronunciation: Sill-van   **Type**: Adjective

Definition: Of, resembling or related to trees and woods.

Example: The **sylvan** smell reminded Toby of his homeland.

Synaesthesia

Pronunciation: Sin-ass-thee-see-ah   **Type**: Noun

Definition: A phenomenon where one or more senses collide with each other, allowing you to experience things with a different sense than you normally would.

Example: Tasting green and seeing musical notes are examples of **synaesthesia**.

Synecdoche

Pronunciation: Sin-eck-duh-key   **Type**: Noun

Definition: A figure of speech where a small part of a thing is used to describe its whole, or vice versa.

Example: If you refer to a person's signature as their John Hancock, you're using **synecdoche**.

Synergism

Pronunciation: Sin-ur-jizz-um   **Type**: Noun

Definition: Another word for "synergy", the state when two individual people or things combine together to produce an effect that's greater than the sum of their parts.

Example: The football team played with **synergism**.

Synonymic

Pronunciation: Sin-on-im-ick   **Type**: Adjective

Definition: Possessing the quality of a synonym – that is, a figure of speech where one word or expression is used as a substitute for another.

Example: The word "chilly" is synonymic with the word "cold."

Syntactic

Pronunciation: Sin-tack-tick   **Type**: Adjective

Definition: Of, relating to or according to syntax[†].

Example: Dane's sentences were always **syntactic** because he spent hour after hour proofreading and sub-editing his work.

Syntax

Pronunciation: Sin-tax   **Type**: Noun

Definition: The arrangement of words and phrases to create correct and well-formed sentences in a language.

Example: Without the correct use of **syntax**, sentences make no sense.

T

Tableau

Pronunciation: Tab-low   **Type**: Noun

Definition: A group of models, statues or other motionless figures that depict[+] a scene from a story or from history.

Example: The visitors were stunned by the rich colours of the **tableau** and didn't know what to make of it.

Taciturn

Pronunciation: Tass-it-urn   **Type**: Adjective

Definition: Quiet, reserved or uncommunicative. This adjective is usually used to describe someone who rarely speaks or who speaks in infrequent short sentences.

Example: After his mother's death, Jack became **taciturn** and inconsolable.

Talebearer

Pronunciation: Tale-bear-ur   **Type**: Noun

Definition: Similar in meaning to "tell-tale," this noun is used to refer to people who spread gossip and rumours.

Example: The gang refused to tell Ray the big secret because he was a **talebearer**.

Tautology

Pronunciation: Tort-ol-oh-gee   **Type**: Noun

Definition: A phrase or expression in which the same thing is said twice but in different ways.

Example: The phrase "going round in circles" is an example of **tautology**, because if you're going round then you're already going in a circle.

Tearaway

Pronunciation: Tear-ah-way   **Type**: Noun

Definition: A young, reckless and impetuous person.

Example: After Tommy broke the window, his grandfather shouted, "Come back, you little **tearaway**, before I tell your mother!"

Technobabble

Pronunciation: Teck-no-bab-ul   **Type**: Noun

Definition: A form of language that uses a large amount of technical jargon, specialised terms and other buzzwords.

Example: Everyone in customer service hated the I.T. department because they only spoke **technobabble**.

Technocracy

Pronunciation: Teck-nock-rass-ee   **Type**: Noun

Definition: A form of control in which a society or an industry is governed or ruled by an elite group of technical experts.

Example: In the future, Earth will become a **technocracy**, and the unskilled will be retired to another planet.

Telegenic

Pronunciation: Tell-uh-jen-ick   **Type**: Adjective

Definition: The televisual equivalent of "photogenic"; possessing an appearance or a manner that's appealing on television.

Example: The new host was more **telegenic** than the old one.

Telegraphese

Pronunciation: Tel-ig-raff-eez   **Type**: Noun

Definition: A type of language that's characterised by terseness and abbreviations, like the language used in telegrams.

Example: Orville Wright's telegram about the first powered flight uses **telegraphese**. "Success four flights Thursday morning all against twenty-one-mile wind started from level with engine power alone."

Teleology

Pronunciation: Tel-ee-ol-oh-gee   **Type**: Noun

Definition: Any philosophical or religious doctrine that explains phenomena[†] by the purposes that they serve, rather than by whatever it is that causes them.

Example: Arguments for the doctrine of intelligent design often rely on **teleology**.

Televangelist

Pronunciation: Tell-iv-an-juh-list   **Type**: Noun

Definition: An evangelical preacher who preaches on television, usually while appealing for funds.

Example: Grandma couldn't afford proper medical care when her arthritis got worse because she'd given her money to the **televangelist**.

Temerity

Pronunciation: Tuh-meh-rit-ee   **Type**: Noun

Definition: An excessive level of boldness, daring or confidence.

Example: No one had the **temerity** to question the end-of-quarter reports, and dozens lost their jobs because of it.

Temperance

Pronunciation: Tem-puh-runce   **Type**: Noun

Definition: Abstinence, moderation or self-restraint, particularly when drinking alcohol or eating.

Example: Mr. Forbes was a firm believer in **temperance** and tried to persuade others to give up drinking.

Temporal

Pronunciation: Tem-por-ul   **Type**: Adjective

Definition: Another example of a word with multiple meanings. This adjective can describe something that relates to time, something that only exists for a short period of time, or something concerned with the present life or the world that we're in, as opposed to the spiritual world.

Example: Janet regretted the **temporal** sins of her youth on her deathbed, but it was far too late by then.

Tenable

Pronunciation: Ten-ab-ull   **Type**: Adjective

Definition: Able to be held or used, or able to be maintained against an attack or objection. The meaning of the word depends upon the context that it's used in.

Example: "I fear it will be difficult to hold a **tenable** position on the matter," the Prime Minister said.

Tenacity

Pronunciation: Ten-ass-it-ee   **Type**: Noun

Definition: The quality or property of being tenacious; doggedness or persistent determination.

Example: The old major was renowned for his **tenacity** because he got things done!

Tendentious

Pronunciation: Ten-densh-uss   **Type**: Adjective

Definition: Expressing approval of or intending to promote a particular cause or point of view.

Example: The teenager's essay was a **tendentious** analysis of the Second World War.

Tenuity

Pronunciation: Ten-yoo-it-ee   **Type**: Noun

Definition: The state of being tenuous, which means to be weak or slight.

Example: Peter struggled to grasp the idea because of the **tenuity** behind the argument.

Tercentennial

Pronunciation: Tur-sen-ten-ee-ul   **Type**: Noun

Definition: The three-hundredth anniversary of something, or the accompanying celebrations.

Example: The sovereign state was celebrating its **tercentennial** when its neighbours launched a surprise attack.

Termagant

Pronunciation: Tur-ma-gunt   **Type**: Noun

Definition: A bad-tempered, violent or otherwise overbearing woman. This noun evolved from the name given to an imaginary deity who often appeared in plays about morality.

Example: The bridegroom refused to marry the **termagant**.

Tessellated

Pronunciation: Tess-ul-ate-id   **Type**: Adjective

Definition: Chequered; shaped like a mosaic or a honeycomb.

Example: The pattern of the **tessellated** floor tiles made Phillip feel ill when he looked at it.

Testaceous

Pronunciation: Test-ace-yuss   **Type**: Adjective

Definition: Of, related to or derived from shells. By extension, this adjective can also describe something that's a dull red colour.

Example: There was a **testaceous** smell in the beach air, and a cold breeze blowing from the north.

Testate

Pronunciation: Test-ate   **Type**: Adjective, Noun

Definition: The adjective is used to describe someone who made a valid will before they died, while the noun refers to a person who died and left behind such a will.

Example:
#1: The **testate** gentleman left all of his money to charity.
#2: The police were as surprised as anyone when they found out that the John Doe was a **testate**.

Tetchy

Pronunciation: Tet-chee   **Type**: Adjective

Definition: Irritable, bad-tempered or easily annoyed.

Example: Karen was a good housemate, but she got **tetchy** when people used her sugar.

Tetrapod

Pronunciation: Tet-ra-pod   **Type**: Noun

Definition: An animal, object or structure with four feet, legs or supports.

Example: Erica was given a **tetrapod** for her birthday.

Teutonic

Pronunciation: Toot-on-ick **Type**: Adjective, Noun

Definition: Of, related to or pertaining to the ancient Teutons or the Germans. The noun refers to their language.

Example:
#1: The **Teutonic** sculpture was badly damaged but still recognisable.
#2: The stranger could only speak **Teutonic** and nobody could understand him.

Thanatology

Pronunciation: Than-at-ol-oh-gee **Type**: Noun

Definition: The scientific study of death and the practices associated with it, including the study of the needs and healthcare of the terminally ill.

Example: The professor of **thanatology** was a sad and lonely man with no time left for the living.

Theocracy

Pronunciation: Thee-ock-rass-ee **Type**: Noun

Definition: A type of government led by priests who rule in the name of a god.

Example: After the civil uprising, the troubled state settled into a **theocracy**.

Theorem

Pronunciation: Thee-or-um   **Type**: Noun

Definition: A formula, rule or mathematic statement that's been deduced from other formulae, propositions or theories. More generally, this noun can also refer to any idea that's accepted or believed to be the truth.

Example: It took the mathematician four years to develop his **theorem**, but he was eventually rewarded with a PhD.

Theosophy

Pronunciation: Thee-oss-oh-fee   **Type**: Noun

Definition: An umbrella term for any type of philosophy which argues that knowledge of god and the divine can be achieved through intuition or spiritual insight.

Example: Everybody thought that the monks were mad and left them to their **theosophy**.

Thermoluminescence

Pronunciation: Thurr-mo-loo-min-ess-unce   **Type**: Noun

Definition: A type of light emission that occurs when certain minerals are warmed or heated.

Example: During the experiment, the minerals showed their **thermoluminescence** and added more light to the room.

Thespian

Pronunciation: Thess-pee-un   **Type**: Adjective, Noun

Definition: The adjective is used to describe something that's related to the theatre, while the noun is another word for an actor or an actress.

Example:
#1 The **thespian** bookshop had every resource an actor could ever need.
#2: The ageing **thespian** returned to the stage for a final bow.

Thrifty

Pronunciation: Thriff-tee   **Type**: Adjective

Definition: This adjective is used to describe a person or their behaviour when they scrimp and save, using money and other resources like food and clothing carefully and without waste.

Example: The family were forced to be **thrifty** in the early days when the father was barely earning enough to pay rent.

Thriving

Pronunciation: Thry-ving   **Type**: Verb

Definition: Growing or developing well; prospering or flourishing.

Example: Arol was **thriving** at his new job. He was receiving a high salary, and he enjoyed the work.

Thrum

Pronunciation: Th-rum   **Type**: Noun, Verb

Definition: The noun refers to a continuous low humming sound, while the verb refers to the action of making such a sound.

Example:
#1: The children found it difficult to sleep at night under the harsh **thrum** of the lighting.
#2: Somewhere in the garden, he heard a nightingale **thrum**.

Tiffin

Pronunciation: Tiff-in   **Type**: Noun

Definition: A term for a light meal or snack, particularly one taken at lunchtime, which originated in British India.

Example: The schoolboys settled down for **tiffin** before heading to the football field.

Timbre

Pronunciation: Tom-bruh   **Type**: Noun

Definition: The unique character or quality of a musical instrument or a voice that distinguishes it from other instruments or voices.

Example: When the record company heard the **timbre** of the young starlet's voice for the first time, they knew they were going to be rich.

Timorous

Pronunciation: Tim-uh-russ   **Type**: Adjective

Definition: Showing signs of nervousness or fear.

Example: The little orphan's **timorous** voice rang out in the market square, but people just walked on by.

Tincture

Pronunciation: Tink-churr   **Type**: Noun

Definition: A medicine that's created by dissolving a drug in alcohol.

Example: The old man drank the **tincture** and prepared for a good night's sleep.

Tinnitus

Pronunciation: Tinn-it-uss   **Type**: Noun

Definition: An irritating and often painful ringing sound in the ears.

Example: After too many years of loud music, Peter suffered from **tinnitus**.

Tintinnabulation

Pronunciation: Tin-tin-ab-yoo-lay-shun   **Type**: Noun

Definition: The ringing of bells.

Example: The **tintinnabulation** of the church's bells could be heard from several streets away.

Tippet

Pronunciation: Tip-it   **Type**: Noun

Definition: A long cape or scarf, often worn by women or as a ceremonial garment in the clergy[†].

Example: He wore a golden **tippet** during the ceremony.

Tiro

Pronunciation: Tie-ro   **Type**: Noun

Definition: Someone who's new to something; a novice.

Example: The young **tiro** had much to learn, and the master wasn't sure if he could teach him.

Tisane

Pronunciation: Tiz-an   **Type**: Noun

Definition: A type of herbal tea, usually consumed because of supposed medicinal properties.

Example: The old man drank **tisane** on his deathbed, but it was far too late for that to save him.

Tittup

Pronunciation: Tit-tup   **Type**: Verb

Definition: To prance around or to walk with a lofty gait, especially in an attempt to impress others.

Example: She watched Gary **tittup** around the cocktail bar in an attempt to make an impression on the barmaid.

Toccata

Pronunciation: Tock-ah-ta   **Type**: Noun

Definition: A type of musical composition that's designed to be played on a keyed instrument to flaunt the performer's ability.

Example: Peter refused to join the band unless he could perform a **toccata** while they took to the stage.

Tocsin

Pronunciation: Tock-sin   **Type**: Noun

Definition: An alarm bell.

Example: Every morning, the sailors woke up to the **tocsin**.

Tome

Pronunciation: Tome   **Type**: Noun

Definition: A large, thick book.

Example: The acolyte[†] flicked through the pages of the heavenly **tome**.

Tonsorial

Pronunciation: Ton-sore-ee-ul   **Type**: Adjective

Definition: Of or relating to hairdressing or hairdressers.

Example: Natalia picked up the **tonsorial** scissors and began to cut the customer's hair.

Tonsure

Pronunciation: Ton-shur   **Type**: Noun, Verb

Definition: A traditional practice in Christian churches where the hair is cut or shaved from the scalp of monks and clerics to leave a bald circle at the centre of the head. The noun refers to the haircut itself, while the verb refers to the process of giving someone such a haircut.

Example:
#1: The locals looked down upon the monk because of his **tonsure**.
#2: Without their razorblades, the monks were unable to **tonsure** the new recruits.

Tope

Pronunciation: Tope   **Type**: Noun, Verb

Definition: A rare example of a word where the noun and the verb have nothing in common. The noun refers to a type of small shark, while the verb means to drink alcohol to excess or to binge†, especially on a regular basis.

Example:
#1: The fishermen spotted a **tope** off the starboard side of the vessel, and he tried to move the boat away from it.
#2: Kevin and his friends liked to **tope** every Friday night.

Toponymy

Pronunciation: Top-on-im-ee   **Type**: Noun

Definition: The scientific or linguistic study of the place names of a region or a language.

Example: Jamie's interest in **toponymy** was first sparked when he discovered that there's a place called Dildo in Newfoundland.

Torpid

Pronunciation: Tor-pid   **Type**: Adjective

Definition: Slow, lethargic or inactive, both mentally and physically.

Example: Alex was always **torpid** in the mornings.

Tortuous

Pronunciation: Tort-yoo-uss   **Type**: Adjective

Definition: Full of twists and turns, or excessively long and complex.

Example: The country roads were **tortuous** and misleading.

Totalitarian

Pronunciation: Toe-tal-it-air-ee-un   **Type**: Adjective, Noun

Definition: The adjective is more commonly seen and is used to describe something that's of or relating to a system of government which has total power and requires complete subservience from its people. The noun refers to a person who believes in, supports or advocates such a government.

Example:
#1: George Orwell's *1984* depicts† a **totalitarian** police state.
#2: The **totalitarian** made no friends at the Labour Party conference.

Tracklement

Pronunciation: Track-ul-munt   **Type**: Noun

Definition: A type of condiment, often chutney or mustard, that's served with meat.

Example: The chef served the roast with a light **tracklement**.

Traditionalism

Pronunciation: Trad-ish-un-ul-iz-um   **Type**: Noun

Definition: The practice of upholding, preserving or maintaining a tradition, particularly when doing so in a conscious effort to resist change.

Example: The Amish community is based on **traditionalism**.

Tragedienne

Pronunciation: Tra-jee-dee-enn   **Type**: Noun

Definition: An actress who specialises in playing tragic roles.

Example: The **tragedienne** died in every play she was in.

Trammel

Pronunciation: Tram-ul   **Type**: Noun, Verb

Definition: The noun refers to a restriction, impediment or barrier to someone's freedom, while the verb refers to the process of depriving someone of their freedom.

Example:
#1: The totalitarian[†] political party acted as a **trammel** for the masses.
#2: The prison warden was determined to **trammel** the leader of the gang of inmates.

Transient

Pronunciation: Tran-zee-unt   **Type**: Adjective

Definition: Fleeting or impermanent; lasting for a short period of time.

Example: The shooting star made a **transient** appearance in the sky.

Transliterate

Pronunciation: Trans-lit-uh-rate   **Type**: Verb

Definition: To write, print or represent a letter or word in a different language, using the closest corresponding letters or symbols.

Example: The professor of Egyptology decided to **transliterate** the hieroglyphs into English.

Transmogrify

Pronunciation: Trans-mog-rif-eye   **Type**: Verb

Definition: To transform in a surprising or a seemingly magical manner.

Example: The illusionist surprised the audience by using his talents to **transmogrify** a hat into a badger.

Trattoria

Pronunciation: Trat-oh-ree-ah   **Type**: Noun

Definition: An Italian restaurant that serves simple food.

Example: The hungry students paid a visit to the **trattoria**.

Travelogue

Pronunciation: Trav-ul-og   **Type**: Noun

Definition: A book, film or other creative piece about a series of places that have been visited and the experiences that the traveller encountered there.

Example: The lecturer showed pictures from his **travelogue** to emphasize the need for people to help the victims of the hurricane.

Trenchant

Pronunciation: Trench-unt   **Type**: Adjective

Definition: This adjective can either be used to describe a sharpness of thought, expression or intellect, or the sharpness of a tool or a weapon.

Example: The soldier cut his finger on his **trenchant** bayonet.

Trepanning

Pronunciation: Trep-an-ing   **Type**: Noun

Definition: A surgical intervention where a hole is drilled into a human skull, either for religious and spiritual reasons or for the treatment of health problems.

Example: The primitive tribe practiced ritualistic **trepanning** to relieve headaches.

Tribulation

Pronunciation: Trib-yoo-lay-shun   **Type**: Noun

Definition: A state of great pain and suffering.

Example: The prophet foresaw a great **tribulation** for the people of Egypt.

Trichology

Pronunciation: Trike-ol-oh-gee   **Type**: Noun

Definition: The medical, cosmetic and scientific study of the hair and scalp.

Example: The professor of **trichology** was concerned about the new brand of hair gel.

Trinket

Pronunciation: Trin-kit   **Type**: Noun

Definition: A small ornament or piece of jewellery that's of little or no monetary value.

Example: John's girlfriend broke up with him after calling the engagement ring an ugly **trinket**.

Trireme

Pronunciation: Try-reem   **Type**: Noun

Definition: An ancient Greek or Roman warship with three banks of oars.

Example: The invaders landed in a **trireme** and began their attack on the fortress.

Triumvirate

Pronunciation: Try-um-vih-rut   **Type**: Noun

Definition: A group of three people, countries or entities that hold power together.

Example: The **triumvirate** ruling the country rarely agreed, as each of the three had their own opinion.

Troglodyte

Pronunciation: Trog-lo-dite   **Type**: Noun

Definition: A person who lives in a cave.

Example: The villagers refused to sell food to the **troglodyte** because they thought it was bad luck.

Troika

Pronunciation: Troy-ka   **Type**: Noun

Definition: A Russian word that originally referred to a vehicle that was pulled by a team of three horses. It's now often used to refer to a group of three people who work together, particularly to run a company, an initiative or a movement.

Example: Larry Page, Sergey Brin and Eric Schmidt were Google's leading **troika**.

Troilism

Pronunciation: Troy-ul-iz-um   **Type**: Noun

Definition: Any sexual activity that involves three partners.

Example: Jennifer was unhappy with her sex life and suggested **troilism** to her husband.

Troubadour

Pronunciation: Troob-ad-or   **Type**: Noun

Definition: A poet who writes verse that's set to music, or a travelling musician who performs such music.

Example: The **troubadour** travelled from town to town, sharing his songs.

Trousseau

Pronunciation: Troo-so   **Type**: Noun

Definition: The clothes, linen and other household items that are collected by a bride for her wedding.

Example: Monica's favourite part of the wedding was the **trousseau** delivered by her in-laws.

Truculent

Pronunciation: Truck-yoo-lunt   **Type**: Adjective

Definition: Quick to argue or fight.

Example: The **truculent** young man was always getting into trouble.

Tryst

Pronunciation: Trist   **Type**: Noun

Definition: A private rendezvous between lovers.

Example: Jack and Jill went up the hill for a midnight **tryst**.

Tumbrel

Pronunciation: Tum-brul   **Type**: Noun

Definition: A large, covered cart, used for carrying dung, moving ammunition and weaponry and ferrying prisoners to the guillotine during the French Revolution.

Example: The peasant was knocked down and killed by a **tumbrel**.

Tumescent

Pronunciation: Tyoo-mess-unt   **Type**: Adjective

Definition: Swollen or puffy. This adjective is often used to describe the male genitals during a state of arousal, but it can also be used to describe language that's pompous or pretentious.

Example: Eleanor gorged on Peter's **tumescent** phallus.

Tumultuous

Pronunciation: Tum-ult-yoo-uss   **Type**: Adjective

Definition: This adjective is used to describe a state of loudness, excitement, uproar or confusion.

Example: The popular orator left the stage to **tumultuous** applause.

Turbid

Pronunciation: Tur-bid   **Type**: Adjective

Definition: Cloudy or opaque. This adjective is usually used to describe a liquid.

Example: The **turbid** water made the villagers ill.

Turgescence

Pronunciation: Turr-jess-unce   **Type**: Noun

Definition: A swollen or enlarged area.

Example: The patient winced when the nurse pressed his **turgescence**.

Turnkey

Pronunciation: Turn-kee   **Type**: Adjective, Noun

Definition: The adjective and the noun have completely different meanings. The adjective is used to describe a product or a service that's ready to use immediately, while the noun is an informal term for a jailer.

Example:
#1: The company bought a **turnkey** graphic design suite and started creating logos almost immediately.
#2: The **turnkey** ordered the leader of the inmate gang to spend a month in solitary isolation.

Turpitude

Pronunciation: Turp-it-yood   **Type**: Noun

Definition: Depravity†, wickedness or immorality.

Example: The whorehouse was in a state of perpetual **turpitude**.

Tweeter

Pronunciation: Tweet-ur   **Type**: Noun

Definition: A type of speaker that's specifically designed to reproduce high frequencies and treble.

Example: At the concert, Karen stood too close to the **tweeter** and went home with a headache.

Tyrannicide

Pronunciation: Ty-ran-iss-ide   **Type**: Noun

Definition: This noun is used to refer to the act of killing a tyrant.

Example: Mr. Vimes was beheaded for treason after committing **tyrannicide**.

Tyrotoxism

Pronunciation: Tie-ro-tox-izz-um   **Type**: Noun

Definition: Poisoning by cheese, milk or any other product containing lactose.

Example: The autopsy determined that Mrs. Arlington died of **tyrotoxism**.

U

Ubiquitous

Pronunciation: Yoo-bick-wit-uss   **Type**: Adjective

Definition: Existing, being or appearing everywhere at the same time.

Example: The earth has a **ubiquitous** supply of oxygen.

Uglification

Pronunciation: Ug-liff-ick-ay-shun   **Type**: Noun

Definition: The act of disfiguring something or of making something ugly.

Example: The supermodel was attacked by a fan who was hell-bent on her **uglification**.

Ululating

Pronunciation: Ul-yoo-late-ing   **Type**: Verb

Definition: Howling, screaming or wailing in profound sorrow, grief or anguish.

Example: The wife of the dead soldier was found **ululating** in the graveyard.

Umbrage

Pronunciation: Um-bridge   **Type**: Noun

Definition: Offence or annoyance, typically as a result of a social snub[†].

Example: Jennifer took **umbrage** at Keith's suggestion that she needed to go on a diet.

Unabashed

Pronunciation: Un-ab-ashed   **Type**: Adjective

Definition: Not embarrassed or ashamed.

Example: Peter was **unabashed** after his daughter wet herself and left a stain on their hostess's carpet.

Unbirthday

Pronunciation: Un-birth-day   **Type**: Noun

Definition: Any day except one's birthday; a neologism[†] coined by C.S. Lewis.

Example: I didn't want to make Joseph a cup of tea, but I felt like I had no choice when he told me it was his **unbirthday**.

Unctuous

Pronunciation: Unk-choo-uss   **Type**: Adjective

Definition: Oily. This adjective can be used to describe anything that's greasy or soapy, and it can also describe someone who's excessively, ingratiatingly or inordinately flattering and complimentary.

Example: I didn't stay at the party for long because Juliette is an **unctuous**

host.

Undulate

Pronunciation: Und-yoo-late   **Type**: Verb

Definition: To move in a smooth, wave-like motion.

Example: The sailor watched the sea **undulate** beneath the stars.

Unearthly

Pronunciation: Un-urth-lee   **Type**: Adjective

Definition: In general usage, this adjective describes something unnatural, mysterious or disturbing. When used to refer to a time, it means that it's unreasonably early or inconvenient.

Example: "Hell no," said David. "No way am I getting up at that **unearthly** hour."

Unfettered

Pronunciation: Un-fett-urd   **Type**: Verb

Definition: Released from restraint, restriction or inhibition.

Example: The fascist grew **unfettered** during his time in Vienna.

Unguent

Pronunciation: Un-joo-unt   **Type**: Noun

Definition: A soft, greasy substance that's designed to be used as an ointment or for lubrication.

Example: The doctor told his patient to start taking a soothing **unguent**.

Unkempt

Pronunciation: Un-kempt   **Type**: Adjective

Definition: Possessing an untidy, uncared for or dishevelled appearance.

Example: Jamie wasn't given the job because he was **unkempt** at the interview.

Unperson

Pronunciation: Un-purr-sun   **Type**: Noun

Definition: A newspeak[†] word from George Orwell's *1984*. An unperson is a person whose existence is denied or ignored, particularly due to a political crime or misdemeanour.

Example: The prole was arrested for having contact with the **unperson**.

Unputdownable

Pronunciation: Un-put-down-ab-ull   **Type**: Adjective

Definition: This adjective is usually used to describe a book that's difficult to put down because it's so engrossing.

Example: *The Lexicologist's Handbook* is so **unputdownable** that Amanda read it three times in a row.

Uppish

Pronunciation: Up-ish   **Type**: Adjective

Definition: Arrogantly self-assertive.

Example: The **uppish** lout often got into fights with the locals.

Ursine

Pronunciation: Ur-sine   **Type**: Adjective

Definition: Of, similar to or related to bears.

Example: The man's back was **ursine** and in desperate need of a shave.

Usury

Pronunciation: Yooz-yuh-ree   **Type**: Noun

Definition: The illegal action of lending money with unreasonably high interest rates.

Example: Dodgy Dave was sent down for committing **usury**.

Uxorious

Pronunciation: Ucks-or-ee-uss   **Type**: Adjective

Definition: Having, possessing or showing an excessive fondness or affection for one's wife.

Example: **Uxorious** as ever, Andrew claimed that Sophie's beauty was woven by angels from silver threads taken from the hearts of stars.

V

Vacillate

Pronunciation: Vass-ill-ate   **Type**: Verb

Definition: To rapidly change or alternate between opinions, or to be indecisive.

Example: Mark annoyed everyone with his tendency to **vacillate**. He could never seem to make up his mind.

Valanced

Pronunciation: Val-unced   **Type**: Adjective

Definition: Framed, particularly a face that's framed with a beard.

Example: The beggar's **valanced** visage[†] was well-known in the village.

Valediction

Pronunciation: Val-uh-dick-shun   **Type**: Noun

Definition: The act of saying farewell.

Example: The pope spread his hands in **valediction** before taking his leave.

Valetudinarian

Pronunciation: Val-it-choo-din-air-ee-un   **Type**: Adjective, Noun

Definition: The adjective refers to the personality trait of showing undue concern and anxiety about one's health. The noun is used to refer to someone who shows this kind of concern.

Example:
#1: "Karen," she said. "You must stop this **valetudinarian** attitude."
#2: The **valetudinarian** arranged his third doctor's appointment of the month.

Variorum

Pronunciation: Vair-ee-or-um   **Type**: Adjective, Noun

Definition: The adjective describes something that contains notes by multiple editors and commentators, while the noun is used to refer to a book of this type.

Example:
#1: The **variorum** manuscript was often difficult to read but gave great insight into the university system.
#2: The **variorum** sold for hundreds of thousands of dollars at auction.

Venal

Pronunciation: Vee-nul   **Type**: Adjective

Definition: Easily corrupted by bribery, or capable of being bought or obtained for money or other valuables.

Example: The pirates were **venal** and susceptible to infighting.

Venereal

Pronunciation: Ven-ear-ee-ul   **Type**: Adjective

Definition: Of or relating to sexual desires, activities, intercourse or diseases.

Example: Chloe first had **venereal** problems at the age of fifteen, and she'd had two children by the time she turned twenty.

Venture

Pronunciation: Vent-chur   **Type**: Noun, Verb

Definition: The noun refers to a risky, hazardous or daring journey, adventure or undertaking, while the verb refers to the act of making such a journey.

Example:
#1: The investors decided to fund the inventor's latest **venture**.
#2: The explorer decided to **venture** out into the storm.

Veracious

Pronunciation: Vuh-ray-shuss   **Type**: Adjective

Definition: Truthful, honest or correct.

Example: The witness's statement was **veracious** and backed up by the evidence.

Verbosity

Pronunciation: Verb-oss-it-ee   **Type**: Noun

Definition: The quality of wordiness.

Example: The old playwright was renowned for his **verbosity**, but his long plays still managed to sell out the theatres.

Verisimilitude

Pronunciation: Veh-riss-im-ill-it-yood　　**Type**: Noun

Definition: The likeness or appearance of being true or real.

Example: The film lacked **verisimilitude** and was universally panned by critics.

Vernacular

Pronunciation: Vur-nack-yoo-la　　**Type**: Adjective, Noun

Definition: The adjective is used to describe a language that's spoken as a mother tongue, while the noun refers to the language or dialect that's spoken in a particular country or region.

Example:
#1: Sophia's **vernacular** English was well-respected in the Far East.
#2: The farmer spoke in a thick **vernacular** that the reporter struggled to understand.

Vicissitude

Pronunciation: Viss-iss-it-yood　　**Type**: Noun

Definition: This noun usually refers to an unwelcome or unpleasant change of circumstances, but it can also refer to alternations or mutations between opposite or contrasting things.

Example: Harold's grandparents struggled through the **vicissitude** of having to take the boy in after his parents died.

Victuals

Pronunciation: Vick-choo-ulls   **Type**: Noun

Definition: Food supplies.

Example: The prisoners were provided with **victuals** twice a day and left to their own devices.

Vigesimal

Pronunciation: Vi-jess-im-ul   **Type**: Adjective

Definition: Characterised by, based on or related to the number twenty.

Example: The shop operated a reward policy for **vigesimal** customers.

Vignette

Pronunciation: Vin-yet   **Type**: Noun

Definition: A brief but evocative[†] depiction[†] or account.

Example: The poet's **vignette** was considered by most to be his greatest work.

Virago

Pronunciation: Vih-rah-go   **Type**: Noun

Definition: A domineering, forceful, violent or ill-tempered woman, or a woman with masculine strength, spirit and attitude.

Example: As embarrassing as it was, John was forced to admit that his wife was a **virago** and that she wore the pants in the family.

Vinification

Pronunciation: Vin-if-ick-ay-shun   **Type**: Noun

Definition: The process by which grape juice or the extract of another fruit or vegetable is turned into wine through fermentation.

Example: The alcoholic waited impatiently for his homebrew to go through **vinification**.

Viridescent

Pronunciation: Vih-rid-ess-unt   **Type**: Adjective

Definition: Green.

Example: Arthur's **viridescent** eyes made him a hit with the ladies.

Visage

Pronunciation: Vize-ij   **Type**: Noun

Definition: A person's face or expression.

Example: Alex's stern **visage** meant trouble for his husband.

Viscera

Pronunciation: Viss-uh-ra   **Type**: Noun

Definition: The internal organs of the body, particularly the intestines.

Example: The horror movie was abundant with gore and **viscera**.

Vitrescent

Pronunciation: Vit-ress-unt   **Type**: Adjective

Definition: Capable of being turned into glass.

Example: The **vitrescent** sand glistened in the moonlight.

Vivarium

Pronunciation: Viv-air-ee-um   **Type**: Noun

Definition: An enclosure, structure or habitat that's been designed for the purpose of housing and raising animals in near-natural conditions for observation or study. It literally means "place of life" in Latin.

Example: The biologist spent a relaxing evening watching the animals at the **vivarium**.

Vivisection

Pronunciation: Viv-ee-sec-shun   **Type**: Noun

Definition: The practice of performing operations on living animals for research or experimentation. The word has evolved to take on a second meaning and can now describe any ruthless piece of analysis.

Example: The animal rights group demanded that the scientists end the practice of **vivisection**.

Volition

Pronunciation: Vol-ish-un   **Type**: Noun

Definition: The ability or power to decide upon or to commit to a course of action.

Example: The judges ruled that Jennifer committed the crime of her own **volition** and sentenced her to six months' probation.

Voluntarism

Pronunciation: Vol-unt-ah-riz-um   **Type**: Noun

Definition: The practice of relying upon voluntary action and voluntary contributions to run an organisation or a not-for-profit.

Example: The not-for-profit relied on **voluntarism** to survive and often recruited people to scour the streets in search of donations.

Voyeur

Pronunciation: Voy-urr   **Type**: Noun

Definition: A person who gains sexual pleasure from spying on or watching others who are naked or having sexual intercourse.

Example: The landlord was a **voyeur** and was arrested for filming his tenants in the shower.

Vulpine

Pronunciation: Vul-pine   **Type**: Adjective

Definition: Of, similar to or related to a fox or a group of foxes. Because of this, the word has taken on a secondary meaning and can also be used to describe someone who's crafty or cunning.

Example: The teacher gave his class a **vulpine** smile when he told them about the homework.

W

Wassail

Pronunciation: Wah-sale   **Type**: Noun, Verb

Definition: The noun refers to a type of ale or wine that's consumed during Christmas celebrations, while the verb refers to the action of merrymaking and drinking lots of alcohol.

Example:
#1: Every Christmas Eve, Jason and his family drank **wassail**.
#2: The students decided to **wassail** the night away.

Weltschmerz

Pronunciation: Velt-schmurtz   **Type**: Noun

Definition: A feeling of sadness, melancholy and apathy.

Example: It took Carol six years to get over her **weltschmerz** after her cat died, and she was never the same again.

Wherewithal

Pronunciation: Ware-with-all   **Type**: Noun

Definition: The things that are necessary for a particular purpose.

Example: Unfortunately, the company didn't have the **wherewithal** to survive the recession.

Whitlow

Pronunciation: Wit-low   **Type**: Noun

Definition: An abscess or lesion in the finger or the thumb.

Example: Stephen found it hard to write because of his **whitlow**.

Widget

Pronunciation: Wij-it   **Type**: Noun

Definition: A small gadget or device. In computing circles, this noun usually refers to a simple application or component that can be used to enhance or improve a larger interface.

Example: The web developer coded a **widget** that allowed people to generate an automatic quotation.

Will-o'-the-wisp

Pronunciation: Will-oh-the-wisp   **Type**: Noun

Definition: A ghostly light seen by travellers at night, usually in the proximity of bogs, marshes, swamps or other wetlands.

Example: The gypsies followed the **will-o'-the-wisp** through the forest and quickly lost their way.

Woebegone

Pronunciation: Woe-be-gone   **Type**: Adjective

Definition: Sad, downtrodden or miserable in attitude or appearance.

Example: The kitten was soaked by the rainfall and looked **woebegone** and bashful when it came in through the cat flap.

X

Xenophobia

Pronunciation: Zen-oh-foe-bee-ah   **Type**: Noun

Definition: An intense[†] or irrational hatred and prejudice towards people from other countries.

Example: The dictator was a believer in **xenophobia** and invaded Poland at the first opportunity.

Xerophilous

Pronunciation: Zeh-roff-ill-uss   **Type**: Adjective

Definition: Adapted to or suited to a dry climate or environment. This adjective is usually used to describe a plant or an animal.

Example: The **xerophilous** cactus could survive for months without water.

Xiphoid

Pronunciation: Zi-foid   **Type**: Adjective

Definition: Shaped like a sword.

Example: The janitor banged his head on the **xiphoid** protrusion.

Y

Yggdrasil

Pronunciation: Igg-drass-ill   **Type**: Noun

Definition: A huge ash tree that, according to Norse mythology, is located at the centre of the Earth. According to legend, the tree has three roots which extend to the underworld, the land of the giants and the land of the gods.

Example: Helga dreamt of the **Yggdrasil** and took it as a sign to switch careers.

Yomp

Pronunciation: Yomp   **Type**: Noun

Definition: A slang term that originated within the Royal Marines to describe a long march carrying full kit.

Example: The privates weren't looking forward to the **yomp** that was scheduled for the morning.

Z

Zany

Pronunciation: Zay-nee   **Type**: Adjective

Definition: Unconventional, strange or idiosyncratic.

Example: Kevin was notoriously **zany** and had a peculiar sense of humour.

Zeitgeist

Pronunciation: Zite-guy-st   **Type**: Noun

Definition: The defining spirit, mood or feeling of a particular period of history, reflected in the ideas and beliefs of the people at the time.

Example: The old-timers missed the **zeitgeist** and camaraderie of the Second World War.

Zenith

Pronunciation: Zen-ith   **Type**: Noun

Definition: A high point, usually an imaginary one that's directly above a particular object or location. Opposite in meaning to nadir[†].

Example: The explorer reached the **zenith** of the mountain.

Zoophyte

Pronunciation: Zoo-fite   **Type**: Noun

Definition: An animal that looks like a plant.

Example: Coral is a classic example of a **zoophyte**.

JOIN THE CONVERSATION

AS ALWAYS, thanks so much for reading my books and supporting my work. I hope you found something here worth taking away with you.

Whether you loved this book or you hated it, please do go ahead and share a short review to Amazon, Goodreads and/or your social networking site of choice.

You can find and follow my writing journey through any of the links below. I hope to see you soon with another book!

danecobain.com

facebook.com/danecobainmusic

youtube.com/danecobain

instagram.com/danecobain

twitter.com/danecobain

MORE GREAT READS
FROM DANE COBAIN

No Rest for the Wicked (Supernatural Thriller) When the Angels attack, there's *No Rest for the Wicked*. Cobain's debut novella, a supernatural thriller, follows the story of the elderly Father Montgomery as he tries to save the world, or at least, his parishioners, from mysterious, spectral assailants.

Eyes Like Lighthouses When the Boats Come Home (Poetry) Eyes Like Lighthouses is Dane Cobain's first book of poetry, distilled from the sweat of a thousand memorised performances in this reality and others. It's not for the faint-hearted.

Former.ly: The Rise and Fall of a Social Network (Literary Fiction) When Dan Roberts starts his new job at Former.ly, he has no idea what he's getting into. The site deals in death. Its users share their innermost thoughts, which are stored privately until they die. Then, their posts are shared with the world, often with unexpected consequences.

Social Paranoia: How Consumers and Brands Can Stay Safe in a Connected World (Non-Fiction) Social Paranoia: How Consumers and Brands Can Stay Safe in a Connected World is the true story of how sometimes the updates that you post come back to haunt you. Sometimes, people really are out to get you. Be afraid. Be very afraid.

Come On Up to the House (Horror) This horror novella and screenplay tells the story of Darran Jersey, a troubled teenager who moves into a house that's inhabited by the malevolent spirit of his predecessor. As tragedy after tragedy threatens to destroy the family, Darran's mother decides to leave the house and start afresh. But is it too late?

Subject Verb Object (Anthology) Eighteen writers from both sides of the Atlantic come together in this genre-bending collection of new writing. Meet Luís da Silva and get (thickly) settled. Get drunk in Cornwall or lose yourself in the Warren. Find out why Pete's remote control keeps disappearing, how

Gary's cat found heaven and what lurks behind Jay's mirror.

Driven (Detective) Meet private detective James Leipfold, computer whiz kid Maile O'Hara and good-natured cop Jack Cholmondeley in the first book of the Leipfold series. A car strikes a woman in the middle of the night and a young actress lies dead in the road. The police force thinks it's an accident, but Maile and Leipfold aren't so sure.

The Tower Hill Terror (Detective) The Tower Hill Terror is on the loose, a serial killer with a grisly M.O., and Maile and Leipfold must work fast to take him down before another body is found. But while the duo are chasing clues on social networking sites and the police are waiting for forensics, the Terror sends a message to the journalists at *the Tribune*. A message written in blood.

Meat (Horror) Veterinarian Tom Copeland takes a job at a factory farm called Sunnyvale after a scandal at his suburban practice. But there are rumours of a strange creature living beneath the complex, accidents waiting to happen on brutal production lines and the threat of zoonotic disease from the pigs, sheep, cows, chickens and fish that the complex houses.

Scarlet Sins (Short Stories) Scarlet Sins is a collection of short stories and songs spanning two decades and taking the reader from the English countryside during the outbreak of World War I to the flower markets of Amsterdam and the depths of the infinite cosmos. *Scarlet Sins: Stories and Songs* is Cobain's first collection of songs and stories and his tenth published work.

Discover more books
at <u>danecobain.com</u>.

Printed in Great Britain
by Amazon